READINGS IN AFRICAN PHILOSOPHY

AN AKAN COLLECTION

Edited by
Safro Kwame

University Press of America, Inc.
Lanham • New York • London

Copyright © 1995 by
University Press of America,®️ Inc.
4720 Boston Way
Lanham, Maryland 20706

3 Henrietta Street
London, WC2E 8LU England

Library of Congress Cataloging-in-Publication Data

Readings in African philosophy / edited by Safro Kwame.
p.   cm.
Includes bibliographical references and index.
1. Philosophy, Akan. 2. Philosophy, African. 3. Akan (African
people).   I. Kwame, Safro
B5619.G4R43   1995   199'.6--dc20   95-6499 CIP

ISBN 0-8191-9910-9 (cloth: alk. paper)
ISBN 0-8191-9911-7 (pbk: alk: paper)

To my teachers,
Wherever they are;
And my students,
Wherever they may be.

Table of Contents

PART II: METAPHYSICS

PART III: LOGIC AND EPISTEMOLOGY

PART IV: MORAL AND POLITICAL PHILOSOPHY

APPROXIMATE PRONUNCIATION OF
AFRICAN/AKAN ('Are-can') NAMES

Abraham ('A'-bra-ham)

Akan (Are-can)

Appiah (Appear-ahh)

Bedu-Addo (Bay-do Are-do)

Busia (Booze-zia)

Danquah (Dan-qua)

Dolphyne (Doll-fine)

Gyekye (Jet-chee)

Kwame (Qua-army)

Nkrumah (In-crew-ma)

Oguah (Oh-goer)

Onyame (Own-yam-me)

Wiredu (Ray-do)

PREFACE

One of the lessons I have learnt in putting together this anthology is that if you take philosophy seriously, it is difficult—if not impossible—to find excuses for not doing it. Further, however tautological the foregoing statement may sound, it is not trivial. I hope you find, in the following pages, an attempt to take African philosophy seriously in spite of the five or so years of frustration in persuading publishers, seeking permissions, soliciting funds, corresponding with scholars and coordinating the efforts of some of Africa's leading philosophers. It ought not be forgotten, however, that to take philosophy seriously is not necessarily to agree with its content nor to presume the infallibility of its advocates. I merely hope you take a critical look at the following pages, with an open mind, from the bottom of your heart; and, above all, you enjoy it. Unlike most of the texts in the field of African philosophy, this anthology includes classics as well as contemporary writings; it deals extensively with philosophical as well as metaphilosophical issues; it covers both traditional and current areas of philosophical research; it presents the same material, essays, and issues at both the introductory and advanced levels in the words of the authors themselves; and it is realistic in limiting the dialogue to those who share a common language and culture.

ACKNOWLEDGEMENTS

To err, as to be in need of help, is human. To receive help when needed and advice and correction when one errs, is to be lucky to be in a truly human community. For that, I am grateful to Kwasi Wiredu, Kobina Oguah, Kwame Gyekye, Anthony Appiah, Emmanuel Abraham, Florence Dolphyne and Dana Flint. I am convinced that without their comments, advice and criticism, this book would never have been better, only worse. Certainly it could not have been better without one of its main contributors, Oguah of Africa, who died in Africa just before its completion. Without the wordprocessing skills of Saudia Grier, Carolyn Staunton-Simpson and my computer fairy-lady, Debbie Carter, this book would never have been finished. My thanks for scanning go to Rodney Brown, Mark Killinger and their collegues at the University of Delaware Graphic and Communications Center. For proofreading, I am indebted to Ezra Engling, Levi Nwackuku, Emmanuel Babatunde and William Dadson. I am grateful for the Lincoln University Research and Publication Grant and for the understanding and help of Michelle Harris and her associates at the University Press of America. To all others who directly or indirectly contributed to the publication of this anthology, I hereby express my appreciation. For ingratitude, in some sense, is inhuman.

Introduction

African Philosophy and the Akan Society: An Introduction

Ɔba nyansafo, wobu no bɛ, na wɔnka no asem. **—You communicate with a wise child in proverbs, not in common parlance. (Akan proverb)**

1. INTRODUCTION

For reasons that will become apparent and significant, presently, this anthology of African philosophy is drawn exclusively from the Akan society in Africa. If one remembers that the main and probably only reason why over 500 million people of different religions, traditions, languages, and shades of color are called Africans is that they all live on the second largest continent on earth, I believe one will not be terribly upset about the fact that this anthology focuses on one of the main, historic, linguistic, ethnic, and cultural groups in Africa. Hopefully it will soon be apparent—if it already is not—that while the closeness in language, tradition, and other aspects of culture is of some philosophical significance, the mere fact that a large group of people lives on the same extensive landmass is in itself of little philosophic significance though it may be of immense geographic significance.

2. THE AKANS

The Akans belong to the Tano language family to the east and west of the Tano river in the coastal and forest regions of the West African countries of Ghana and La Cote d'Ivoire (Ivory Coast). In Ghana, the Akans are found mostly to the east of the Tano river in the Ashanti, Brong-Ahafo, Central, Western and Eastern regions of the country.

They constitute about fifty percent of the 14 million or so citizens of Ghana and the biggest ethnic group in that country. They speak dialects such as Akuapem, Asante, Fante, Kwahu and Akyem, collectively called the Akan language, part of which is more popularly known as Twi. To the best of my knowledge, all the authors included in this anthology speak the Akan language as a first language or as well as those who do; and all of them are Ghanaians who belong to the Akan ethnic group. Hence, they belong to a closely knit linguistic and cultural group.

The origin of the Akans is a mystery. It has been suggested that they migrated from the ancient empires of Ghana, Libya, Egypt or Abyssinia possibly 1,000-2,000 years ago. According to the Ghanaian historian, Adu Boahen, they migrated in two groups from the Savannah region, in the area of the Black Volta and the Comoe rivers between 1,000-1,300 A.D.[1] On Boahen's account, the two large groups of Akan families and clans moved southwards until they reached the coastal regions of modern Ghana between the late thirteenth century and early fourteenth century.[2] Here, in the forest and coastal regions of modern Ghana, they culturally assimilated the pre-existing Guan people. Additionally, they developed the Akan language, a seven-day calendar, eight partrilineal clans and eight matrilineal clans; and, also, a matrilineal system of inheritance.[3] According to Boahen, the extent to which they succeeded in absorbing the various groups of Guans accounts for the present linguistic differences among the Akans.[4]

Trading and other activities between the fourteenth and nineteenth centuries led to the rise and fall of a succession of Akan kingdoms starting with Bono-Tekyiman and including Banda, Twifo, Adansi, Denkyira, Fante, Akyem, Akwamu and the Asante kingdoms. These early groups of kingdoms ended with the fall of the Asante empire in the wake of the Anglo-Asante war of 1874 in which the British defeated the Asante people and formed the British Crown colony of the Gold Coast in July 1874, though resistance continued thereafter. The scramble by Britain, France, Germany, Portugal and other European powers for colonies in Africa led to the Berlin conference from 15th November 1884 to 30th January 1885 and the partition of Africa. Colonial rule prevailed for the first half of the twentieth century until Ghana's independence on 6th March 1957 as a result of the anti-colonial activities of Akans, such as Joseph Boakye Danquah and Kwame Nkrumah, and of non-Akans too.

3. AN INTRODUCTION TO AFRICAN PHILOSOPHY

On 6th March 1957, the British Colony of the Gold Coast officially became known as modern Ghana and the first post-colonial nation-State in Africa south of the Sahara. At the beginning of Ghana's independence day, Black Africa's first post-colonial prime minister (and, later, president), Kwame Nkrumah, observed that "our independence is meaningless unless it is linked up with the total liberation of the African continent."[5]

There have been various interpretations of and suggestions for "the total liberation of the African continent."[6] Apart from the obvious suggestions about fighting and eradicating colonialism, apartheid and neo-colonialism all over the African continent, there have been suggestions concerning what people like Ngugi Wa Thiong'o term 'decolonising the mind'[7] or, in Kwasi Wiredu's phrase, 'conceptual decolonization.'[8] Both political and conceptual decolonization have been suggested as preconditions for achieving total liberation in Africa.

Thus the kind of nationalism and independence movement led by Akans like Danquah and Nkrumah, among others, and resulting in mass independence in Africa, also led to a debate about African philosophy. The reasons are obvious. First, African philosophy is seen as needed to replace, wholly or partly, the European philosophy and philosophers that were imposed by the colonial masters as part of the curriculum for African students and also as means of governing and organizing African societies. Secondly, it is perceived as providing the means for conceptual decolonization; in other words, freeing the minds of Africans from the categories, concepts, and logic embedded in the European languages used to educate Africans.

4. TWO VIEWS OF AFRICAN PHILOSOPHY

There have been two main views of African philosophy. One looks back to the pre-colonial, traditional, African society for African philosophy. On this view, African philosophy is contained in, found in, or constructed out of the proverbs, folklore, art, aphorisms, fragments, rituals, traditions and collective wisdom of the African people; and African philosophy so discovered or constructed is comparable to Western philosophy (without necessarily being, significantly, the same). On this view, the lack of writing in large areas of traditional Africa is not sufficient for denying the existence of a traditional African philosophy that is comparable to Western philosophy. The general reasoning for this traditional approach to African philosophy seems to be that the post-colonial African society has been so Westernized that any authentic African philosophy must be rooted in the pre-colonial society. This is the way Gyekye puts it in his book *An Essay on African Philosophical Thought: The Akan Conceptual Scheme:*

> ...It is indeed a mistake to maintain that the term "African philosophy" should be used to cover only the philosophy, that is, the written philosophy, that is being produced by contemporary African philosophers. For philosophy, whether in the sense of a worldview or in the sense of a discipline—that is, in the sense of systematic critical thought about the problems covered in philosophy as worldview—is discoverable in African traditional thought...Consequently a distinction must be made between traditional African philosophy and modern African philosophy: The latter, to be African, and have a basis in African culture and experience, must have a connection with the former, the traditional.[9]

From the second, more forward-looking point of view, this traditional approach to African Philosophy merely produces ethnography with philosophical pretensions or, in short, ethnophilosophy. On this view, African philosophy consists of the post-colonial, literary works of individuals connected to the African continent. According to those who adopt this view, the reason for this approach to African philosophy is that real or serious philosophy is not a collective activity by the whole society as is apparently suggested by some who use the so-called ethnophilosophical approach. On this view, philosophy is an individual and literary activity; hence, writing is necessary for philosophy. Additionally, they note that, until the European colonial masters introduced writing on a mass scale in Africa, much of Black Africa lacked a tradition of writing and, hence, the absence of traditional African philosophy.

While Kwasi Wiredu's views are not the same as those identified above and the differences will become obvious as we proceed, I believe that on some interpretations, his views have some affinities with those characterized above. "African philosophy as distinct from African 'traditional world-view,'" Kwasi Wiredu writes, "is the philosophy that is being produced by contemporary African philosophers."[10] He adds, "it is still in the making."[11] As Wiredu explains, in making this remark he is talking not about the present but the future "when the phrase 'African philosophy' will refer simply to the African tradition of written philosophy."[12] In his opinion, there is a need to recover,

interpret and record traditional thought but there is a more urgent need
to fashion philosophies based on contemporary African experience:

> ...there is a need, possibly more urgent, to fashion philosophies based upon
> contemporary African experience with its many-sidedness. From this point
> of view, one might suggest without being whimsical that the term 'African
> philosophy' should be reserved for the results of that enterprise.[13]

It may be more appropriate to characterize the two main views as two
extreme positions on a continuum in which others beside Gyekye and
Wiredu are represented. These others include John Mbiti of Kenya who
believes that "philosophical systems of different African people have not
yet been formulated, but some of the areas where they may be found
are in the religion, proverbs, oral tradition, ethics and morals of the
society concerned."[14]   According to Kobina Oguah, many Western
philosophical doctrines are expressed in Africa "not in documents but
in the proverbs, ritual songs, folktales and customs of the people."[15]
Odera Oruka of Kenya, like W. Emmanuel Abraham of Ghana, denies
that literacy or writing is necessary for philosophy but, at the same
time, dissociates himself from the works of Gyekye and Olubi Sodipo
as being "unable to get out of the anthropological fog."[16] According to
Abraham, one "can find all over Africa specimens of what might be
called a public philosophy, usually tracing out the theoretical
foundations of the traditional society" and "also the private
philosophy...which is more the thinking of an individual than a
laying-bare of the communal mind."[17]   V. Y. Mudimbe prefers to call
traditional thought 'gnosis,' on the grounds that "it is only
metaphorically, or, at best, from a historicist perspective, that one would
extend the notion of philosophy to African traditional systems of
thought, considering them as dynamic processes in which concrete
experiences are integrated into an order of concepts and discourses."[18]

5. FOUR QUESTIONS ON AFRICAN PHILOSOPHY
In characterizing the views of these scholars on the continuum, it is
important that we distinguish between four questions. The questions
concern (1) whether there are traditional African philosophers, (2)
whether there is a traditional African philosophy, (3) whether there is
a modern or contemporary African philosophy, and (4) how to define
African philosophy. There is almost universal agreement concerning the
existence of modern or contemporary African philosophy. We have

adduced evidence above to suggest that even Gyekye who comes as close as possible to adopting the first view of African philosophy acknowledges the existence of a contemporary African philosophy. It is doubtful that even Mbiti who is characterized as an ethnophilosopher 'par excellence' denies the existence of contemporary African philosophy. Recall, for example, his above-quoted statement on philosophical systems. There may be some disagreement about the existence of traditional African philosophers. But even that is not a subject on which there is strong disagreement. Both Wiredu and Oruka, who disagree with Mbiti and (to some extent) Gyekye, acknowledge the existence of traditional African philosophers. Both Paulin Hountondji of Benin and Abraham believe that there could have been African philosophers without an African philosophy.[19] Hountondji's argument is that "thousands of Socrates could never have given birth to Greek philosophy...so thousands of philosophers without written works could never have given birth to an African philosophy."[20]

There is much more disagreement among these scholars with regard to the existence of a traditional African philosophy. It is interesting to note that both Wiredu and Kwame Appiah of Ghana acknowledge the existence of a traditional African philosophy in at least some sense. However, both of them may be characterized as adopting part of the second view of African philosophy. Together with Peter Bodunrin of Nigeria and Hountondji, they belong to the so-called camp of professional, rationalist, neo-logical-positivist philosophers or what I call the individualist-literary school of thought. Traditional African philosophy, on Appiah's account, is folk rather than formal philosophy; for reasons having to do with the lack of a tradition of writing. Literacy, according to Appiah, "is not a sufficient condition for formal philosophy, but it certainly seems to be necessary."[21] "If instead of asking, 'Is there an African philosophy?,' it had been asked, 'Is there an African traditional philosophy,' it would have been clearly unproblematic to answer in the affirmative," Wiredu writes.[22] "If the phrase 'African philosophy' is interpreted in the way that the phrase 'British philosophy' is (quite legitimately) construed," he adds, "then it might begin to seem that some skepticism is in order, for in most parts of Africa we do not have a substantial tradition of written philosophy."[23] It is exactly in this kind of context that it is useful to distinguish between a traditional (unwritten) philosophy and a nontraditional (written) philosophy.

In my opinion, there are three main factors that account for the differences or similarities of opinion on the existence of traditional African philosophy. They are (1) the status of traditional beliefs, (2) the fairness of comparison and (3) the definition of African philosophy. These factors will be discussed presently. Meanwhile, it is worth noting that, to some extent, the issue of whether or not there is a traditional African philosophy is the main bone of contention and accounts for where we place individual scholars on the continuum constituted by the two main schools of thought. While the two schools of thought on African philosophy tend to coincide or correlate with the two views of African philosophy spelt out earlier, they are not synonymous. My suggestion is that there is a tendency for people like Mbiti, Gyekye, and Oguah in the traditional or so-called ethnophilosophical school of thought to adopt or use the first view of African philosophy which identifies or constructs African philosophy from the proverbs, customs, traditions and folk beliefs of African societies. They may have other views apart from this and they need not be the only ones who use this view. Similarly there is a tendency for people like Wiredu, Hountondji, Bodunrin, and Appiah in the individualist-literary or the so-called professional or rationalist, positivistic school of thought to adopt or use the second view of African philosophy. This is the view which identifies African philosophy with the literary works of contemporary philosophers. Here, again, I wish to stress that this need not be the exclusive view of this group. Both Wiredu and Gyekye use traditional Akan proverbs and beliefs for their respective philosophies which may be the construction of traditional or contemporary African philosophy. Additionally, it is important to remember that these two views are ideal views which the two schools of thought approximate. Strictly speaking, the class of those who adopt either view of African philosophy may be empty.

In any case, one of the three factors that I perceive to account for the differences and similarities between the members of the two schools of thought with regard to the existence of a traditional African philosophy is the status of traditional African beliefs. As I see it, part of the difference in the two schools of thought on African philosophy has to do with whether they take the statements expressing traditional African beliefs as premises or conclusions. There is a tendency for the traditional or so-called ethnophilosophical school of thought to take those statements as conclusions (on the basis of the evidence available to them) and, hence infer that there were unrecorded or unknown but reconstructible statements that constitute premises for those conclusions.

On the basis of the evidence available to them, the individualist-literary school of thought tends, instead, to consider those traditional African belief-statements as premises to be used by contemporary philosophers to draw conclusions or construct arguments and contemporary philosophies.

The second factor with regard to the status of traditional African philosophy has to do with the issue of fairness in comparing traditional African philosophy as the dominant or popular view of African societies with Western philosophy as criticism or dissensions of individuals who disagree with the popular view. There is a tendency for the individualist-literary school of thought to think that such comparisons are unfair or inappropriate. They tend to think that it is rather like trying to compare two different things—apples and oranges—which are incommensurable. Some of them believe that what has been considered as philosophy in the West, from Socrates to Bertrand Russell, has mainly been objections to the dominant beliefs in the society and have been deviations from them. On the other hand, the traditional or so-called ethnophilosophical school of thought tends to think that such comparisons are not improper, since some of the philosophies in the West have been attempts to articulate and defend the prevailing or dominant beliefs in society. In any case, because of the absence of writing in most of these traditional societies, their philosophies —whether or not they are dissensions—are bound to be included in the oral tradition. The traditional school of thought in question tends to believe that because of this special or peculiar situation, it is not unfair to compare African philosophy so interpreted with Western philosophy.

6. ON DEFINING AFRICAN PHILOSOPHY

The third factor that accounts for the differences in schools of thought and in belief in a traditional African philosophy is the definition of philosophy in general and of African philosophy in particular. It will be recalled that this problem of the definition of African philosophy was identified earlier on as the issue at stake in one of the four main questions about African philosophy. There is no doubt that the definition of African philosophy is related to the question of whether there is a traditional African philosophy. Here are just two definitions of African philosophy from the so-called professional or, better still, individualists-literary school of thought. The first one is by Paulin Hountondji of Benin in West Africa from his book *African Philosophy: Myth and Reality*. He defines African philosophy in terms of (i) intentions (to create philosophy), (ii) location (i.e. geography or nationality of the person), and (iii) the medium used (i.e. writing):

> By 'African philosophy' I mean a set of texts, specifically the set of texts written by Africans and described as philosophical by their authors themselves...In other words, we are concerned solely with the philosophical intention of the authors not with the degree of its effective realization, which cannot easily be assessed. So for us African philosophy is a body of literature whose existence is undeniable, a bibliography which has grown constantly over the last thirty years or so...The essential point here is that we have produced a radically new definition of African philosophy, the criterion now being the geographical origin of the authors rather than an alleged specificity of content.[24]

The second definition, extracted from comments by the Nigerian philosopher Bodunrin on the activities of certain sages and professionals, focuses on (i) the location (i.e. place of origin or work), (ii) the (nature of the) action, (iii) the intention (of the author) and (iv) the medium used (i.e. writing):

> They are doing African philosophy only because the participants are Africans or are working in Africa and are interested in a philosophical problem from an African point of view...Philosophy is a conscious creation. One cannot be said to have philosophy in the strict sense of the word until one has consciously reflected on one's beliefs...Even if writing cannot be a precondition for philosophy, nevertheless, the role of writing in the creation of a philosophical tradition cannot be underrated.[25]

This is a slightly more relaxed version of Hountondji's definition. In this case there is more emphasis on philosophy as an activity and less emphasis on writing as a medium. Besides, location is not restricted to nationality. One does not have to be an African to produce African philosophy. One may satisfy the 'location-requirement' by merely working in Africa. Further, 'intention' is interpreted broadly as 'consciousness' and not specifically in terms of being conscious of your attempt to produce (nothing but) philosophy.

In a narrower (exclusive) sense, then, African philosophy may be seen as consisting in:

1. The documented (written) ideas or techniques of people in or from Africa for   philosophical purposes.   This definition still

focuses, broadly on location, intentions and writing, and captures much of Hountondji's and Bodunrin's definitions. In a broader sense, African philosophy may be perceived as follows:

2. The distinctive or characteristic way that Africans or people associated with Africa do philosophy by focusing on, say, certain particular questions, answers, issues, or techniques. This (second) definition stresses uniqueness and location, but not intentions or writing. It is slightly broader than the first, because in addition to not emphasizing writing or intentions, it does not restrict African philosophy to those who are—in some way—from Africa. They merely have to be associated with Africa in some way, since it leaves 'association' undefined; provided the philosophy produced stands out or can be differentiated from other kinds of philosophy (e.g. Indian, Chinese, American, and European philosophies).

There is a more inclusive definition of African philosophy that is offered in Chapter 2 and may be contrasted with the first two above. On this, third, conception, unlike the last (i.e. second) one above, African philosophy need not be completely unique. Further, unlike Hountondji's and Bodunrin's or the first definitions listed in the last paragraph, *African philosophy may be conceived mainly in terms of actions and consequences regardless of the medium, intentions, or place of origin or work.* The two-part definition of African philosophy I have in mind is along the following lines:

3. (a) Consequences: An African philosophy is the work or end-product of a person in his or her role as an African philosopher.
(b) Actions: An African philosopher is a person of whatever sex, race, or color who brings his or her peculiarly African experience (of, say, language, examples, topics, or beliefs) to bear, significantly, on the treatment of a philosophical question, issue or problem.

What remains undefined, here, because of the large number of alternative conceptions and approaches, is 'philosophy.' If it is permissible to reveal my biases here and now, I would have to say that philosophy is, from my point of view, deep and critical thinking about basic concepts or fundamental issues involved in any kind of activity or study.   It is, in my opinion, the use of arguments to address fundamental issues or concepts about life and/or knowledge. Alternatively, in a more historical and concrete perspective, it is a tradition of inquiry associated with—among others—ancient Greek scholars such as Socrates, Plato, Aristotle and their counterparts, predecessors, and successors, or, in short, those who think and act (generally but significantly) like them. It ought to be noted that even though this alternative conception of philosophy uses Greek scholars like Socrates and Aristotle as examples of philosophers, it does not restrict philosophical activity to Greece or Greeks.

7. AFRICAN PHILOSOPHY AND THE AKAN SOCIETY

Those whose works are collected in this anthology are all African philosophers in the third sense outlined above (as the bearing of African experiences on philosophical issues) or at least in one of the three senses outlined above. Hopefully this anthology qualifies as African philosophy in the third sense, even if it fails in the two more exclusive senses. The main advantage in limiting this anthology to African philosophers who work primarily in just two (Akan and English) languages of the approximately one thousand languages[26] used in Africa, is that it makes for cohesiveness, coherence, unity, and better dialogue. Further, if both the analytic (linguistic)[27] and post-analytic (hermeneutical)[28] philosophers are right in their claim that logic and philosophy are closely related to language or culture, this limitation of languages should be conducive to the production of better philosophy and, hence, better African philosophy. As we mentioned at the onset, all those included in this anthology are Ghanaians who belong to one ethnic group and speak the Akan language as a first language or as fluently as those who do.

The criterion used in the selection of authors in this text ensures that these authors are (i) Akan and, hence, African people who are philosophizing about various issues, or (ii) people who are philosophizing with or about Akan and, hence, African concepts, beliefs, issues, etc. Simply stated, since Akans constitute one of the main ethnic groups in Africa, it is philosophy by Akans and, hence, by Africans or philosophy about Akans and, thus, about Africans or, as is often the case, both.

This book is divided into four parts. The first part gives a general account of philosophy and a comparison of Western and African philosophical ideas with particular reference to the Akan society. Kwame Appiah attempts a characterization of philosophy, and Safro Kwame uses Appiah's characterization to address issues about the existence of African philosophy while taking issue with some of Appiah's conclusions. W. E. Abraham gives an account of the Akan worldview, and Kobina Oguah compares Akan theories with Western ones. Part II deals specifically with metaphysical issues such as the concepts of God, mind and persons. In this part, Boakye Danquah characterizes the Akan conception of God differently from Abraham, Amo Afer takes issue with Descartes' conception of mind, and Kwasi Wiredu presents an account of the Akan conception of mind that is opposed to Gyekye's as well as Oguah's. In part III Wiredu and Bedu-Addo debate the Akan conception of truth, and Gyekye compares Akan language and logic with those of English and Greek. Part IV deals with moral and political issues in Africa as a whole and the Akan society in particular. In this part of the text, Kwame Nkrumah argues for socialism in Africa and Kofi Busia argues against it, while Florence Dolphyne and Safro Kwame deal with feminism and business ethics in Akan and African societies. Note that 'Kwame' is, in Akan society, merely the name—usually though not always a middle name—of a male child born on a Saturday. Hence the relatively large number of 'Kwames' listed in this anthology merely indicates the—coincidental—'bias' in the editor's sample.

Each reading or chapter is preceded by an introduction (a prologue) which consists of (i) an editorial summary and (ii) an abridged version of the main arguments in the author's own words. The editorial summary is intended to outline the argument from the editor's point of view and provide the reader, especially the undergraduate student, with a general introduction to the text. The excerpts used to provide an abridged version of the argument are intended for undergraduates such as freshmen or freshwomen and sophomores who may want to read the original works themselves but find the full text either too long or too difficult. The full text is provided for seniors, graduate students, professional philosophers and others who may want to read the whole argument in its original form for themselves.

NOTES

1. *Topics in West African History* (London:Longman Group Limited, 1966), 58.
2. 'Asante and Fante A.D. 1000-1800' in *A Thousand Years of West African History,* edited by J.F. Ajayi and Ian Epie, (Ibadan: Nigeria:Ibadan University Press and Thomas Nelson and Sons Ltd, 1969), 166.
3. *Topics in West African History, op. cit.,* 59.
4. 'Asante and Fante A.D. 1000-1800' *op. cit.,* 167.
5. 'Extract from the Midnight Prouncement of Independence' in *Revolutionary Path* (London:Panaf Books Ltd., 1973), 121.
6. *ibid.,* 121.
7. On pages 16 and 28, respectively, of *Decolonising the Mind: The Politics of Language in African Literature* (Portsmouth, New Hampshire: Heinemann, 1986), Ngugi writes: "the domination of a people's language by the language of the colonizing nations was crucial to the domination of the mental universe of the colonized." "I believe that my writing in Gikuyu language, a Kenyan language, an African language, is part and parcel of the anti-imperialist struggles of Kenyan African people."
8. On page 6 of 'Philosophical Research and Teaching in Africa: Some Suggestions Towards Conceptual Decolonization,' *Proceedings of International Conference on Philosophy* 1980, Wiredu writes: "to decolonise our philosophical thinking means divesting our thought of all undue influences from the modes of thought of our erstwhile colonizers." (Page reference is to the original unpublished manuscript).
9. *An Essay on African Philosophical Thought: The Akan Conceptual Scheme* (New York: Cambridge University Press, 1987), 11-12.
10. *Philosophy and an African Culture* (Cambridge: Cambridge University Press, 1980), 36.
11. *ibid.*
12. 'On Defining African Philosophy' in *African Philosophy: The Essential Readings,* edited by T. Serequeberhan (New York: Paragon House, 1991), 97.
13. *Philosophy and an African Culture, op. cit.,* 36.
14. *African Religions and Philosophy* (Nairobi: Heineann Educational Books, 1969), 2.
15. 'African and Western Philosophy: A Comparative Study' in *Journal of African Studies* Vol. 4 No. 3, Fall 1977, 281. Reprinted in Chapter 4 of this volume.
16. *Sage Philosophy,* (Nairobi: ACTS Press, 1991), 9.
17. *The Mind of Africa,* (Chicago: The University of Chicago Press, 1962), 104.
18. *The Invention of Africa: Gnosis, Philosophy, and the Order of*

Knowledge (Bloomington & Indianapolis: Indiana University Press, 1988), ix.

19. See footnote 17 above and 20 below.

20. *African Philosophy: Myth and Reality* (Bloomington: Indiana University Press, 1983), 106.

21. *Necessary Questions: An Introduction to Philosophy* (Englewood Cliffs: Prentice-Hall Inc., 1989), 210. Reprinted in Chapter 1 of this volume.

22. 'On Defining African Philosophy,' *op. cit.*, 96.

23. *ibid.*, 97. Similarities between Wiredu's position and Appiah's are presented in Appiah's more complicated account in *In My Father's House* (New York: Oxford University Press): "If it means 'Is there folk philosophy in Africa?' the answer is: 'Africa has living people and cultures and therefore, of necessity, folk philosophies.'" (91). "Going beyond the descriptive project of ethnophilosophy is the real challenge of philosophers engaged with the problems of contemporary Africa; like Wiredu—and Hountondji—I aspire to a more truly critical discourse." (106).

24. *African Philosophy: Myth and Reality* (Bloomington: Indiana University Press, 1985), 33 & 66.

25. 'The Question of African Philosophy' in *African Philosophy: An Introduction,* edited by Richard Wright (Lanham, Maryland: University Press of America, Inc., 1984), 9 & 10.

26. According to the *Encyclopedia Britannica*, "the peoples inhabiting Africa probably speak more separate and distinct languages (800-1,000) than those of any other continent." See the *New Encyclopedia Britannica* 15th Edition, Volume 1, (Chicago: Encyclopedia Britannica, Inc., 1990), 131.

27. "Philosophy," Ludwig Wittgenstein for example writes on page 27 of *The Blue and the Brown Books* (London: Basil Blackwell), "may in no way interfere with the actual use of language; it can in the end only describe it."

28. Hermeneutics or, at least, one version of it claims that all thoughts, meanings and understanding are linguistically and historically conditioned. As Brice Wachterhauser points out, on page 6 of *Hermeneutics and Modern Philosophy* (New York: Albany State University of New York Press, 1986) it is the institution of language which ensures that all our understanding is historically mediated. Note, however, that even if both the analytic and hermeneutic philosophers are right, it does not mean that, ideally, philosophy, philosophical theses, and truths should be relative to language. The fact that they are often so conditioned, does not mean that they ought to. Indeed one suggestion is that the philosophic goal is to rise above the cultural and

linguistic pulls in an attempt to reach and grasp a relatively unconditioned truth or approximations of 'the absolute truth.' "If you wish to be a philosopher," Bertrand Russell writes in *The Art of Philosophizing and Other Essays* (New York: Philosophical Library Inc., 1989),(4), "you must try, as far as you can, to get rid of beliefs which depend solely upon the place and time of your education, and upon what your parents and schoolmasters told you." He continues: "No one can do this completely, and no one can be a perfect philosopher, but up to a point we can achieve it if we wish to." (*ibid.*, 4),(New York: Cambridge University Press), 11-12.

Correspondence

African Philosophy and the Akan Society: A Correspondence

Ti koro nkɔ agyina. **—One head does not hold a discussion. (Akan Proverb)**

PROLOGUE

The following pages contain some of the correspondence I had with Professors Kwasi Wiredu, Kwame Gyekye, Emmanuel Abraham, Kwame Appiah and Kobina Oguah between 1991 and 1994. They constitute a discussion on the concept and definition of African philosophy before Oguah's untimely death in Egypt in December 1994. Much of the correspondence consists of comments on and objections to the foregoing introduction titled "African Philosophy and the Akan Society." It starts with Wiredu's comment on a quotation which I made use of in section 4 of my introduction. The quotation in question is from Gyekye's *An Essay on African Philosophical Thought* asserting that "...it is indeed a mistake to maintain that the term 'African philosophy' should be used to cover only the philosophy...that is being produced by contemporary African philosophers." I hope the reader will find the correspondence helpful in understanding both the introduction and the perspectives on the question of the nature of African philosophy implicit in the contributions gathered in this volume.

Comments on African Philosophy and the Akan Society

Kwasi Wiredu

In remarking that "...it is indeed a mistake to maintain that the term 'African philosophy' should be used to cover only the philosophy...that is being produced by contemporary African philosophers,"[1] Kwame Gyekye is thinking of a statement I made in "On An African Orientation in Philosophy,"[2] that from the point of view of the imperative to "fashion philosophies based upon contemporary African experience with its many-sidedness" the term "'African philosophy' should be reserved for the results of that enterprise" etc.[3] Gyekye and others regularly omit the qualification "from this point of view," and assume that I am saying here that we cannot speak of traditional African philosophy. This in spite of the fact that on a previous page I had said "our peoples have their own traditional philosophies..."[4]

There is a flexibility in the use of phrases like 'African philosophy,' 'British philosophy,' 'American philosophy' etc. of which one can easily lose sight. The context of a particular use of such a phrase can affect its reference. If one is talking from the point of view of constructing philosophies for contemporary African living, then 'African philosophy' will refer to the activities of contemporary African philosophers. But this cannot possibly mean that there is no such thing as traditional African philosophy or that the contemporary African philosopher should not take account of it. On the contrary, in the article in question, I say he should.

Both Gyekye and I believe that African philosophy includes traditional African philosophy. We also both believe that it includes modern philosophizing which has a basis in our traditional thought, even if such philosophizing exploits some non-African intellectual resources. The difference between us is only that I believe that it can also include modern philosophizing by an African which does not have a basis in our traditional thought and Gyekye denies this. Thus my view does not include less; it includes more than Gyekye's. Gyekye and I would have the same position except for his insistence that if a philosophical effort does not have a basis in (traditional) African culture and experience then it does not belong to African philosophy. This requirement is needlessly restrictive, for African culture and experience have not remained the same as in olden times. Gyekye himself is a

Christian. That implies that a tremendous set of foreign metaphysical conceptions have become part of his intellectual make-up. Shouldn't modern African philosophy, among other things, examine those conceptions as part of its task?

On another matter, I absolutely do not subscribe to the view that the study of traditional African philosophy merely produces ethnography with philosophical pretensions, that real or serious philosophy cannot be a collective activity, or that writing is necessary for philosophy. The "collective" philosophy is the result of the thought of individual traditional African philosophers.[5] I have said in a number of places that there is a philosophical component to our traditional thought.[6] There is an inappropriate way of approaching it which might produce an ethnography in the guise of a philosophy, but I think that our traditional philosophy is very important for us, and I have said so. I do not hold that writing is necessary for philosophical thinking;[7] it is necessary for developing philosophy as an academic discipline, but that is not the same thing.

NOTES

1. *An Essay on African Philosophical Thought: The Akan Conceptual Scheme* (New York: Cambridge University Press, 1987), 11.
2. *Philosophy and an African Culture* (Cambridge:Cambridge University Press, 1980).
3. *ibid.*, 36.
4. *ibid.*, 28.
5. See, e.g., my 'On Defining African Philosophy' in *African Philosophy: The Essential Readings* edited by T. Serequeberhan, (New York: Paragon House, 1991), 96.
6. *ibid.*, 96-97.
7. *ibid.*, 94-95.

Comments on African Philosophy and the Akan Society

Kwame Gyekye

With regard to Safro Kwame's characterization of my position on African philosophy, he seems to think that I belong to what he calls the 'traditional' or 'ethno-philosophical' school. First, I do not properly understand the term 'ethnophilosophy,' and did not use it in my book. I have the impression, however, that those who use this term tend to assume or imply that African traditional philosophy is a 'collective' thought, that it is the work of an 'ethnos,' a collectivity, a group. While I believe in the existence of philosophy in the traditional setting of Africa, I reject without reservation the characterization of that philosophy as 'collective' (See pp. 24-29, 44-47 of my *An Essay on African Philosophical Thought*) and hence as 'ethnophilosophical.' My position is that traditional thought, *as* thought, is—and can only be—the work of individual intellects; it resulted from the activity of individuals whose names we simply do not know.

Second, I do not, as a corollary of the foregoing, understand why Kwame uses the terms 'traditional' and 'ethnophilosophical' disjunctively (See his introduction) as if the two terms can be used interchangeably. My view, to repeat, is that a traditional thought is not necessarily ethnophilosophical. Thus, the so-called 'individualist' elements that are harped upon by people like Hountondji, Appiah, Bodunrin, etc. as the main or only yardstick of philosophizing are not, to my mind, absent form the traditional genre of thought. This view of mine derives from the logic of the concept of thought itself. I do belong to the "traditional school" if by that he means those who believe that African traditional philosophy can be explored through a study of proverbs, myths, language, beliefs, institutions; yes. I do not belong to the traditional school if by that he means those who believe that traditional African thought is collective or 'ethnophilosophical' and totally lacks the 'individualist elements.'

Wiredu misinterprets me somewhat: I do not say that African philosophy should have a basis only in 'our traditional thought' or 'traditional African culture and experience.' My position is that philosophy is a cultural phenomenon, and I do not anywhere imply that that phenomenon is to be restricted to the traditional. I fully agree with Wiredu that "African culture and experience have not remained the same as in olden times." This of course is indisputable; it is in fact very obvious. My position is that for a contemporary (modern) philosophical work also to be considered 'African,' it must have a basis in African culture and experience. By 'African culture' here, I mean the contemporary culture, including the changes traditional values are going through in the wake of the pressures being pounded on them by the ethos of contemporary life, and would naturally include alien metaphysical systems that have gained *footing* in our pristine culture. On p. 39 of my book, *An Essay on African Philosophical Thought*, I write: "Given the dynamic nature of culture and experience, however, philosophy cannot ossify. For this reason, and in view of the relevance of philosophy to the affairs of men and society, it must be considered as a conceptual response to basic human problems at different epochs." Note my words 'dynamic,' 'different epochs.' These terms surely imply that I do not mean African culture to be limited to the traditional, or to be taken as, in Wiredu's words, "the same as in olden times." Also, on p. 42 I write: "Thus, a modern African philosophy would comprise the conceptual response to the problems and circumstances of modern African societies as well as, interpretations...of concepts in African traditional thought." In my published Inaugural Lecture (*The Unexamined Life: Philosophy and the African Experience*. Accra: Ghana Universities Press, 1988, 13-14) I write: "It is the task of modern African philosophers to use philosophy constructively not only to deal with the consequences of colonialism on African society and culture, but also to face squarely the challenges of industrialization and modernization. To do this most effectively it is imperative that they philosophize with the contemporary situation in mind, that they give conceptual interpretation to contemporary experience." Africa's contemporary experience is of course a many-sided experience. On the whole, I think Wiredu and I are in much agreement. But I strongly believe that for a modern philosophy to count as African philosophy, it must have a basis in African culture as such (but not just traditional culture). It seems to me that the view of philosophy as a cultural phenomenon is a widely accepted view. This should be so, for all philosophizing starts out from a culture and an experience.

Additional Comments on African Philosophy and the Akan Society

March 2, 1992

Dear S. Kwame,

At the end of my rejoinder to Wiredu's rejoinder, I said: "On the whole, I think Wiredu and I are in much agreement." One should consider the implications of the phrases "on the whole" and "in much agreement." I do not accept the view put forward by Hountondji in his book *African Philosophy: Myth and Reality* (Bloomington: Indiana University Press, 1983) that if an African philosopher writes on Plato or Marx he is producing an authentic African work. I do not know Wiredu's attitude to this proposition of Hountondji's, for instance.

Yours sincerely,

Kwame Gyekye, FGA.

November 8, 1994

Dear S. K.,

(a) My attitude to Hountondji's position is expressed explicitly in "On defining African Philosophy." See Serequeberhan (editor) *African Philosophy: The Essential Readings,* pages 92 and 93, where I say: "Among the writings he [Hountondji] cites to illustrate his point are a number of my articles, including my "Kant's Synthetic A Priori in Geometry and the Rise of Non-Euclidean Geometries," but I hope it is not ungracious on my part to urge a qualification. If an interest in the sort of problems in the philosophy of mathematics that I discussed in that article never develops in African thought, and no tradition emerges on our continent into which my article might naturally fit, then it would not be unjust to exclude it from African Philosophy. The philosophy of a people is always a tradition; and a tradition presupposes a certain minimum of organic relationship among (at least some of) its elements. If a tradition of modern philosophy is to develop and flourish in Africa, there will have to be philosophical interaction and cross-fertilization among contemporary African workers in philosophy. Of course, since the future is infinite, there is always the possibility that, however isolated a part (or the whole) of a person's philosophical work may currently be in the context of the thought of his own area of origin, it might eventually come to have a place in it. But if, at this particular point in time, the question is raised whether the article in question can be said to be 'part and parcel' of African philosophy, the answer must be, I suggest, that, while it is certainly 'part and parcel' of the existing corpus of African writings in philosophy, the question is nevertheless somewhat premature, since the African tradition of modern philosophy is still in the making."

  (b) If Gyekye does not insist that if a philosophical effort does not have a basis in (traditional) African culture and experience then it does not belong to African philosophy, that is a welcome change from some of the things he said in his *Essay*:

(i) By modern African philosophy I refer to the philosophy that is being produced by contemporary African philosophers, but which *reflects* or has a *basis* in African experience, thought categories, and cultural values (p. 32).

(ii) …if a philosophy produced by a modern African has no basis in the culture and experience of African peoples, then it cannot appropriately claim to be an *African* philosophy, even though it was created by an African philosopher (p. 33).

(iii) [...a distinction must be made between traditional African philosophy and modern African philosophy.] The latter, to be African and have a basis in African culture and experience, must have a connection with the former, the traditional (p. 12).

  Assertions (i) and (ii), which are equivalent, together with (iii), without a doubt, yield the condition under discussion. Even with the most progressive construal of the phrase 'African culture and experience,' the requirement that there must be 'a connection with the traditional' was still too restrictive. But, given, Gyekye's present remarks, I am glad to acknowledge that, 'on the whole,' he and I are in 'much agreement.'

Sincerely,

Kwasi Wiredu.

(By the way, I always thought that I agreed a hundred percent with Abraham on these matters.—K. W.)

December 23, 1994.

Dear Dr. Kwame:

Very many thanks for sending me part of Wiredu's communication of November 8, 1994 that relates to my conception of the nature of modern African philosophy. The remarks in my correspondence of December 23, 1991 do *not* in any way imply a change in my position on the nature of a genuine African philosophy, as Wiredu thinks. The reason is that I had not maintained in my *An Essay on African Philosophical Thought* that modern African philosophy must be tethered to African traditional thought. So, I do not, on my part, see the "welcome change" he sees in the remarks of my 1991 communication.

Of the many statements I make in *An Essay* that express my position on what a genuine African philosophy should be, Wiredu fastens on the one on p. 12 which appears to require "a connection with the traditional" as condition for a piece of modern philosophical work to be African. It must be recalled, however, that the context of that statement was a critical response to the view held by Wiredu, Bodunrin, and Hountondji that African philosophy (in their own words, respectively) "is still in the making", or "is yet in the making," or "is yet to come" (see *An Essay*, p. 8)—a view which implies the nonrecognition of the philosophical component of African traditional thought. (Wiredu, in his communication of November 6, 1991 has clarified his position here). It, thus, also implies a rejection of African traditional philosophical thought as part of the *history* of philosophical thought in Africa.

For me, however, a history of African philosophy will have to include the philosophical productions of the past African traditional thinkers (or, sages). Second, it is an indisputable fact that a good many of the elements of traditional culture (including thought categories) have been accepted into modernity; this is true also of Western modernity. As I pointed out on p. 42 of *An Essay*, "most of the traditional concepts and values have, generally speaking, not relaxed their grip on modern African life and thought." After asserting that "...modern African philosophers must try to provide conceptual responses to the problems confronting contemporary African societies; their philosophical output or a greater part of it—if it is to be African—must reflect the contemporary situation," I add "But modern philosophers cannot afford to neglect the concepts and values in African traditional life and thought, which after all constitute the background of the modern African cultural experience" (p. 40; see also, pp. 32-33). Thus, by "connection"

I am only calling for some analytic attention to be paid to the traditional thought categories, values, outlooks, and so on—but not, of course, to the neglect of nontraditional (modern, contemporary) concepts or issues, as a way of providing a continuity in the African philosophical trajectory. Note that the expression "must reflect the contemporary situation" in a foregoing quotation does not in any way suggest a "connection" with the traditional.

I did not intend to make this concern for continuity—for history—part of the criteria for what would, in my view, count as genuine modern African philosophy. In fact Chapter One of *An Essay* where the statement about the "connection" is made is not at all intended to provide criteria for an authentic African philosophy; it is subsequent chapters that do so. It was not my intention to imply that every piece of philosophical work by the modern African philosopher should involve inquiry into, or reference to, the traditional: such a position would have been inconsistent with my emphasis on the need to perceive philosophy as a 'conceptual response' to basic human problems at different epochs (*An Essay*, pp. 39, 40, 42); some of the modern philosophical issues or concepts may not have occurred to the traditional thinker.

My substantive position on what I, on my part, would count as a genuine African philosophy is stated in detail in Chapter 2.4 (i.e. pp. 32-43), subtitled, quite significantly, as "On defining African philosophy: some proposals" (see also, pp. 211-212, well at the end of the book). My position, already articulated in *An Essay* (and not in the communication of December 1991) has been that a modern African philosophy must be linked to African culture and experience. I do not think that such a position is "too restrictive" of the nature or scope of modern African philosophy. For, when I speak of African culture, I have in mind the ideas, beliefs, values, practices, outlooks, habits, and institutions endogenously created or exogenously inherited, the latter (however) having *taken root* in the entire way of life and thought of the African people, having, thus, become part of an African tradition (*An Essay*, p.37). I am making an elaborate analysis of the notions of culture and tradition in a forthcoming book now under preparation.

All the best.

Yours sincerely,

Kwame Gyekye, FGA.

April 11, 1992

Dear Dr. Kwame,

I noticed in your discussion with Professor Wiredu your expression of uncertainty as to my views on the fact of an African philosophy. You will notice from my 'African Philosophy: its proto-history and future history' in G. Floistad's *Contemporary Philosophy: A New Survey* Vol. 5, if you have had a chance to glance at it, that I do very much believe that there is an African philosophy, and hold that the disagreements on that question result principally from adherence to different paradigms of the subject. In fact, to-day, as in the very beginning, philosophers hold to conflicting paradigms; it is only a matter of decades ago that practitioners of analytical philosophy and continental philosophy looked upon each other with considerable suspicion.

Sincerely,

W. Emmanuel Abraham.

April 16, 1992

Dear Safro,

I have made some of the points that Kwame Anthony Appiah makes in *In My Father's House* (New York, Oxford University Press, 1992) about ethnophilosophy, by which he means 'folk philosophy' or 'collective philosophy' which he thinks, like I do, as against Hountondji, should be made the starting point of a contemporary philosophizing in Africa. Hountondji seems to think that the so-called ethnophilosophy is good for nothing. Appiah does not think that way, even though he urges a more critical approach to the study of it.

In my book (*An Essay on African Philosophical Thought: The Akan Conceptual Scheme*, New York, Cambridge University Press, 1987), I do attempt evaluation of African (Akan) concepts, values etc. This is probably the reason why it does not come under attack in Appiah's book. But surely we need to understand the ideas and arguments of thinkers before we launch critical/evaluative attacks on them, if necessary. A critique of Aristotle's conception of the soul, for instance, will misfire if that conception is misinterpreted or misunderstood.

When all is said and done, the emergence of African philosophy will, in my view, depend on individual African philosophers' critically examining concepts and values in African thought and culture, including a philosophical reflection on contemporary experience of the African people. Hitherto most of us have been talking about African philosophy, instead of *doing* African philosophy.

Yours sincerely,

Kwame Gyekye, FGA.

June 30, 1992

Dear Safro:

I do basically think Gyekye's book, *An Essay on African Philosophical Thought* (New York, Cambridge University Press, 1987), does critically evaluate as it proceeds, so that I do not think that my sterner criticisms (in *In My Father's House*) apply to him at all. All I would say in partial disagreement is that the idea of an Akan view still strikes me as wrong, for reasons I give in the book (*In My Father's House*). One way to put it would be this: I like what he does, but I don't agree with his meta-philosophical account of what he is doing. I think what he is doing is using resources within Akan culture for thinking about certain important questions, identifying a cluster of views associated with elders in a certain part of the culture, and exploring them. He expresses himself, for example, as a dualist who finds a monistic mind-body scheme: and this is not just exposition of somebody's ideas but critical analysis.

With all good wishes,

K. Anthony Appiah.

September 29, 1992

Ɔpanyin Kwame,

In all fairness, these criticisms referred to by Appiah in *In My Father's House* (parts of which are reprinted in Chapter 5 of this volume), must not be confined to African Philosophy but also to (a) Indian Philosophy, (b) Chinese Philosophy, (c) Islamic Philosophy, (d) Jewish Philosophy, (f) the pseudo-psychological observations of Descartes, Locke, Hume, etc., and (g) Pre-Socratic Philosophy. He appears dangerously close to decertifying all philosophical systems except Analytical Philosophy. I cannot protest much, since I similarly erred as a younger man.

Kobina Oguah.

Chapter 1

Philosophy and Necessary Questions

Kwame Anthony Appiah

Asɛm nko, nyansa nko. —It is one thing to make a statement and another, to express wisdom. (Akan proverb)

PROLOGUE

Kwame Anthony Appiah is a native of the Ashanti region of the Akan society in Ghana. He grew up in that region of Ghana where he had his early studies before studying philosophy at Cambridge University in England. Upon graduating, he went back to Ghana in 1975 to teach philosophy at the University of Ghana, Legon. He then returned to Cambridge to do his doctoral research in the philosophies of language and mind. He moved to the United States in 1981, teaching African and African-American Studies and philosophy at Yale, Cornell and, now, at Harvard University, where he is a Professor of African-American Studies.

According to Anthony Appiah, philosophy concerns itself with questions which are necessary because they are (1) questions which are in fact answered in all cultures, and (2) questions which ought to be answered in order to gain a general and systematic understanding of the central problems of human life. Answers to necessary questions in the first case constitute folk philosophy and need not be justified, consistent, or written down. Answers to questions in the second case constitute formal philosophy and require justification by evidence and reasons, consistency and, hence, writing.

Here is a summary of his argument in his own words:

"I shall be arguing that many problems that trouble us in ordinary life—down in the city, rather than up in the tower—can only be answered if we first ask the more fundamental questions that are the hallmark of philosophy...In one sense, the philosophy of a person or group is just the sum of the beliefs they hold about the central questions of human life; about mind and matter, knowledge and truth, good and bad, right and wrong; about human nature and the universe we inhabit...There are many continuities between conversation about these universal questions—what we might call folk-philosophy—and the kind of discussion that has filled the chapters of this book...If any thought about these questions counts as philosophy, then philosophy is likely to be found in every human society, past and present—wherever there are people struggling to live and make sense of their lives...And, as we shall see, much of what we take to be typical of formal philosophy derives in large measure from the fact that formal philosophy, unlike folk-philosophy, is written...Writing makes possible a kind of consistency that pre-literate culture cannot demand...Without literacy it is hard to see how formal philosophy could have got started: it is not a sufficient condition for formal philosophy, but it certainly seems to be necessary...The questions I have asked in this book are some of those that are important to philosophy now...If you share our vision of a general and systematic understanding of the central problems of human life, they are questions you will want to ask also. I hope I have persuaded you that you do share that vision. And if you do, you will be irresistibly drawn to the questions of philosophy. In that sense they are, indeed, necessary questions."

Philosophy and Necessary Questions

Anthony Kwame Appiah

1. INTRODUCTION

In many a village around the world, in cultures traditional and industrialized, people gather in the evenings to talk. In pubs and bars, under trees in the open air in the tropics, and around fires in the far North and South of our globe, people exchange tales; tell jokes; discuss issues of the day; argue about matters important and trivial. Listening to such conversations in cultures other than your own, you learn much about the concepts and theories people use to understand their experience, and you learn what values they hold most dear.

It would be natural enough, as we built a picture of those values, theories, and concepts in another culture, to describe what we were doing as coming to understand the philosophy of that culture. In one sense, the philosophy of a person or a group is just the sum of the beliefs they hold about the central questions of human life; about mind and matter, knowledge and truth, good and bad, right and wrong; about human nature and the universe we inhabit.

At their most general, as I say, these beliefs are naturally called "philosophy" and there is nothing wrong in using the word this way. There are many continuities between conversation about these universal questions—what we might call folk-philosophy and the kind of discussion that has filled the chapters of this book.

All human cultures, simple or complex, large or small, industrial or pre-industrial, have many of the concepts we have discussed—or, at least, concepts much like them. Issues about what is good and right, what we know and mean, what it is to have a mind and to think, can arise for people living in the simplest of societies. Indeed, at least some of the problems of the philosophy of mind, of epistemology, and of ethics surely do arise naturally for any curious member of our species. We might suppose, as a result, that people have reflected on these questions everywhere and always. If any thought about these questions counts as philosophy, then philosophy is likely to be found in every human society, past and present—wherever there are people struggling to live—and make sense of—their lives.

But it is important, too, that there are discontinuities between folk-philosophy and the discussions of this book. Philosophy, as it is practiced and taught in modern Western universities, is a distinctive institution that has evolved along with Western societies. I mentioned that science—unlike minds and knowledge and language—has not existed in every human culture. The problems of the philosophy of science occur only in cultures that have the institution of science: and just so, political philosophy and the philosophy of law raise questions that only matter if you live—as not all human beings have lived—in a society organized as a state.

The differences between folk-philosophy and the discussions of this book are not, however, simply differences in subject matter. Along with the new problems of the philosophy of science and law, social change has also produced new ways of tackling the old problems. One way to focus on what we have learned about the character of modern Western philosophy, the kind of philosophy that I have tried to introduce in this book, is to contrast it both with the folk-philosophy of other cultures and with other styles of thought in our own culture. In doing this it will help to have a name for the style of philosophical thought that I have been engaged in. I suggest that we call it formal philosophy, to contrast it with the informal style of folk-philosophy.

In the next few sections I am going to contrast formal philosophy with the traditional thought of pre-literate cultures, with Western religious thought, and with science. Each of these contrasts will allow us not only to learn more about philosophy, but also to ask some important philosophical questions.

2. TRADITIONAL THOUGHT

If you have ever read any anthropology, you are bound, I think, to be struck by the astonishing range of ways in which human beings have tried to understand our world. The Mbuti [of Zaire], for example, think of the forest around them as a person—what we might call a god—and they think that the forest will take care of them. If they have a run of bad luck in their hunting, they suppose not that the forest is trying to harm them, but that it has lost interest in them; that it has, as they say, "gone to sleep." When this happens they try to waken the forest by singing for it, and they believe that if their songs please the forest, their luck will turn.

Not only do most Westerners find such beliefs surprising, they are likely to think that they are unreasonable. Why should a forest care about anything, let alone human singing? And even if it did, how could it determine the success of a hunt for honey or for game?

This sense that Mbuti beliefs are unreasonable is likely to grow when you are told that the Mbuti know very well that other people who live nearby, people with whom they have complex social relationships, believe quite different things. Their neighbors, in the villages on the edge of the Ituri rain-forest where they live, believe that most bad luck is due to witchcraft—the malevolent action of special people whom they regard as witches. In these circumstances, it is surely very curious that the Mbuti do not worry about whether they are right.

Both the fact that the Mbuti know that other people believe different things, and the fact that this does not seem to concern them, mark their way of thinking off from that of Western cultures. Most Westerners would worry if they discovered that people in the next town got on very well without believing in electricity. We think our general beliefs can be justified: and if others challenge our beliefs, we are inclined to seek evidence and reasons for our position and to challenge their reasons and their evidence in response. The anthropologist and philosopher Robin Horton has used the term **adversarial** to describe this feature of Western cultures. We tend to treat our intellectual disputes like our legal disputes, trading evidence and argument in a vigorous exchange, like adversaries on a field of intellectual battle. Horton uses the term adversarial to contrast this Western approach to argument with what the Nigerian Nobel Laureate, Wole Soyinka, calls the **accommodative** style of many traditional cultures. Traditional people are often willing to accept and accommodate the different views of other groups.

Indeed, the Mbuti, like many traditional peoples, tend not to give the justification of their general beliefs much thought at all. If we asked them why they believed in the god-forest, they would probably tell us, as many people in many cultures have told many anthropologists, that they believe it because it is what their ancestors taught them. Indeed many traditional cultures have proverbs which say, in effect, "everything we know was taught us by our ancestors."

Justifying beliefs by saying they have the authority of tradition is one of the practices that demarcates traditional cultures from formal philosophy. Even where I have cited distinguished philosophical authorities from the past—the "ancestors" of Western philosophy like Plato and Descartes—I have considered their arguments and tried to understand and criticize them. The fact that Plato or Descartes or Kant said something is not, by itself, a reason to believe it.

We should be careful, however, not to exaggerate the differences in the way Mbuti people and Westerners *ordinarily* justify their beliefs. Most of what you and I believe, we too believe because our parents or teachers told it to us. Some of the differences between the Mbuti and formal philosophy reflect differences not so much between traditional and Western people, as between formal and informal thought.

Nevertheless, Westerners (and Western-trained people generally) are more likely to ask even their parents and teachers not just *what* they believe but *why* they believe it. And when Westerners ask why we should believe something, what they want is not just an authority, but some evidence or argument. This is especially true in formal philosophy. Throughout this book I have tried to offer and examine reasons for believing the claims I have made; and the philosophers I have discussed have done the same.

I have also tried to proceed *systematically*. I have tried, that is, to connect arguments made on one subject—fallibilism, for example—with other apparently remote questions —the inevitability that our courts will sometimes punish the innocent, the underdetermination of empirical theory. And this shows up another contrast with traditional thought. Though anthropologists often try to make a system out of the thought of traditional peoples, they do not usually get much help from the people whose thought they study.

Sir Edward Evans-Pritchard, one of the founders of modern cultural anthropology, attempted, in his book *Witchcraft, Oracles and Magic Among the Azande* to explain the theory of witchcraft implicit in the practice of the Azande people of southern Sudan. But when he discovered inconsistencies in their claims—it turned out that if you followed the Zande beliefs about the inheritance of witchcraft through, everybody was a witch!—they didn't seem to be very concerned about it.

The urge to give arguments and evidence for what you believe, and to make your beliefs consistent with each other so that they form a system, is one of the marks of formal philosophy. We can say that formal philosophy aims to be systematic. But though this urge to theorize is important to philosophy, it is also central, as we saw, to science; and it is not hard to see that it is central to the whole range of modern intellectual life. In short, the systematic character of philosophy is not special to the subject. It is an outgrowth of the systematic nature of our current modes of thought.

The reason why the Azande did not theorize systematically about witchcraft in the way that Evans-Pritchard did is that they did not want to. Their lives made sense to them in terms of the theories they had, and, so far as they could see, there was plenty of evidence for their beliefs. The evidence that witchcraft exists was as obvious to them as the evidence that electricity exists no doubt seems to you. People who were ill got better after the application of spiritual medicines; people died regularly after their enemies had appealed to powerful spirits. Of course, not everyone who is treated with spiritual medicine gets better; but then the lights don't always go on when you turn on a switch! The reason why the Zande did not think much about the evidence for their theories, in other words, is that they had no reason to suspect that they might be wrong.

Now I imagine that you have been supposing that it is quite obvious that the Azande not only *might* be wrong, but that they *are*. You probably also think that your belief that they are wrong is one that you can justify with evidence and reason, and that Azande people who respected rational argumentation and sensible principles of evidence would eventually come to agree with you.

If I had started not with Zande beliefs about witchcraft but with their moral beliefs, by contrast, I suspect you would suppose that the same would not apply. I suspect, in other words, that you probably believe there is some truth in moral relativism but none in relativism about such factual questions as whether there are any witches. Yet just as moral relativists hold that what is good depends on who you are or where or in what culture or when you live, so some people have recently argued that what is true about factual questions depends on who you are (or in what culture or when you live).

Relativism about factual matters is usually called *cognitive relativism*; and if you are not a cognitive relativist, then it is an important philosophical question whether you can defend your position. Relativism is important because its truth would set limits on the role of evidence and reason; and evidence and reason are central to formal philosophy. So it is important, too, that it turns out to be harder than you might think to defend the non-relativity of factual beliefs: and if we imagine what it would be like to argue with a convinced Azande, we shall see why.

3. ARGUING WITH THE AZANDE

Azande beliefs about witchcraft were rich and complex; but it does not take more than a brief summary to get to the heart of the difficulty I want to address. So, let me try to give you an idea of their main beliefs in a brisk summary. The Azande believed that *mangu*—which is the word that Evans-Pritchard translated as "witchcraft"—was a substance in the bodies of witches. *Mangu* produced a spiritual power that could cause ill-health or other misfortune to its victims, even without the conscious intention of the witch. *Mangu's* physical manifestation was supposed to be a black substance—perhaps in the gall-bladder—which was inherited from males to males and females to females.

Witches were supposed to do their evil in two major ways. Sometimes the soul of a witch travelled through the air—visible in the daytime only to other witches but at night visible to all as a flame—and devoured the "soul of the flesh of the victim. On other occasions, witches projected "witchcraft things" into their victims, causing pain in the relevant place; but this substance could be removed by the professional healers and seers whom Evans-Pritchard called "witch-doctors."

These witch-doctors were experts in the use of various kinds of Zande magic; but most ordinary Zande people knew many spells and rituals that were intended to help them control their world by, for example, bringing rain, curing disease, ensuring success in hunting or in farming, or guaranteeing the fertility of men and women.

Witchcraft, for the Azande, was involved in the explanation of all those unfortunate happenings that do people harm. But the Azande did not deny the role of other kinds of influence. They understood the interaction of witchcraft and other causes of harm through an analogy with hunting. When they went elephant hunting, they called the man who plunged in the second spear *umbaga*: and he and the man who plunged in the first spear were held to be jointly responsible for the elephant's death. The Azande compared witchcraft to *umbaga*. When, for example, a man was killed by a spear in war, they said that witchcraft was the second spear: for sometimes a spear thrust does not kill its victim and the "second spear" is needed to explain why, in this case, the man died.

If you asked the Azande what evidence they had for the existence of witchcraft, they would point, first, to many of the misfortunes of human life, and ask how else they could be explained. But they would also tell you that they had a number of ways of discovering more precisely how witchcraft operated and these various ways of finding out about witchcraft they called *soroka*, which Evans-Pritchard translated as "oracles."

The Zande used many kinds of oracles: ways of finding out what was going on in the world of spirits, in general, and witchcraft, in particular. They regarded dreams about witchcraft as oracles, for example. But the highest in the hierarchy of oracles, in terms of reliability, was their "poison oracle;" and they used it regularly in their attempts to discover who had bewitched them.

The oracle involved administering a special poison to young chicks: and then questions were put to it and whether the chicken died determined the answer. In a typical case an Azande man—and, in Zandeland, it always was an adult male—would administer the poison to a chicken and ask the oracle whether So-and-so had bewitched them. If the fowl died, the accusation was confirmed but the question had now to be put the other way round, so that, on the second test, it was the fowl's *survival* that confirmed that there had been witchcraft. Thus, on the first test, the oracle's operator might say "Have I been bewitched, oracle? If so, kill the chicken." And on the second test, he would say "Have I been bewitched? If so, save the chicken."

Even given this little sketch of some Zande beliefs, you might think that you had enough to begin to persuade a reasonable Zande person that they were wrong. After all, surely, on many occasions, the oracle would give contradictory answers. Suppose someone put the two questions I just suggested to an oracle and the chicken died both times? Wouldn't that show the oracle was unreliable?

Unfortunately, things are not so simple. Like many traditional people, the Azande believed that there were many taboos that should be observed in every important area of their lives; and the oracle was no exception. If the operator had broken a taboo—for example, by eating certain prohibited foods—the oracle was supposed to lose its power. So, if an oracle proved unreliable, they could say that one of the operators had broken a taboo. But they also believed that powerful witchcraft could undermine the working of the oracle: that would be another possible explanation for the failure. In short, when an oracle failed the Azande had plenty of resources within their theories to explain it.

Evans-Pritchard noticed this feature of Zande thought; and he said that the reason why they didn't notice that their oracles were unreliable was that they were able to make these explanatory moves, which he called *secondary elaborations*. And Evans-Pritchard observed that "the perception of error in one mystical notion in a particular situation merely proves the correctness of another and equally mystical notion." The problem is that it is not so clear that, in making these secondary elaborations, the Zande were being unreasonable.

For, as Evans-Pritchard noticed, the system of witchcraft, oracles and other kinds of magic formed a coherent system of mutually supporting beliefs.

> Death is proof of witchcraft...The results which magic is supposed to produce actually happen after the rites are performed... Hunting-magic is made and animals are speared...Magic is only made to produce events which are likely to happen in any case—e.g. rain is produced in the rainy season and held up in the dry season...[Magic] is seldom asked to produce a result by itself but is associated with empirical action that does in fact produce it—e.g. a prince gives food to attract followers and does not rely on magic alone.

And he also gave many more examples of the ways in which they can explain failures when they occur.

Consider, now, for the sake of comparison, what you would say if you did a simple experiment in chemistry which came out differently on two successive occasions. You would say, quite reasonably, that you had probably not done the experiment quite the same way both times. Perhaps one of your test-tubes wasn't quite clean; perhaps you hadn't measured the reagents quite carefully enough; and so on. In other words, it would take systematic observation, experimentation (where possible) and thought.

Now why shouldn't an Azande say to you that your explanation here is just as much a case of defending one mystical notion—the idea of chemical reactions—in terms of another—the idea that there is an invisible quantity of some reagent in the test-tube? Your theory, too, constitutes a set of "mutually supporting beliefs": and that, far from being an argument against it, seems to be a point in its favor. Nevertheless, unless you already have some faith that the world is made of atoms and molecules which react according to definite rules, there is no obvious reason why a few experiments should persuade you of this general theory. And, similarly, there is no reason why the failure of even a good number of experiments should make you give it up.

At this point you may recall... that our theories are **underdetermined** by the evidence for them. This meant that the contents of our empirical beliefs are not fully determined by the evidence we have for them. I argued also that much of the language we use for describing the world is theory laden the way we commit ourselves to the existence of objects and properties beyond our sensory evidence is partly determined by the theories we happen to have. What Evans-Pritchard noticed was, in effect, a consequence of the fact that Zande observation was theory-laden also. They interpreted what they heard and saw in terms of their belief in witchcraft. But if theory-ladenness is a feature their theories share with our scientific beliefs, that fact is not, by itself, an argument against them.

In practice, then, we should have to do more than point to a few cases where the oracle seemed to give inconsistent results if we were to persuade a reasonable Azande person that their theory was wrong. What more would it take?

The answer, surely, is that it would take the collection of a lot of data on oracles; examining carefully the question whether anyone had broken a taboo: looking to see if we could find grounds to support the claim that witchcraft was interfering in those cases where the oracle failed and no one had broken a taboo; checking to see that the reason one chicken on this day died and the other did not was not that different quantities of poison had been administered; and so on.

Notice that we could do all this, while still using the language of the Azande to describe what we were doing. We would not need to assume our own theories were correct. We could use our theories in order to see if we could construct cases where the oracle would fail; but we would still leave it up to the actual experiments to decide whether we were right. Because we share with the Azande some of the concepts we use for describing the world—*chicken, person, death*—we could agree that, in some cases, the results had come out in ways that didn't fit Zande theory; in others, that it had come out in ways that didn't fit ours.

In the long run, after much experimentation of this kind, some Azande might come to give up their theory. But there is no guarantee that this would happen. For, just as it is always possible for us to explain away experimental results by supposing that something—though we are not sure what—went wrong, so this move is open to the Azande, also. Nothing I have suggested presupposes that it has to be us that raise doubts about Azande beliefs. Because the problem of consistency with the evidence can be put without presupposing that Zande theory is false, it would have been open to them to carry out these experiments.

So, perhaps, if the Azande were wrong, they could have found it out for themselves.

I shall return to the question of whether we should expect the Azande to come, after experiment and systematic thought, to agree with us; and not simply to assume a development of their own witchcraft theory. But it is worth spending a little time first to consider why it is unlikely that the Azande would have done either of these things on their own. For even if the Azande of Evans-Pritchard's day had started to worry about their beliefs, they would have been severely limited in their ability to theorize about them and to carry out these sorts of experiments—not because they were not clever enough, but because they lacked at least one essential tool. For the Azande did not have writing. And, as we shall see, much of what we take to be typical of formal philosophy derives in large measure from the fact that formal philosophy, unlike folk-philosophy, is written.

4. THE SIGNIFICANCE OF LITERACY

It is very striking that the founders of Western philosophy—Socrates and Plato—stand at the beginning of the development of Western writing. There is something emblematic in the fact that Plato, the first philosopher whose writings are still important to us, wrote dialogues which reported in *writing* the *oral* discussions of Socrates. Plato made Socrates important to us by writing down his thought. The fact that formal philosophy is written is tremendously important, and it pays to think about why this is.

Imagine yourself in a culture without writing and ask yourself what difference it would make to your thought. Consider, for example, how you would think about some of the questions we have discussed in this book. Could you remember every step in any of the arguments I gave for the claim that knowledge is not justified true belief, if you were not able to read and re-read the examples, to think about them and then read them again? Could you check, without written words to look at, that what you had decided about the nature of the mind was consistent with what you thought about knowledge?

Writing makes possible a kind of consistency that pre-literate culture cannot demand. Write down a sentence and it is there, in principle, for ever: and that means that if you write down another sentence inconsistent with it, you can be caught out. It is this fact that is at the root of the possibility of the sort of extended philosophical argument that I have made again and again in this book. Philosophical argument, is rooted in a philosophical tradition. But this is possible only because we can re-read—and thus re-think—the arguments of our philosophical forebears.

It is this fact that is at the root of the possibility of our adversarial style. How often have we seen Perry Mason ask the stenographer to read back from the record? In the traditional culture the answer can only be "What record?" In the absence of writing, it is not possible to compare our ancestors' theories in their actual words with ours. Given the limitations of quantity imposed by oral transmission, we do not even have a detailed knowledge of what those theories were. We know more of Plato's thought two millennia ago about epistemology than we know about the views of the entire population of the Azande a century ago about anything.

The Azande would have had great difficulty in testing their system of beliefs in the way I have suggested because they had no way of recording their experiments and their theorizing about the world. That is the main reason why systematic theorizing of the kind that we have been engaged in would have been difficult for the Azande.

But literacy does not matter only for our ability to examine arguments over and over again and to record the results of experiment and experience. It has important consequences also for the style of the language that we use. Those of us who read and write learn very quickly how different in style written communication is from oral. Indeed, we learn it so early and so well that we need to be reminded of some of the really important differences.

Consider, for example, the generality and abstractness of many of the arguments I have offered and how much these features depend upon writing. A simple example will help make this dependence clear.

Suppose you found a scrap of paper, which contained the following words:

> On Sundays here, we often do what Joe is doing over there. But it is not normal to do it on this day. I asked the priest whether it was permissible to do it today and he just did this.

A reasonable assumption would be that someone had transcribed what someone was saying. And why? Because all these words—"I," "here," "there," "this," "today," and even "Joe" and "the priest"—are what logicians call **indexicals**. You need the context in which the sentence is uttered to know what they are referring to: you need to know who the speaker or writer was to know what "I" refers to; you need to know where that speaker was to know where "here" refers to; and so on.

When we write we have to fill in much of what context provides when we speak. We must do this not only so that we avoid the uncertainty of indexicals, but also because we cannot assume that our readers will share our knowledge of our situation; and because, if they do not, they cannot ask us. We can now see why trying to avoid these possibilities for misunderstanding is bound to move you towards abstract and general questions, and away from questions that are concrete and particular. The need for generality becomes dear if we consider the difference between the judgments of a traditional Zande oracle, and those of experts in a written tradition. A traditional thinker can get away with saying that if three oracles have answered that the carver, Kisanga, has stolen a chicken, then he has. But in a written tradition, all sorts of problems can arise.

After all, everybody knows of cases where the oracles have been wrong three times because they were interfered with by witchcraft. On a particular occasion, where the possibility of witchcraft has not been raised, it will seem silly to raise this objection. But if we are trying to write an account of the oracle, we shall have to take other cases into account. The literate theorist has to formulate principles not just for the particular case, but more generally. Rather than saying
Three oracles have spoken it is so
he or she will have to say something like this:

> Three oracles constitute good *prima facie* evidence that something is so: but they may have been interfered with by witchcraft. This is to be revealed by such and such means. If they have been interfered with by witchcraft, it is necessary first to purify the oracle...

Literate theorists, in other words, will have to list those qualifying clauses that we recognize as the mark of written scholarship.

Literacy forces you to consider general claims, because it requires you to make claims that are relevant beyond the particular conversation you are having. And it is easy to see that literacy also encourages abstraction in your language. Consider a traditional proverb that has been orally transmitted. Take this proverb from the Akan region of Ghana:
If all seeds that fall were to grow, then no one could follow the path under the trees.

When someone says this they are usually expressing the view that if everyone were prosperous, no one would work. But the proverb is about seeds, trees, and paths through the forest. The message is abstract, but the wording is concrete. The concreteness makes the proverb memorable —and in oral tradition nothing is carried but what is carried on in memory. But it also means that to understand the message—as I am sure only Akan speaking people did before I explained it—you have to share with the speaker a knowledge of his or her background assumptions.

The proverb works because, in traditional societies, you talk largely with people you know; all the assumptions that are needed to interpret a proverb are shared. And it is because they are shared that the language of oral exchange (including, of course, the conversation of literate people) can be indexical, metaphorical and context-dependent.

Once you are writing, therefore, the demands imposed by trying to cater to an unknown reader move you towards both greater generality and greater abstraction. Because readers may not share the cultural assumptions of writers, written language becomes less metaphorical in contexts where communication of information is important. This is another reason we are less able to get away with the inconsistencies of our informal thought.

For if we speak metaphorically, then what we say can be taken and reinterpreted in a new context; the same proverb, precisely because its message is not fixed, can be used again and again. And if we can use it again and again with different messages, we may fail to notice that the messages are inconsistent with each other. After all, the proverb is being used in this situation, and why should we think now of those other occasions of its use?

Evans-Pritchard wrote:

> [Although] Azande often observed that a medicine is unsuccessful, they do not generalize their observations. Therefore the failure of a single medicine does not teach them that all medicines of this type are foolish. Far less does it teach them that all magic is useless... Contradictions between their beliefs are not noticed by the Azande because beliefs are not all present at the same time but function in different situations... Each man and each kinship group acts alone without cognizance of the actions of others. People do not pool their ritual experiences.

But we can now see that, without literacy, it would be very hard indeed to generalize in this way; or to bring beliefs from different situations together to check their consistency; or to share the full range of Zande ritual experience.

Neither the impulse towards universality and abstraction and away from metaphorical language, nor the recognition of inconsistencies of the traditional world view, leads automatically to formal philosophy. But without literacy it is hard to see how formal philosophy could have got started: it is not a sufficient condition for formal philosophy, but it certainly seems to be necessary. And, as we have seen, it is literacy that explains some of the features of formal philosophy...

5. PHILOSOPHY AND RELIGION

The distinguishing marks of formal philosophy that I have so far identified are marks of intellectual inquiry in a literate culture. Like all such intellectual inquiry, it involves systematic, abstract, general theorizing, with a concern to think critically and consistently: sometimes in the company of thinkers long dead. These features reflect the fact that formal philosophy involves not just a way of thinking, but also a way of writing. The systematic character of philosophy shows up quite clearly as we think philosophically about philosophy's own character: **meta-philosophy**—systematic critical reflection on the nature of philosophy—is itself part of the philosophical enterprise.

I have argued that evidence and reasons are central to this systematic enterprise, even if they are not sufficient to pick one conceptual scheme as the only correct one. Even as the Azande became literate, they might have developed a style of thought with the marks of literate intellectual life, while still having a conceptual scheme different from ours.

But the development of literacy would almost certainly have one other important consequence for them, which it has had for the Western intellectual tradition. It would lead to an intellectual division of labor. Just as, in industrialized societies, there has been an increasing specialization of material production—think how many different skills go into the design, the making, the distribution and the sale of a car—so there are many different skills, trainings and institutions involved in the production and transmission of ideas. Even within, say, physics, there are not only many subdivisions of subject-matter—astronomy, particle physics, condensed matter theory—there are also many jobs within each of the fields—laboratory technicians, theorists, experimentalists, teachers, textbook authors, and so on. The division of labor in the West is so highly developed that, as the American philosopher of science

Hilary Putnam has pointed out, we even leave the task of understanding some parts of our language to experts: it is because words like "electron" have precise meanings for physicists that I, who have no very good grasp of their meaning, can use them, and the same goes for the word "contract" and lawyers. These words, as my tool, only do their business for me because their meanings are sharpened by others.

One of the ways in which our high degree of intellectual division of labor shows up is in comparison, once more, with the intellectual life of the Azande. They did not have this substantial proliferation of kinds of theoretical knowledge. Though they did have what Evans-Pritchard called "witch-doctors," any adult male could conduct an oracle or perform magic or hunt, because most people shared the same concepts and beliefs. Any senior person in Zande society would be a source of information about their beliefs about gods, spirits, witchcraft, oracles and magic.

In the Western tradition, by contrast, many of our central intellectual projects are carried out by specialists. Questions about God—which, if there is a God, are as important as any questions could be for us—are studied in our culture by a variety of different sorts of experts. Though the philosophy of religion, for example, addresses theological questions, it shares that task with theology and with other kinds of Western religious thought. Similarly, theories of the ultimate constitution of nature are central to any folk-philosophy; and, once more, though metaphysics and the philosophy of science address these questions, they share them with the natural sciences.

But, unlike Zande religion, Western religions—Christianity and Judaism—are deeply bound up with writing: and, without writing, physics would be impossible. If literacy and its consequences mark formal philosophy off from traditional thought, how can we distinguish Western philosophy from Western religion and Western science?

It is easy enough to point to one thing that distinguishes formal philosophy from Western religion as a whole. Religion involves not only theories about how the world is and should be, but also specific rituals—the Jewish *Seder*, the Catholic Mass, the Protestant Lord's Supper—and practices such as prayer. These are all practices a philosopher could engage in: but in doing so, he or she would not be acting as a philosopher but as a believer.

But there is, of course, a reason why it is so natural to think of philosophy and religion together: a reason that is connected with what I said at the beginning of this chapter. All religions—even those, like

Buddhism, that believe neither in God nor in systematic theory—are associated with a view of human life, of our place in the world, and of how we ought to live. And such a connected set of views is often called a "philosophy of life." The philosophy of life of a modern woman or man is, in effect, the folk-philosophy of a literate culture.

The questions formal philosophers ask are relevant to these issues: studying formal philosophy can change your philosophy of life. For a literate intellectual, it is natural to think systematically about these questions. But if one is also religious, that systematic thought will involve not only the sorts of philosophical questions I have raised, but questions of theology also. It is important, therefore, to distinguish philosophy from theology, the critical intellectual activity that is a part—but only a part—of modern religion; as, indeed, it was only a part of the religion of the European Middle Ages.

One crucial difference between philosophy and most theology is that, in philosophy, we do not usually presuppose the truth of any particular religious claims. When philosophers address questions central to Christianity—the existence of God, or the morality of abortion—they do so in the light of their religious beliefs, but with a concern to defend even those claims that can be taken, within a religious tradition, for granted. But theologians, too, offer evidence and reasons for many of the claims they make about God. They are often concerned not only with setting out religious doctrines, but with systematizing them and relating them, through the use of reason, to our beliefs about the natural world. When this happens it is hard to tell where theology ends and the philosophy of religion begins.

Though there are, then, some ways of distinguishing most theology from most philosophy of religion, they have not so much to do with subject matter as with issues that have, in the end, to do with the way in which philosophy and theology have been institutionalized as professions. Philosophy of religion addresses religion with the training of philosophers that means, in part, that it uses the same tools of logic and semantics, the same concepts of epistemology and ethics, that philosophers use outside the philosophy of religion. Christian theology, on the other hand, is closely bound both to traditions of interpreting a central text, the Bible, and to the experience of the Christian church in history. Jewish religious writing is similarly tied to the *Torah* and to other texts; and rooted, similarly, in its history. But because the central questions of theology are crucially relevant to the central questions of human life, it should not be a surprise that philosophers and theologians often come to ask the same questions. Someone who cares—as, surely, we should—about whether religious claims are true may want to follow both these routes to a deeper understanding of religion.

6. PHILOSOPHY AND SCIENCE

The distinction between philosophy and science is sometimes held to be, by comparison, a simple matter. Though Isaac Newton called his *Principia*, the first great text of modern theoretical physics, a work of natural philosophy, many philosophers since would have said that it was not a work of what I have called formal philosophy. The reason they would have given is that Newton's work was about (admittedly, very abstract) empirical questions—questions to which the evidence of sensation and perception is relevant. Formal philosophy, on the other hand, deals with questions which are conceptual—having to do not with how the world happens to be, but with how we conceive of it.

But this way of making the distinction between philosophy and science seems to me to be too simple. Much theoretical physics is very difficult to connect in any straightforward way with empirical evidence and much philosophy of mind depends on facts about how our human minds happen to be constituted. It will not do, either, to say that the use of empirical evidence in science involves experiments, while in philosophy it does not. For thought experiments play an important role in both science and philosophy; and many branches of the sciences—cosmology, for example—have to proceed with very few, if any, experiments, just because experiments would be so hard to arrange. (Imagine trying to organize the explosion of a star!)

Nevertheless, there is a difference—which, like the difference between philosophy and theology, is by no means absolute —between philosophy and physics and it has to do with the fact that the kind of empirical evidence that is relevant to the sciences must usually be collected a good deal more systematically than the evidence that is sometimes relevant in philosophy.

Even this difference is a matter of degree, however. In the philosophy of language—in semantics, for example—we need to collect systematic evidence about how our languages are actually used if our theories of meaning are to be useful; and, the discovery of cases like the ones that Gettier thought up can play a crucial role in epistemology. But there is a pattern in the history of Western intellectual life, in which problems that are central at one time to philosophy become the basis of new, more specialized sciences. Thus, modern linguistics grows out of philosophical reflection on language, just as economics and sociology grew out of philosophical reflection on society, and physics grew out of Greek, Roman and Medieval philosophical reflection on the nature of matter and motion. As these special subjects develop, some of the problems which used to concern philosophers move out of the focus of philosophical attention. But the more conceptual problems remain.

This pattern is reflected in the fact that where philosophy and the specialized sciences address the same problem, the more empirical questions are usually studied by the scientists and the less empirical ones by the philosophers. That is the sense in which philosophy really is a primarily conceptual matter.

The division of labor between science and philosophy has been productive. While philosophical work has often generated new sciences, new philosophical problems are also generated by the development of science. Some of the most interesting philosophical work of our day, for example, involves examining the conceptual problems raised by relativity and quantum theory. To do this work—or, at least, to do it well—it is necessary to understand theoretical physics. But it also requires the tools and training of the philosopher.

7. THE SPECIAL CHARACTER OF PHILOSOPHY

What can we say we have learned about the distinctive style of philosophical work? The first lesson, as I have just argued, is that philosophy, even when it is answering apparently particular questions—What is the difference between M and my mother?— approaches them in the light of broadly conceptual, abstract considerations, even though it would be foolish to do philosophy without one eye on the empirical world. That is why philosophical reasoning is so often *a priori*; for truths about conceptual matters can be discovered by reason alone. Nevertheless, as I have insisted, there is no sharp line between philosophical questions and those of other specialized areas of thought, such as theology or the sciences.

Another lesson, confirmed many times in this book, is that there is no area of philosophy that is independent of all the others. The subject is not a collection of separate problems that can be addressed independently. Issues in epistemology and the philosophy of language reappear in discussions of mind, morals, politics, law, science and, in this chapter, of religion. Questions in morals—When may we take somebody's property against their will?—depend on issues in the philosophy of mind—Are interpersonal comparisons of utility possible?;

and are further dependent on metaphysical questions—What is consciousness?

What is at the root of the philosophical style is a desire to give a *general* and *systematic* account of our thought and experience, one that is developed critically, in the light of evidence and argument. You will remember that John Rawls used the notion of **reflective equilibrium** to describe the goal of philosophical thought. We start with an intuitive understanding of a problem, seeing it "through a glass, darkly;" and, from these intuitions we build a little theory. The theory sharpens and guides our intuitions, and we return to theorizing. As we move back and forth from intuition to theory, we approach, we hope, a reflective equilibrium where theory and intuition coincide.

If the history of philosophy is anything to go by, one person's reflective equilibrium is another person's state of puzzlement. Cartesianism seemed to many seventeenth century thinkers a reasonable way of understanding the mind and its place in the world. To modern behaviorists, on the other hand, and to functionalists, it seems to raise too many philosophical difficulties. Perhaps the history of the subject is better represented by the picture suggested by the great German philosopher, Georg Wilhelm Friedrich Hegel.

Hegel thought that the life of reason proceeded by a continuing sequence of ideas. First, someone would develop a systematic theory—which Hegel called a *thesis*. It would then be denied by those who supported the *anti-thesis*; and, finally, a new view would develop which took what was best of each to produce a new *synthesis*. That is what we saw in the movement from Cartesianism to behaviorism to functionalism in the philosophy of mind; or from realism to emotivism to prescriptivism in moral philosophy. But this is not the end of the process. On a Hegelian view, a synthesis can itself become the thesis for some new anti-thesis.

Hegel also thought, however, that this process was tending toward a final goal, in which philosophy approached ever closer to the absolute truth. But if, as I have argued, both fallibilism and weak relativism are true, we need not accept this part of his view. As our understanding of the world changes, as we find new ways to live our lives, there will be new problems to address, new questions to ask, new syntheses to be created. Because fallibilism is (probably!) true, we will never be sure that our theories are right. And because weak relativism is true, it really will be a task of creation—the invention of concepts—as well as a voyage of discovery. As a result, philosophy, along with other intellectual specializations, can change both its tools and its problems.

In this chapter I have looked at the character of philosophy and suggested some contrasts between it and traditional thought, religion and the sciences. But the problems we have discussed in this book are explored with *all* the resources of literate culture. Thus, literature, too, examines moral and political ideas and the novel explores the nature of human experience in society, and, sometimes—as in some science fiction—our understanding of the natural world. To claim that philosophy is important and enjoyable is not to say that we should not learn from and enjoy these other styles of thought, these other kinds of writing.

The questions I have asked are some of those that are important to philosophy now. I have addressed them with some of the intellectual tools that philosophers now find useful. If you share our vision of a general and systematic understanding of the central problems of human life, they are questions you will want to ask also. I hope I have persuaded you that you do share that vision. And if you do, you will be irresistibly drawn to the questions of philosophy. In that sense they are, indeed, necessary questions.

Questions for Chapter 1
Philosophy and Necessary Questions

1. TRUE OR FALSE?

   a. According to Appiah, the difference between folk and formal philosophies is simply a difference in subject-matter.
   b. According to Appiah, one of the differences between philosophy and religion is that religion does not address central questions.
   c. According to Appiah, one of the differences between philosophy and science is that philosophy does not deal with facts.
   d. According to Appiah, an examination of the proverbs of the Akans of Ghana shows that writing is important.

2. According to Appiah, which of these is not a mark of formal philosophy?

   (A) System.
   (B) Writing.
   (C) Experimentation.
   (D) Justification.

3. In what sense does Appiah believe that the questions of philosophy are necessary, and in what sense does he believe that writing is necessary for answering these questions?
   Do you agree with him on both counts?
   Give reasons for your answer.

4. 'On Appiah's account, there is no African Philosophy.'
   Discuss.

Chapter 2

Necessary Questions and African Philosophy

Safro Kwame

Wonkɔɔ obi afum da a, wuse: "Me nko ne kuafo." —If you have never been to another person's farm, you say "I am the only farmer." (Akan proverb)

PROLOGUE

Safro Kwame is a native of the Akuapem region of the Akan society. He was born in Accra, Ghana on October 31, 1953. He received most of his higher level education at the University of Ghana at Legon where he received instruction from Kwasi Wiredu, Kwame Gyekye, Kobina Oguah, and Kwame Appiah, among others. He is currently an assistant professor of philosophy at Lincoln University in Pennsylvania. Before that he was a lecturer in moral and political philosophy at the University of Ghana (1980-1982) and a Charles Phelps Tafts Graduate Fellow at the University of Cincinnati (1987-1989).

Kwame argues that if philosophy consists of answering necessary questions then there is an African philosophy in both the folk and formal senses; partly because thinking but not writing is necessary for answering necessary questions. Further, he argues that unless we presume that there is agreement about the definition and ownership of philosophy, the claim that there is or there is no African philosophy is meaningless.

Here is part of Kwame's argument:

"If one denies that a non-literate people ever thought deeply or critically about fundamental issues of life, he or she will either have to be familiar with the details of their entire history or have to deny that they are human; since, from my experience, human beings have fundamental problems of life and think about them if they are sensitive and have thinking faculties. But one cannot be familiar with the details of the long history of non-literate Africa because, 'ex hypothesi', we have no written record of it. Neither can one consistently deny that a people, however illiterate, consists of human beings or even that these, human beings, if they are normal, have problems on and about (fundamental issues such as) life. Note that thinking is not the same as writing; and to admit that any people think about life, is to admit that they think deeply or critically about fundamental issues which, essentially, is philosophy. To think about life—what life is, whether there is life after death or whether a life is worth taking or preserving, etc.—is not to take life for granted; it is being critical, and thinking deeply about very fundamental issues and necessary questions. No one that I am aware of denies that traditional Africans have a conception of a person, life after death, whether it is right or wrong to take or preserve human life, etc. Neither does anyone I know of deny that these 'metaphysical' or 'ethical' conceptions are the product of deep or critical thinking about fundamental issues of life, or that metaphysics and ethics are by themselves sufficient indicators of the presence of philosophy. I am consequently amazed that these same people deny the existence of traditional African philosophy, philosophers or philosophizing in any but the most naive and unphilosophical sense."

Necessary Questions and African Philosophy: How to Bury the Problem of the Existence of African Philosophy

Safro Kwame

1. INTRODUCTION

Anthony Appiah in his recent *Introduction to Philosophy* advocates the necessary-questions conception of philosophy. Yet he seems to shy away from advocating the existence of a traditional African philosophy that is comparable with ancient or modern Western philosophy. I wish to pursue the necessary-questions conception of philosophy further, because I see in it an interesting account of philosophy that is simple but useful to the college freshman or freshwoman and to the discussion of African philosophy. In particular, I wish to show that on this and other popular conceptions of philosophy, there is a traditional African philosophy. Lastly, I wish to show that, since not everyone accepts this or any other conception of philosophy, even those who argue that the existence of African philosophy is undeniable are faced with a dilemma of sorts based on certain questionable assumptions about philosophy. Hopefully, when all is said and done, the problem of the existence of African philosophy would be seen as a pseudo-problem which needs to be buried.

2. NECESSARY QUESTIONS & POSSIBLE ANSWERS

If philosophy is an attempt to answer necessary questions, we shall have to say it merely provides possible answers to these fundamental but difficult questions. Further, for reasons that would be apparent later on, we seem compelled to note that, on this conception of philosophy, it is doubtful that any elaborate culture of long standing lacks philosophy or a philosophical tradition. I believe that, if philosophy is concerned about necessary questions, it can only provide possible answers for the following reasons. In the first place, philosophy, unlike the physical and social sciences, is not primarily interested in recording or describing facts and, hence, capturing what is actually or descriptively true or false. If it were, philosophy will be identifiable with science in this sense; but it is not. Secondly the primary vehicle of philosophical knowledge is *logic* which is *merely the study of consistency*. While logic can show us what is possible (consistent) or impossible (inconsistent), it cannot tell us what is actually the case or is in fact true or false. If the impossible is ruled out on pain of contradiction and the actual is beyond the realm of philosophy, then philosophy is concerned with the realm of possibilities as the only remaining option.

In applying this conception of philosophy, African philosophy may be perceived as the set of possible answers to fundamental or, in Appiah's terminology, necessary questions provided by Africans or even non-Africans on the basis of their African experience. It is the collective wisdom of Africa, so to speak. In extended but more concrete terms, an African philosopher is a person of whatever sex, race, or color, who brings his or her peculiarly African experience (of, say, language, examples, topics, or beliefs) to bear, significantly, on the treatment of a philosophical question, issue, or problem.

3. NECESSARY STATEMENTS & NECESSARY QUESTIONS

I am not opposed to Appiah's idea of explaining philosophy in terms of necessary questions. In fact, I am very much sympathetic. However, the concept of a necessary question, unlike that of a necessary statement, is not an entirely clear concept. On Saul Kripke's characterization, necessity may be identified by determining whether whatever is said to be necessary could have been otherwise. If, for example, "two plus two equals four" is really necessary, then two-plus-two cannot be equal to something other than four. In other words, in every possible world we can think of, "two plus two equals four" would be true. The question to ask in determining necessity is this:

> Is it possible that, in this respect, the world should have been different from the way it is? (Kripke 1972, 261).

"If the answer is 'no'," Kripke remarks, "then this fact about the world is a necessary one," (ibid., 261). If this characterization were applicable to the claim that a question is necessary, then we would have to say that a necessary question is such that, in respect of its being asked, it is impossible that the world should have been different. In other words, in this sense, *a necessary question is a question which would be asked even if the world were different from what it is.* Unfortunately on this conception of necessity, it is doubtful that there are necessary questions; for one could imagine a coherent world in which these philosophical questions were not asked. In a world in which there were no human or intelligent beings, these questions would not be asked; because in this world—as differently characterized—there would be no one to ask them.

It seems obvious that the problem, here, arises, not from Kripke's test of necessity, but rather his conception of necessity. For Kripke, necessity is about statements that are true in every possible world not about questions or our knowledge of these statements (i.e. how we come to know that those statements are true). To say that a statement is 'a-priori' is, for Kripke, to say that it is known independently of experience not that it is necessary in the sense that it is true in every possible world. Kripke concludes that "the terms 'necessary' and 'a-priori', then, as applied to statements are not obvious synonyms" (ibid., 263). Unfortunately Kripke does not tell us much about necessity as applied to questions. In any case it is noteworthy that, in some respects, Appiah seems to be in agreement with Kripke concerning the use of necessity. "What is true in every possible world," Appiah notes, "is what is necessary" (1989, 75).

However, questions unlike statements, are neither true nor false. To predicate truth or falsity of a question is no less a misnomer than to predicate truth of a command or request. Neither of them asserts or denies anything. It would seem that to predicate necessity of a question is, by implication, no less a misnomer and the concept of a necessary question is a confused one; unless it is used in a very different sense. In this different sense, even though necessity concerns what happens in various possible worlds, it is associated with (a) only worlds in which there are human beings, (b) empirical—not 'a-priori'—knowledge and (c) conditional—not categorical—statements. Let us note how Appiah characterizes it.

4. A CONCEPTION OF PHILOSOPHY

In the last chapter of his book *Necessary Questions* (reprinted as Chapter 1 of this text), Appiah notes that philosophy consists in "universal questions" that have been addressed in various cultures around the world (op. cit., 200). These questions about mind and matter, knowledge and truth, good and bad, right and wrong, human nature and the universe, are "the central questions of human life" (ibid., 200). "If any thought about these questions count as philosophy," Appiah continues, "then philosophy is likely to be found in every human society, past and present—wherever there are people struggling to live—and make sense of their—lives" (ibid., 200-201). In this sense, necessary questions—as universal questions—are, apparently, questions that are raised in every possible world. But questions unlike truths or facts seem to require human or other kinds of minds. These questions, to use the possible-world model of necessity, would be questions that are raised not in every possible world but only in worlds in which there are humans or beings of that sort to raise them.

This is not to suggest that every human being who raised these questions would find them necessary. As most philosophy teachers including Appiah are well aware, to most college freshmen and freshwomen, these are unnecessary questions which seem not to be universal until they are pointed out. Further as comparative philosophers such as Kwasi Wiredu are aware, some philosophical questions, though fundamental, arise from the natural languages of specific cultures and hence are not universal (Wiredu 1985, 43-54). The examples given by Wiredu include questions about how true propositions are related to facts, whether the relationship between "p if and only if p" and "if p then q, and if q then p" is really one of equivalence, and whether the correspondence and identity theories are acceptable.

The conditional nature of the necessity of these questions is more pronounced in Appiah's closing remarks. These questions, he remarks, are questions that must be addressed if we—as he presumes we do—share in the vision of a general and systematic understanding of the problems of human life:

> If you share our vision of a general and systematic understanding of the central problems of human life, they are questions you will want to ask also. I hope I have persuaded you that you do share that vision. And if you do, you will be irresistibly drawn to the questions of philosophy. In that sense they are, indeed, necessary questions (Appiah 1989, 220).

If Wiredu is right, this modification of the necessity of philosophical questions does not go far enough. In any case, if it is reasonable to assume that any arbitrarily selected individual (who happens to read or hear Appiah's book read) aspires to an understanding of human life, then philosophy is, as Kwame Gyekye, Frederick Copleston, and Brand Blanshard indicate, truly human in the sense that it is not restricted to men or non-Africans. A little reflection and empirical observation, Copleston points out, is enough to convince anyone that the harsh reality of death, for example, stimulates profound thought in any human society (Copleston 1980, 2). Philosophy, Blanshard remarks, is best understood as part of an older and wider enterprise of understanding the world (Blanshard 1975, 163). Where there is life, he adds, there is philosophy, for the effort to understand is central to the very nature of the existence of human beings (ibid., 177).

5. WESTERN & AFRICAN PHILOSOPHIES

Even though Appiah shares Blanshard's type of premise about philosophy being part of a wider enterprise, he seems to reject Blanshards' conclusion that real philosophy exists everywhere on the grounds that (for Appiah) only written thought is real philosophy. Using the Akans of Ghana (op. cit., 209), the Mbuti of Zaire (ibid., 201) and the Azande of Sudan (ibid., 210) as examples, Appiah distinguishes between (formal) philosophy and traditional (folk) thought on the grounds that writing is also a necessary condition for 'real' or formal philosophy (ibid., 207). According to Appiah, the special chapter of philosophy is to be found in its literary style—a style that characterizes formal philosophy but is conspicuously absent in folk philosophy:

> What is at the root of the philosophical style is a desire to give a general and systematic account of our thought and experience, one that is developed critically, in the light of evidence and argument (ibid., 219). The urge to give arguments and evidence for what you believe, and to make your beliefs consistent with each other so that they form a system, is one of the marks of formal philosophy (ibid., 203)...Much of what we take to be typical of formal philosophy derives in large measure from the fact that formal philosophy, unlike folk-philosophy, is written (ibid., 207). And we have seen; it is literacy that explains some of the features of formal philosophy (ibid., 210).

This places Appiah in the camp of Wiredu, Oruka, Bodunrin, and others who believe that, even though there was some amount of reflection on fundamental issues going on in traditional African societies, it is not comparable with the kind of activity that goes on in Western philosophy. These professional philosophers—in what I call the individualist-literary camp—attempt to resolve the apparent tension in their thesis by making individual, personal, writing necessary or, in the case of Paulin Hountondji, maybe even sufficient for real philosophy. "What remains certain," Hountondji writes, "is that the first and most basic requirement of philosophy as of science (in the strict sense of these words), is the broad democratic practice of writing—a necessary, if not sufficient condition" (Hountondji 1983, 101).

Opposed to those who use the individualist-literary approach are those whom Oruka and Hountondji characterize as taking an ethnophilosophical approach to traditional African philosophy, (See Oruka 1978, & Bodunrin 1984, 1-2). These so-called ethnophilosophers assert the existence of traditional African philosophy in unambiguous terms; apparently, for the same reason that people like Appiah and Wiredu acknowledge the existence of traditional African folk thought. I find myself drawn to the so-called ethnophilosophical camp into which people like Kwame Gyekye, Kobina Oguah, Alexis Kagame, John Mbiti, and Leopold Senghor are lumped. Basically, my reason is that it is inconsistent to maintain a necessary-questions conception of philosophy even in Appiah's limited sense and deny Africans philosophy. As Kwame Gyekye and others have pointed out, some traditional African proverbs, aphorisms, fragments, and folklore provide independent confirmation of the existence of traditional African philosophy (Gyekye 1987, 10). Philosophy consists in thinking, rather than writing, about certain basic concepts and issues in life; such as, the fundamental questions about what is right, what is truth, or what is a person. To assert anything to the contrary is to confuse literature with philosophy, writing with thinking, and records with facts.

6. THE QUESTION & DILEMMA OF AFRICAN PHILOSOPHY

I do not intend to dwell at length on the metaphilosophical issue of the existence or nonexistence of African philosophy, for two reasons. First, as I have tried to suggest, whether or not there is an African philosophy is, unlike the question of the knowledge of necessary truths, ultimately an empirical question. Ultimately, it is only empirical observation that will confirm the assumption concerning necessary questions; namely every culture, whether of a male or female society, raises those basic questions of life that characterize philosophy to the level of profound reflection. Note that it is not necessary that all philosophical questions be raised in a particular society for it to have philosophy. If Wiredu is right, some—but not all—philosophical questions are so tied up to a natural language that they are unlikely to arise naturally in other languages and societies. It is sufficient that at least some philosophical questions be raised and answered in a society for that society to have philosophy. Those questions will include those that are truly human, universal and necessary as well as those that arise from the peculiarities of that culture.   Secondly, the whole debate between the so-called ethno-philosophers (who assert the existence of African philosophy in almost all senses) and the so-called professional or individualist-literary philosophers (who deny it in all but the least serious sense) rests on a simple constructive dilemma that is generated by untenable assumptions.

With regard to the origin of the dilemma, it would suffice to note that when philosophy as we know it is appropriated by one race, the peoples of other races—in particular, the black race or those of African descent—are forced to come up with something that is either different or, else, not different from philosophy as we know it. Enthymematically stated, the dilemma is this: If Africans come up with something that is not different from philosophy as it is popularly known around the world, they cannot be said to have philosophy since philosophy as it is popularly known has become the possession of another race or civilization (i.e. the Western World, in particular Euro-Americans).   If on the other hand, Africans come up with something very different from the one which is popularly known around the world, it is unlikely to be accepted as philosophy; because it is different from philosophy as it is popularly known.   The untenable assumptions are that, contrary to the lack of a consensus on the definition of philosophy, we are agreed as to what philosophy is, and that we are agreed on whom philosophy belongs to—as if philosophy is an individual possession or private property. If we assumed rather plausibly, I think, that we know neither whether philosophy is a property of one race nor exactly what philosophy is, the problem of philosophy ceases to be a serious one. By 'knowledge,' here, I mean 'agreement.'   Professional philosophers do not agree on what philosophy is and they do not agree that philosophy belongs to one and only one race or gender.

7. CONCLUSION

Given the multiplicity of definitions, it is difficult to rule out the existence of philosophy in one culture or society merely because no such activity exists in that society to meet the requirements of philosophy as specified by one or two definitions. Indeed, in the light of the lack of agreement on the definition of philosophy by professional philosophers in any culture, it is reasonable to conjecture that philosophy exists in every culture or human society according to one definition or another used by some popular philosopher in the Western world. Yet the disagreements about the existence of African philosophy and the many attempts to solve the problem seem to be meaningful only within the context of a dilemma that is founded on the untenable assumptions that we are agreed as to what philosophy is and to whom it belongs. If the foregoing account of the so-called problem of the existence of African philosophy is correct, it comes very close to a postmortem examination of what seems to be a dead issue. The reason is that, as we explained earlier, the problem arises because of a dilemma and the dilemma arises because of certain assumptions about philosophy. But those assumptions, we noted, are false; and, if they are false, the dilemma does not really arise and, hence, the problem too does not arise.

NOTES

1. Raymond Bradley and Norman Swartz in *Possible Worlds* (Hackett, 1979 pp. 3-4) are at pains to point out that even though possibility and conceivability are closely connected, they are not synonymous since possibility is not a mere function of human psychology. Yet they acknowledge that the attempt to distinguish possibility from conceivability by defining possibility in terms of coherent conceivability generates a circularity that can only be avoided by citing examples of what we mean by possible and impossible worlds.

2. Kwasi Wiredu in his much publicized but very controversial and hotly-debated paper 'Truth as Opinion' reprinted in *Philosophy and an African Culture* (Cambridge, 1980, p. 115) suggests that the existence of truths require human minds, since truth is merely an opinion advanced from someone's point of view. The problem with this thesis, as I see it, is that it ignores the distinction between metaphysics and epistemology. Even though claims about truth are commonly advanced as opinions by individuals, they are advanced as attempts by human beings to gain knowledge of things that (are assumed to) exist independently of our cognition. The problem that arises, here, is not metaphysical i.e. it is not a problem about whether truths exist, because the one who attempts to tell the truth assumes that truths exist. It is an epistemological problem i.e. a problem about how we know that the opinions that we put forward from our point of view as truths really capture the truths that we seek. Wiredu, it seems to me, takes truths to be opinions because he treats an epistemological problem like a metaphysical one.

3. Wiredu in *Philosophy and an African Culture* (Cambridge, 1980) acknowledges the existence of traditional African thought but not a traditional African philosophy that is comparable with ancient or modern Western philosophy.

BIBLIOGRAPHY

1. Appiah, Anthony *Necessary Questions.*   Englewood Cliff, NJ.: Prentice-Hall Inc., 1989. Reprinted as Chapter 1 of this text.
2. Blandshard, Brand 'The Philosophic Enterprise' in *The Owl of Minerva* by C. Bontempo & S. Odell (eds.). N.Y.: The Viking Press, 1975.
3. Bodunrin, P. O. 'The Question of African Philosophy' in *African Philosophy: An Introduction* by Richard Wright (ed). Lanham: University Press of America, 1984.
4. Copleston, F. C. *Philosophies and Cultures*. Oxford: Oxford University Press, 1980.

5. Gyekye, Kwame. *An Essay on African Philosophical Thought.* New York: Cambridge University Press, 1987.

6. Hountondji, P.J. *African Philosophy: Myth and Reality.* Bloomington: Indiana University Press, 1983.

7. Kripke, Saul. 'Naming and Necessity' in *Semantics of Natural Language* by D. Davidson & Hurman (eds). Boston: D. Reidel, 1972.

8. Oruka, H. O. 'Four Trends in Current African Philosophy.' Presented at the William Amo Symposium in Accra, Ghana, July 1978.

9. Wiredu, Kwasi. 'The Concept of Truth in the Akan Language' in *Philosophy in Africa: Trends and Perspectives*, by P. O. Bodurnrin (ed). Ile-Ife, Nigeria: University of Ife Press, 1985.

Questions for Chapter 2
Necessary Questions and African Philosophy

1. TRUE or FALSE?

    a. Safro Kwame, is opposed to Appiah's idea of explaining philosophy in terms of necessary questions.

    b. Safro Kwame is in the professional (individualist-literary) camp of African Philosophers.

    c. According to Safro Kwame, if philosophy is an attempt to answer necessary questions then its answers are to be found in necessary statements.

    d. According to Safro Kwame the question about whether there is an African philosophy is an empirical question.

2. According to Safro Kwame, the concept of a necessary question is definitely:

    (A) a misnomer.

    (B) confused.

    (C) explained by Kripke.

    (D) none of the above.

3. State the dilemma of African philosophy and evaluate Safro Kwame's attempt to deal with it.

4. Do you agree that, according to Safro Kwame, there is no problem of African philosophy?
Give reasons for your answer.

Chapter 3

A Paradigm of African Society

W. Emmanuel Abraham

Nsɛm nyinaa ne Nyame. —Everything is God. (Akan proverb)

PROLOGUE

W. Emmanuel Abraham is a native of the Fanti group of Akans. He was born in Lagos and studied philosophy at the University of Ghana at Legon and Oxford University. He is a classmate of Kwasi Wiredu's and, in the 1960's he was the chairperson of the Philosophy Department at the University of Ghana, Legon. He has held teaching appointments at Liverpool University, Indiana University, MaCalester College, Stanford University, University of California at Berkeley, and is currently a professor of philosophy at the University of California at Santa Cruz.

According to Abraham, the Akan society is a typical African society to which most African societies bear a family resemblance. In such a society, the world is metaphysically conceived, to be explained, in its general features, in mythic not scientific ways. All other things including morality, politics and medicine are explained in terms of the existence and operation of the so-called spiritual or religious entities. What he means is that these explanations take into account a belief in the existence of non-manifest, sacred and quasi-sacred entities (as well as their interests and operations.) These entities are not radically different from other entities in the Akan hierarchy. Altogether, they form a contiguous order with no unbridgeable distance between the various entities that exist in the world. From the Akan point of view,

God exists not as the sky-god or shining one but as a masculine being whom we weakly resemble. We are the beings he sends into this world with individual destinies. Science and preventive medicine exist in Akan society as non-metaphysical aspects and solutions to some problems in Akan society. In spite of the lack of writing, the traditional Akans propound philosophical ideas or clusters of ideas. They appeal to these ideas in their most general explanations and express them in their art.

Abraham's essay covers many areas and issues in Akan society. Here are some of his arguments on several aspects of African philosophy as represented in Akan thought: "According to the Akan's metaphysical view, the world is rationalist philosophical. Relations between ideas take on body and flesh in the relations between things in nature. According to such a view, therefore, the true metaphysics must be a deductive system. And morality, politics, medicine are all made to flow from metaphysics. From this point of view, science with its experimentalism becomes a simulation of stupidity...Though the world was metaphysical to the Akan mind, not all problems admitted of metaphysical solutions. Hence, it is wrong to infer that the Akan had neither science nor technology. Nor, however, is this a greedy attempt to have it both ways. The Akan had iron and steel enterprises...Because we were all religious objects, there was not sufficient externality and profundity to call for worship and religion in that sense. As men, that is to say, as accidents, we owed our existence to God; as spirits, that is to say, in our essence, we were uncreated. For this reason, even as men, we were said to be not God's creatures, but his messengers. God himself was well to the fore of Akan thinking. He luxuriated in various by-names, of which *Onyame* seems to be central. Quite a few writers, Westerman, Rattray, and latterly Meyerowitz among them, have sought to identify *Onyame* or *Nyame* as a sky-god, because of a supposed etymology...I do not, in fact, believe that *Onyame* means the shining one either. If it meant the shining one, this would be the sun. At least God would then have to be associated with temporal epiphanies or associated—what is more far-fetched—with a shining domicile. Neither of these hypotheses is in fact fulfilled among the Akans; for on the one hand *Onyame* is thought to be invisible and not to have any epiphanies (it is indeed for this reason that he has no images or shrines). On the other hand he is not held to live in the sky by name, but simply above, up there...Most philosophical theories can usually be stated in a few sentences. A great deal of philosophical writing consists, according to a colleague, Kwasi Wiredu, of anticipation of the objections of half-wits and replies thereto. Much also comprises explanations of the statement of the theories themselves, and of course arguments for them. The absence of a body of writing among the Akans does not in itself, therefore, mean the absence of philosophical ideas. As the Akans could not write, they expressed their philosophico-religious ideas through art, through the timeless, immemorial, silent, and elemental power so characteristic of African traditional art."

A Paradigm Of African Society

W. Emmanuel Abraham

1. SIMILARITY BETWEEN CULTURES

Each culture, while remaining the same, passes through different successive *milieux*, phases. Each culture has a number of basic aspects each of which has the possibility of becoming dominant. A *milieu* or phase of a culture is determined by that aspect of the culture to which greatest emphasis is currently given, while the other aspects are kept in mild abeyance. This possibility of a culture, which passes through a succession of *milieux* or phases, nevertheless remaining the same is that which enables one to give a certain kind of account of the culture. This kind of account is correct in its own way, though hardly reflecting any particular phase of the culture. The possibility of so presenting a culture is the possibility of putting forward its framework, the range within which each phase of it is set. Much controversy about culture in fact boils down to a discussion in favour of this or that phase of the culture. Thus, one might say that F. R. Leavis would like the puritanic streak in British culture to become dominant at this moment, to become thematic of it. If the puritanic element should become dominant, one could then say of British culture that it had entered its puritanic phase or *milieu*. The totality of streaks, which limits the possibility of phases, is all there all the time, and there is an abiding open possibility of any one of the streaks becoming dominant, thematic. It is like the legs of an insect; they are all there, but the insect can be picked up by a different leg each time.

2. AFRICAN CULTURE

In this chapter I shall attempt to present what I grasp to be the typical range of African cultures. The central feature of the type to which African cultures belong is that there is a certain world-view to which can be related all other central concepts, including those of religion and theology, morality and social organisation. I therefore propose to give some account of this world-view, and to illustrate the way in which all

Reprinted by permission of the author and publisher from *The Mind of Africa*, by W. E. Abraham, Chicago: The University of Chicago Press (44-59 & 103-115), © 1962 by W. E. Abraham.

other central aspects of the traditional African society flow from it. In order to do this, I shall choose a given African society. My paradigm will be the Akan of Ghana.

The Akan of Ghana represent some two-thirds of the fourteen million people of Ghana. They are to be found in Ashanti and to the south, and in Axim and to just west of Accra. They speak a cluster of languages which have a family resemblance but are not related as language to dialect.

In introducing the idea of a paradigm, it is not my intention to suggest that all African cultures, or even the majority of them, share a certain identity of principles and a certain identity of detail. Every culture has its sanctions. It is these sanctions which indicate what general value statements are within that culture reasonable. Such general value statements affect law, ethics and social organisation. And they are commonly held to be incapable of non-circular proof. Even in a Kantian sort of framework, in which general normative principles are founded on edicts of the reason, sooner or later one reaches practical principles which are held to be imposed by reason upon itself. Elsewhere, it can only be with reference to individual cultures that these general value statements are held to become reasonable or valid.

It is of course possible for two cultures to share the same general values. Where this happens, the institutions expressing the values could still be different from place to place. And each of the cultures would also have several cultural phenomena which will not be directly linked with any particular general values. This section of a culture, which includes the phenomena not directly linked with any particular general values, may be referred to as the mannerisms of the culture. In that case where two cultures share the same inspiration, their mannerisms may still be different. Mannerisms would most obviously include those objects which are subject to taste. Indeed, the cobwebby saying *"de gustibus non est disputandum"* may itself be said to be a confession that tastes, in so far as they are mannerisms of a culture, are not directly linked with its higher general values. Nevertheless, tastes lend themselves to use as auxiliary devices for supporting a cultural phase or *milieu*.

So far it has been suggested how instances of the same type-culture may differ. But one also expects resemblances between them. The resemblances are, however, not the kind which one, so to say, finds between sentences of different languages expressing the same thought. Cultures which belong to the same type could still be in different *milieux* or phases. Their mannerisms could be different; and so more obviously could their institutions be. The resemblances between cultures of the same type are rather to be thought of in terms of family likeness. Here the same culture could markedly resemble different cultures of the same type in different ways—like the members of a family.

This is what justifies the substantial treatment of an individual culture treated as paradigmatic of a type. It would be unsatisfactory to attempt to present the schema of the type itself.

3. AKAN WORLDVIEW

The Akan thought very much about the world, not, indeed, as the world *inside* which he found himself, but as the world of which he formed a part. The Akan did not have an attitude of externality to the world. For him the world was metaphysical, not scientific. Properly to understand this view, it is necessary to think that modernity consists in the assassination of ideas, in the whittling down of the extent to which the conception of the relations between ideas determines the content and nature of the world. In Europe this is now held to be possible only in the field of thought and action. In Europe, the world is for the rest hardly an intellectual world; and it is of the essence of research, for example, that whoever made the world was not a rationalist philosopher.

According to the Akan's metaphysical view, the world is rationalist philosophical. Relations between ideas take on body and flesh in the relations between things in nature. According to such a view, therefore, the true metaphysics must be a deductive system. And morality, politics, medicine are all made to flow from metaphysics. From this point of view, science with its experimentalism becomes a simulation of stupidity.

With the growth of science and technology in Europe the scope of morality as the implicate of metaphysics has dwindled; one finds morality yielding to medicine, the relation between thought and action giving ground to that between cause and effect, by way of motives and childhood antecedents. Evil-doers and sinners masquerade as sick men and invalids. But to the Akan, the distinction between wrong and sin was hardly there, the same word, *ebon*, casting the same kind of gloom over wrongs and sins. It is as though instead of wrong and sin, one used the word, evil. Sin was the counterpart in human activity of contradiction in human thinking. Since contradiction paralyses thought, it follows that sin or evil would be heavily punished. Since metaphysics spewed out morality, politics, medicine, theory of social organisation, *et cetera*, the consequences of an error in metaphysics could well be grave. And this is possibly that which explains that severity of punishment among the Akans which has appeared as barbarity. What the growth of science does is to anthropologise morality and politics. Morality comes to be based on that complex which suits men in their present circumstances, or on the consensus of human opinion. A sort of utilitarianism and naturalism in ethics would then be almost inevitable. Politics come to emphasise institutions with but scant mention of their ideals. This is borne out by contemporary European and American discussions on ethics and politics. On the one hand, it is suggested that to call something good is really to recommend it: that, rather than any possible intended naturalistic description, being held to be the point of calling it good. On the other hand, it is also suggested that all ideals which are realisable have certain specific institutions geared on to them in a proprietary manner. The question of the practicability of the ideals is then identified with the question of the acceptability and efficacy of the named institutions. Identifying those two questions leads to much controversy, for the propriety of such a step is indeed questionable. In a sense, even, the disputes in religion, literature, philosophy are finally the same, corresponding in their basic features to the distinction between nature and supernature. Philosophy can be seen as the secularisation of such a distinction. That is, in philosophy, the distinction is discussed without reference to that antenna of recommendation which ideals hang out. The distinction is made cold, even brutal. In philosophy, the dispute reaches its critical point when art is identified with reality, supernature with nature itself, ideals with mere truths, fiction with history. And this interlocking is generalised in that account which alleges that what is said to be objective is nothing but the reconciliation or coincidence of many subjective views, or in that account of reality which treats it as the way things appear in normal and standard conditions. Here appearance and reality incontinently interlock. Reality becomes appearance, so to say, in Sunday clothes. History becomes a kind of fiction in so far as creative imagination is given play in it. This is Trevor-Roper's recommendation. Fiction in comparative mythology is treated as being in its essence history. Ideals become truths to which attention needs to be drawn, and those who do not share the ideals are called perverse or blind. Art becomes a deep reality, the artist a kind of scientist using different apparatuses, and speaking different languages. Ideals, fiction, art, all come to be said to be true; and so do truths, history, science. Morality, what the people want or say, instead of making out the voice of the people to be the voice of God by a sort of oxymoron makes out the voice of God to be the voice of the people. And God becomes one of us again. All this is only a by-product of the rise of science and technology.

Though the world was metaphysical to the Akan mind, not all problems admitted of metaphysical solutions. Hence, it is wrong to infer that the Akan had neither science nor technology. Nor, however, is this a greedy attempt to have it both ways. The Akan had iron and steel enterprises. Iron and steel implements have been discovered; and the sites of some foundries have also been unearthed. They had brassware, some of which seems however to have been imported. They had precious metal ornaments and their artistry and skill in the treatment of gold and jewellery impressed the early European visitors. With the possible exception of preventive medicine, medicine too was not for them a question of the analysis of concepts. The operation of metaphysics here was not in prognosis, diagnosis, or prescription. These questions were settled through naturalistic means. And herbal treatment was developed to a high degree of efficacy. To this day, this is the form of treatment to which by far the larger part of the population has reasonably easy access. When, however, questions of prognosis, diagnosis, and prescription had been solved, there was recognised a residual question, the question of that particular conjunction of circumstances, which, in the particular case of the patient, constituted his disease. The way in which this became a question was evidently through its being regarded as unique, that is, through the thought that the individual affected is a constant, not a variable in the disease situation. When the individual, as well as the conjoining circumstances, is regarded as a variable and not a constant in the disease situation, experiments become *theoretically* justified, the individual case acquires not a holy interest but a scientific curiosity-value, and the stage is set for a naturalistic theory of disease. In such a case, sacrifices, by way of thanksgiving, will not be any longer called for. Though an avoidance of the conjunction of circumstances which constituted the disease situation was traditionally recommended by the Akans, and though sanitary measures, both private and public, and also regulated feeding and drinking had always been counsels of prudence, the uniqueness of the patient, which the metaphysical view postulated, created in them a sense of the possibility of divine intervention. Hence it was to human interest that sacrific and prayers should be offered for regained or continued good health.

One aspect of this view is the limitation which is involved on the operation of the concept of accidents. The occurrence of accidents was not itself denied. The world admits of accidents both as a scientific corpus and as a metaphysical corpus. Accidents in a scientific corpus include conjunctions for which no law is known; in the metaphysical corpus, they include conjunctions the concepts of whose elements are held to be irrelevant to each other. And though relevance in the one view can be established through empirical (even statistical) evidence, in the other view it is exclusively through the analysis of concepts.

Gods, in such a view as the Akans had, were not an invention of priests and priestesses. It is grossly wrong to think that here nature is spiritualised. Nature was in fact relatively insignificant. To state the metaphysical view in terms of a spiritualising of nature is to falsify the view altogether. It is to try to state it in terms of a position with which it is in radical conflict, for in the Akan view, nature was, if you like, supernature, antecedently spiritual.

In the Akan metaphysic, what is is in the first place spirit. Spirits exist in a hierarchy because the primary properties of spirits are qualities, those which are called moral: intelligence, courage, virtues, *et cetera*. There is of course a distinction between properties and qualities, properties being neutral and germane to descriptions, while qualities are tendentious, and germane to appraisals. Properties may be said to be naturalistic, and qualities to be moral. This distinction, however, is naturally a distinction of analysis, not of being, for the same aspects of an object may be properties now, and now qualities. The existence of a purpose, for example, is often sufficient to turn properties into qualities; thus, the properties of steel may be its qualities for some specific purpose. The purpose makes properties subject to suitability appraisals, and so makes them qualities. This distinction is possible only in a language in which the sense of the naturalistic is quite strong. In a metaphysical view, the feasibility of the distinction varies inversely with the dominance of metaphysics. In any case, there are in this view, qualities which have not become qualities; that is, qualities which are qualities, not in relation to some specific purpose or variable end, but are, in a way of speaking, qualities in their own proper being, either as ends in themselves, or as eminently suitable to fixed and unchanging ends. In brief then, any property could become a quality, but some qualities have never been properties. One point which emerges from this is that in the Akan metaphysics, certain entities have qualities for their properties and this immediately introduces a hierarchy of beings, and also determines the positions of objects in this hierarchy according as they have qualities or properties. Nonliving things belong to the lower ends of the hierarchy. Objects associated with spirits, including the human body, belong to the middle portions. And spirits, including that spirit which is proper to man, belong to the upper reaches. The whole forms one internally contiguous order. The contiguity of the order in which living beings are placed in a hierarchy immediately poses problems for religion. And to this attention may now be turned.

4. ITS SUPERNATURAL ASPECT

The Akan State was a sacred state in the sense that it was conceived as falling inside a world inhabited by human beings as well as spirits and gods, to whom human beings owed specific duties discharged through appropriate rites, and with whom human beings were in constant communion on the grounds of kinship. Spiritual kinship was the central form of kinship among the Akans and can even be used to explain their matrilinearity. A human being was for them an incapsulated spirit, and not an animated body as the Genesis story has it. The obligations of spiritual kinship took precedence over those of biological kinship, and the matrilineal descent is an expression of this hierarchy of kinship with its obligations. In what way it expresses it will become clear when the Akan family is discussed.

Living men too were essentially spirit, even if encased in flesh for a time. This has consequences for religion. Either the State itself is said to be religious because composed in the main of spirit, or the worshipful attitude of men becomes limited because they are themselves spiritual. It is when man is regarded as a substantive species in himself that the worshipful attitude has its best chance of occurrence. When man is regarded as partaking of the nature of the object of worship, then the actual degree of his worship must be lower than if he were not. Indeed, if a distinction can be drawn between worship and serving, then the Akans never had a word for worship. Worship is a concept that had no place in Akan thought. It was more completely absent among the Akans than among even the ancient Greeks who worshipped standing, on the grounds that only slaves bent their backs. Furthermore, the Akan theory of destiny even more thoroughly than their theory of the essence of man hampered worship. Each man was a spirit sent into the visible and natural world to fulfil a particular mission. This was not a point of view attained through reflection on human inequalities, though indeed one might argue that human inequalities become so startling that they are suggestive of fatalism. Rather, the Akan view of destiny was simply consonant with their idea of the perfectly integrated and cohesive society in which men have a place somewhat comparable to the parts of a machine. Their place is appointed in it, and in that place they function for the total harmony and well-being. With the Akans it is nearer the truth to describe the State itself as being religious. The Akans did not conceive the world in terms of the supposition of an unbridgeable distance between two worlds, the temporal and the non-temporal, in terms of the supposition that of the two the latter was infinitely the better and the more important; in terms of that idea of some presence outside religious practitioners at which they aim, and which gives rise to a certain type of feeling including the feeling of reverence and self-abasement, characteristics ingredient in the worshipful attitude. Because we were all religious objects, there was not sufficient externality and profundity to call for worship and religion in that sense. As men, that is to say, as accidents, we owed our existence to God; as spirits, that is to say, in our essence, we were uncreated. For this reason, even as men, we were said to be not God's creatures, but his messengers.

God himself was well to the fore of Akan thinking. He luxuriated in various by-names, of which *Onyame* seems to be central. Quite a few writers, Westerman, Rattray, and latterly Meyerowitz among them, have sought to identify *Onyame* or *Nyame* as a sky-god, because of a supposed etymology. It is thought by them that *Nyame* is derived from *nyam* or *onyam*. There is indeed a verb *nyam* in Akan, usually used of witches. In this use, it refers to their rapid and phosphorescent movements this way and that when performing. But this can hardly be the derivation of the name of the Supreme Being. Also, there is a noun, and a cognate adjective, *onyam* meaning dignity, majesty, glory. These are all epithet nouns which admittedly are applied in Akan theology to God. But it is arbitrary to insist that they have an origin in the sun. The Christian or Moslem God is no more a sky-god than the Akan, because the same epithets apply. The identification of the Akan God with a sky-god is encouraged by the lexicographer Chrystaller's rendering of *Onyame* in his great Akan-English dictionary. Here he conjectures that *onyame* is the Akan word for heaven, sky. He invokes a comparison between *nyam* and the root *dio* in Sanscritic languages. Here, he suffers himself to be misled by Sanscritic languages which he assumes, without offering any reason, to be similar to the otherwise disparate Akan in the derivations of the name of God. What he does is, therefore, in effect to have a name for God's abode but no name for God, for Chrystaller himself allows the other bynames of God to be of *subsequent* origin to *onyame*. Now, the word *onyame* does not itself mean sky, heaven, at all, but is only used by metonymy to refer to heaven, just as 'heaven' is sometimes used to refer to, but does not mean, God. In Chrystaller's own translation of the Bible into Akan, not once is *onyame* used for the heavens. He always uses the proper Akan word for it: *osor*. In his dictionary, he gives the correct Akan word for sky: *ewim* (i.e. the regions of the sun).

I do not, in fact, believe that *onyame* means the shining one either. If it meant the shining one, this would be the sun. At least God would then have to be associated with temporal epiphanies or associated—what is more far-fetched—with a shining domicile. Neither of these hypotheses is in fact fulfilled among the Akans; for on the one hand *Onyame* is thought to be invisible and not to have any epiphanies (it is indeed for this reason that he has no images or shrines). On the other hand he is not held to live in the sky by name, but simply above, up there. An Akan myth about the location of heaven seems to connect it, though not to identify it, with the sky. The sky is conceived as an object, a sort of ceiling to the world, perhaps, even, the floor of heaven. According to this myth, once upon a time, when our ancestors were young, God lived very close to us. One day, however, a certain old woman, who was pounding her *fufu* (a plantain meal) with pestle and mortar, struck heaven with her pestle. Whereupon God said to her: 'Why do you do this to me? Because of what you have done, I am taking myself far up.' And, true to his word, as was to be expected, God betook himself far up. The myth goes on to present a sort of Tower of Babel story with a more tragic ending. The old woman, regretting that God was no longer near to man, asked all her children to gather together all the mortars they could find, and by building them one upon another, reach up to God on high. The children were dutiful enough, but found that they were one mortar short. The old woman, evidently quite senile by now, having taken thought, spoke again thus: 'Children, remove the bottom-most mortar, and by placing it on the top one so reach God at last.' Once more the dutiful children did as they were bidden. But now all the mortars collapsed, rolled to the ground, and all the children perished. A remarkable story, but it does not identify God's dwelling-place with the sky, though it connects them.

If *Onyame* is the central name of God, then it must express a strikingly theological meaning. And, from the proliferation of minor deities which the Akans claimed to be an avenue to God's munificence and bountiful protection, I am led to believe that the correct and proper derivation of *Onyame* or *Nyame* is *nya*: to get or *onya*: fortunate possession and *mee*: be satisfied, want nothing. This derivation would appear to be confirmed by the assiduity and frequency with which the Akans appealed for all sorts of help to minor deities whom they conceived as lieutenants of the Supreme Being, almost even as the expression of his omnipotence.

Some writers who have been struck by the Akan conception of the Supreme Being as the one true God have claimed, mistakenly, that he was imported from Europe. But the perspicuous Rattray has already refuted this opinion. *Onyame* is too central to the speech and thought of the Akans, he figures in the immemorial prologue to Akan ceremonial drumming, and he was well-known in the deepest fastnesses of the forest where missionary zeal had not been. If he were of European import, the amount of diffusion which would have to be supposed to explain the thorough permeation of thought and speech by '*Onyame*,' would properly belong to the realm of fantasy. Indeed the Akans believe the knowledge of God to be intuitive and immediate. This is suggested by the adage: '*Obi nnkyere abofra Nyame.*' 'No-one teaches a child God.'

The properties of God were signalised in his other by-names, chief of which was *Onyankopon* or *Nyankopon*. This is usually said to mean one-who-bears-the-weight-of-others-without-crooking. The idea is that the word is derived from *nya*: one, he; *nko*: alone; *mmpon*: crook not, bend not. But Rattray reports that the word among the Akims, a sub-group of the Akans, was in his time *Onyame-nko-pon*, which means the alone great God. There is also a third account which is somewhat bizarre, according to which the proper derivation is from *onyan*: brightness; *koro*: city; *pon*: great, the great sky city. The method of teaching, that of oral instruction, would seem to make the occurrence of *Onyame-nko-pon* significant. It suggests this as the original form from which *Onyankopon* was contracted. In that case, the intended meaning of the latter would be the meaning of the former. Some confirmation may be seen for this in the occurrence of another by-name of God, *Twereduampon*, or, among the Fantis, a coastal sub-group of the Akans, *Twereampon*. The suggested derivation is *twere*: lean on; *dua*: tree; *ammpon*: bend not. Hence the idea of God as that on whom one leans with safety is already explicit in this by-name. Here again the more explicit form would be the older one. Now if in this by-name of God he is explicitly said to be dependable for leaning on, then in view of the rival etymologies suggested for *Nyankopon*, it would not be reasonable to hold it too as expressing the same dependability. I myself am drawn to the meaning, the alone great God. He is also called *Otumfuo* (the mightiest and most powerful by right and fact); *Odomankoma* (Prometheus, Inventor); *Onyankopon Kwame* (Onyankopon, whose day is Saturday); *Borebore* (maker of things). God is invisible, but is everywhere, and is directly accessible. The Akans say that if you wish to say something to God, tell it to the wind.

It has often been said by European writers on the Akan that *Nyame* has no interest in morality. This remark can only have arisen out of ignorance. *Onyame* is conceived by the Akans to be so interested in justice that he gave two different names to two different things that there might not be injustice. He is full of love, and is even said to pound *fufu* for the cripple. This compares with the saying that God cares for the tailless animal. He is, however, at the same time unchangeable, though subject to his own laws. He is the appointer of destiny, and there is a saying that there are no sidepaths from the destiny which God appoints. Finally, to sum up the attitude to God, one might quote the Akan saying according to which the earth is vast, but God is the chief. He is said to be always creating.

The proliferation of gods that one finds among the Akans is in fact among the Akans themselves superstitious. Minor gods are artificial means to the bounty of *Onyame*. They are instituted by priests between man and God, with the explanation that they are portions of God's virtue and power sent to men for their speedy comfort through the exclusive intervention of the priests who also are their guardians. If one thinks of saints and priests in Christianity, one is enabled to form a quick idea of the artificiality of minor deities among the Akans. Intercession through the saints is comparable in intention to intercession through the minor deities. This comparison has in fact been made by Arthur Ramos and Bastide in discussing syncretism in South America. The Christian God has no feast-day, except, doubtfully, the Sunday of Holy Trinity. Similarly, *Onyame* has no feast-day. Feast-days belong to the minor deities. In ritual, the gods are in fact enslaved, for when the correct rite has been performed, the recipient of the rite is left little choice. Ritual is a quasi-magical set of exercises. The institution of minor deities thus appears as an attempt to make sure of God's succour and even influence it. For this reason, there are no rites for *Nyame*, and it would be impious to set oneself up as his priest, the man who has a private extension to him, and who knows his special magical rites. For the same reason, *Nyame* has no altar. To address him, you speak to the wind.

The priest, by claiming special connections with minor deities and hence indirectly with God, was enabled to become oracular. In this way, his influence spread from the religious to the purely social. Omniscience is not a widespread property of man, and the priest became consulted as a supposedly unfailing source of information. People came to appeal to him as one might appeal to the Encyclopaedia or the Criminal Investigation Department. The Criminal Investigation Department is a profane organisation, and its profanity consists in the declared method of operation. The sacredness of the priest too consisted in his declared method of operation, a hand-dip into the omniscience of *Odumankoma*, God. The real method of operation of the priest was, however, as profane, if not as fruitful, as that of the Criminal Investigation Department. He organised scouts who made enquiries and collected pieces of gossip and practically maintained extensive dossiers.

The minor deities were always associated with a focus to which they could be summoned at will. They are said by the priests to be sent by God himself, usually in a blinding flash of lightning. The priest, if he is alert enough, catches this piece of God's omnipotence, and imprisons it in a gourd—until he can prepare a proper focus for it, usually fashioned out of stone or wood, which is acceptable to it. After this, it becomes an intermediary between man and God. This focus is not in itself sacred, but becomes so only during those periods in which the minor deity enters it, whether summoned or not. The priest, of course, claims to be able to summon it to its focus, and the deity indicates his arrival through the priest's body being thrown into a fit of trembling. The priest is frequently a woman, and training before ordination takes two to three years.

That this was a superstitious corruption of the relation between man and God is evident enough from the theology of God. The priest as a mouthpiece of God (*Onyankupon Kyeame*) is an arrant blasphemy. To make this clear, one may consider that there is an Akan saying that no man's path lies in another's. This saying is linked with Akan views on destiny. It is believed that there is an aspect of man called *ɔkra* (literally, mission) which represents the destiny that God has appointed for him. Each man's spirit gives an account to *Nyame* at death, and might be allowed to come into the world of flesh again, or he might be detained at *Samanadze* where the spirits of the dead wander. That the relation between each man and God is direct and exclusive is further suggested by the sayings that when one's spirit takes leave of God to become a man, there are no witnesses; nor are there sidepaths to the destiny that God has appointed for one; a sensible man does not try to change the words that God has spoken beforehand; if God has not fixed one's death, and a human being tries to kill one, one does not die; and if God fills one's cup with wine and a mortal stumbles over it, God fills it up for one again. These sayings fully suggest the fatality and loneliness of life. And the resort to priests and their minor deities appears as an attempt to derive some comfort in face of this fatality and loneliness of life. This spiritual atomism is in direct contrast with the social organisation of the Akan. The latter will be taken up in its place.

God was mainly put to two kinds of use. Supplications could naturally be addressed to him directly, and the satisfaction which he gave was thought to be complete. Each household had a *Nyame Dua*, which was a forked post. On the fork was fitted a pot or bowl containing a stone axe-head, never used as an axe but believed to be planted in the earth by lightning. In the pot was also some water containing specific herbs. The courtyard and even the people were sprinkled with the water in the morning as a prayer for God's continued protection. The *Nyame Dua* is a sign of acknowledgement of our dependence on God. Along with the idea of destiny, God was also used to explain striking talents and special aptitudes. Thus, there is a saying that one does not teach the son of the smith how to forge, God does. And again, if God did not give the remarkable swallow anything, at least he endowed it with swiftness in turning. The occasions on which God is invoked are many and diverse. But in particular he is invoked at the installation of chiefs and in the official drummer's preface.

5. ITS ETHICS AND METAPHYSICS

Most philosophical theories can usually be stated in a few sentences. A great deal of philosophical writing consists, according to a colleague, Kwasi Wiredu, of an anticipation of the objections of half-wits and replies thereto. Much also comprises explanations of the statement of the theories themselves, and of course arguments for them. The absence of a body of writing among the Akans does not in itself, therefore, mean the absence of philosophical ideas. Griaule and Balandier have put questions to sage Africans and elicited from them statements and views which are without doubt philosophical. The Abbé Alexis Kagame wrote a doctoral thesis on the concept of being among the Ruanda-Urundis. Father Placide Tempels sketched the world view and the ethics consequent on this among the Balubas of the Congo. Dr. Danquah in Ghana has done extensive work on the concept of God among the Akans. Intense as some of these works have been, they have been quite sporadic in incidence, and have not been quite clearly seen as forming efforts in a recognisable field of African philosophical speculation.

There are, of course, two main aspects of such a field, the public aspect and the private. Workers in the field can find all over Africa specimens of what might be called a public philosophy, usually tracing out the theoretical foundations of the traditional society. There is also the private philosophy, however, which is more the thinking of an individual than a laying-bare of the communal mind. Without any doubt, much of Kagame's work and also Griaule's is of this latter kind. Griaule, it might be said, found in his blind hunter an individual African philosopher rather than a repository of the public philosophy.

At the same time, the question whether there is an African philosophy must be distinguished from the question whether there are African philosophers. Though a negative answer to the latter implies a negative answer to the former, a positive answer to it leaves the former question still open. The question of the existence of an African philosophy is not a 'uniqueness' question. There is no reason why, in order that there should be an African philosophy, it has to be different from every other philosophy. It is sufficient that philosophy should occur in Africa such that it is not derived from outside Africa.

Some of the problems raised in philosophy elsewhere have answers in African thought. One might take theory of knowledge as an example. Theory of knowledge, speaking roughly, concerns the conditions of knowledge in general, an attempt to fix the limits of the human understanding and its avenues to knowledge of different types, a type of knowledge being in fact constituted a type in virtue of the avenue which the understanding has to it. But theory of knowledge also concerns itself with particular items of knowledge, especially those the application of whose concept-term is also an appraisal situation. Professor Ryle's success-verbs come under this heading. But so do many terms which feature in ethics, like voluntary, excuse, deliberate, willed, intention, *et cetera*. The concept of motive alone, for example, involves the concept of a reasonable man. Whether a man is said to have a motive or not does not depend crucially on his own admissions or the fruit of his introspection. He is not thought to be a privileged observer of his own motives. What motives he is credited with or accused of depend on the general features of his behaviour and the public idea of the reasonable man in his situation. But the public image of the reasonable man is itself heavily infected by the organisation of society and its theoretical foundations. This is why the reasonable man so nearly corresponds everywhere to the ethical man. But if the image and deportment of the reasonable man in being reasonable, depend on the kind of society in which he is located, it is clear that resolutions of ethical problems which are in fact only quasi-theoretical are going to reflect differences in types of societies. To conclude the example, even if catalogues of motives are the same, the ascription of motives will be affected by the theory of society current. Philosophical positions concerning them will show parallel differences. The resort of linguistic philosophers to what we say or do is not, therefore, shortsighted. This is where relativism might affect philosophy.

The limits of the human understanding and of knowledge have been differently drawn by different peoples, and the cleavage between rationalism and empiricism reflect such a difference. This kind of difference does not often reveal itself in the vocabulary, but more often in redefinitions and explications. In the rationalist traditions, for example, in order to explain one thing in terms of another, one must be able to establish an inference from the one to the other. Mere invariant succession is inadequate, and so far from providing an explanation, it itself calls for one. Hence some accounts which in an empiricist tradition would be of the nature of an explanation would in a rationalist tradition be neither correct nor incorrect, but the wrong kind of thing to call an explanation at all. This kind of difference over the notion of explanation already indicates an acceptance of some general concepts and classification of experience. And this introduces metaphysics. The fundamental classification of experience *prima facie* offers various possibilities. The study of philosophical models is itself parasitic on this *prima facie* possibility, for what a philosophical model presents is an epistemological ontology, the general categories of being and their constitution, which form a conceptual framework for apperception of the world. In the West, the bifurcation into matter and spirit is no longer a burning question, the possibility that quality might be founded on quantity causes few nightmares, the explication of spirit into dispositions, and minds into abilities, the founding of individual identity on characteristics of body and relations of bodies, these are philosophical delicacies which strike sourly on the Akan philosophical palate. The questions are philosophical, and so equally are the verbal reactions to them.

Concerning spirit and matter, we have said that the Akans drew a distinction, but did not regard the two categories as being co-ordinate; that the Akans distinguished a number of spiritual factors in a man, that though a body could be identified through physical characteristics, an individual did not so hold his personal identity. Personal identity was traced to the identity of the *ɔkra*. Clan identity was traced to the *mongya*. The *sunsum* was held to be responsible for character, and the identity of character depended on the exclusion of possession by an alien *sunsum*. Thus, a non-dispositional view of character was held in Akan thinking. Moral defects were spiritual flaws, and almost sinful. They were thought to be removable by, so to say, spiritual surgery.

Because morality was so based on metaphysical beliefs, the ethics of the Akans was rationalistic. Since the moral sanctions were spirit-regarding, with a little casuistry they came to accommodate much that was barbarous and cruel. They are the same metaphysical colour notwithstanding, which explains the sense of outrage that the Akans had about moral aberrations. Traditionally, it was not merely a disgrace to be immoral, it was almost sinful, for immorality was held to jeopardise spiritual welfare. The rationalistic, and so absolutist nature of the ethics, also explains the reluctance to admit degrees of gravity of the same misdeed. The classification of the misdeed was held to be formal and defining, and so to admit of no degrees. Punishment did not often in consequence reflect any differences in degree of seriousness of the offence in its severity. An empiricist attitude towards crime and punishment works for humaneness in the latter.

The distinction between spirit and matter, the most fundamental in Akan metaphysics, is reinforced by their distinction between quality and property. Whereas property might come to be founded on the quantitative, in Akan thinking no room was left for quality also being resolvable.

Still philosophy was never scholastic among the Akans, and might Spinozistically be said to be the idea of that of which society was the body. Just as the traditional society has receded into the Akan village, so has the traditional public philosophy. This philosophy fixed the Akan religion and the Akan morality, and indeed often inspired Akan law. The souls of men were members of a spiritual republic, sojourning for a while in flesh, and the rites that an individual had to perform, like those of the washing of the soul, were intended to be phenomenal marks of spiritual states, in order that the society at large might thereby be afforded an insight into its condition as a spiritual entity.

Akan law could be conceived as a sort of supplement to ethics. The retribution that followed moral evil was often slow to come, and when it did come, it was held to express either the displeasure of *Nyame*, who was said to abhor evil, or the atonement which a troubled spirit wreaked on itself. This sort of retribution, because it could be slow in coming, was not always clearly enough seen to be connected with evil-doing. Wicked men might therefore be tempted to great activity. To limit this, systems of man-made law were created which prescribed visible punishment, lest the wicked should seek to profit from the slowness and long-suffering of *Nyame* or the indulgence of one's own soul. Naturally, law had also a purely temporal inspiration.

Social rules were more or less informal and further regulated the association between people. Without being completely rigid, they tended to confirm status.

It is with the culture that I have barely described that the Western culture has unilaterally interacted. Very few elements of Akan culture have been transmitted to the West. On the other hand, Western cultural influence has been channelled along imperialist, commercialist and missionary lines. As long as the imperialistic design might be thwarted by the unifying and binding power of culture, it became of interest to imperialism to weaken this culture. The initial outrages towards the Golden Stool of Ashanti could only be explained in this way. As long as the Golden Stool existed and was in their keeping, the Ashantis, it was thought, were bound to defend their nation against all aggression. With the entry of Rattray into the field, he quickly persuaded the Colonial Office that any direct move against the Golden Stool was bound to be lustily resisted. When Ashanti was settled, the women made a silver stool, not out of a feeling of subjection, but out of friendship, and presented it to Princess Mary. A passage of the speech delivered to Governor Guggisberg by the Queen Mother of Ashanti went like this.

We pray the great God Nyankopon, on whom men lean and do not fall, whose day of worship is a Saturday, and whom the Ashantis serve just as she [Princess Mary] serves him, that He may give the King's child and her husband long life and happiness, and finally, when she sits upon this silver stool, which the women of Ashanti have made for their white Queen

Mother, may she call us to mind.

The missionaries too were guilty of their own acts of vandalism. Thinking that the Akans and other Africans worshipped their objects of art, they collected a great many such objects with great assiduity and consigned them to the flames. It is a miracle that some specimens have survived.

A major vehicle of westernisation was, of course, the formal school. It was ridiculously easy for it to take place for the reason that the formal school was largely unknown to Africa. Though it therefore totally lacked conditions from which to grow naturally, there was, at the same time, little in the *status quo* with which the formal school could be incompatible. The prestigious benefits attending a Western education in an African setting decidedly seduced quite a few persons, some of whom marvellously had their nationalism thereby only made doubly articulate. The representatives of the metropolitan countries carried their culture into the colonies, and those of their subjects who were absorbed into the new administrative and new cultural whirl sought a place in the new glowing cultural sun. The reorientation started in the schools where even the folktales children were told were other folks' tales, not theirs. The standards of passable behaviour and possible ideals embedded in these tales could not always be assumed to be local, and in this way, from the beginning, children were encouraged to live, in addition to an outward life, an inner life that was apart from that of their relations and people; to lose their feeling for that complex from which they had sprung. They were instead encouraged to exploit the startling abilities of the European, his technology, his resourcefulness, his cheeky but rewarding curiosity about nature, and the impression this had made on Africans, in a bid to divert to themselves in a vicarious way something of the reputation of the white man. This was so much accepted in the north of Nigeria, for example, that Africans who today do the jobs Europeans did yesterday are there called white men.

Through the orientation of the formal school, a great opportunity for enriching African cultures was thrown away, for there was no organised and purposeful drive to borrow and adapt, urged by a sense of needs and capacities, a process which would have meant an interweaving of elements of Western cultures with African cultures in an understandable and digestible form.

By means of commercial activity, new tastes and new processes of economic activity were introduced; with these came Western systems of law and mechanisms of government. These did not however seek thoroughly to transform the whole scene; the latter were kept at a minimum, while the former thrived in a riotous way.

Though the vandalism of missionaries has been referred to, artistic expression is perhaps the side of the traditional life which was least shaken. Dance music and literature have continued in strength; and even though the vulgar tourist art has been taking the place of traditional sculpture, the talent for the latter continues to be in evidence.

The patronage which the traditional plastic artists enjoyed was given by chiefs and heads of families, and also by the priesthood. Religious and secular art could be distinguished not so much according to their content as according to their use. Religious art may be said to have included figures and figurines of gods and ancestors. The masks which were put to a magical use would have occupied a role half-way between the religious and the secular. Secular art itself was mainly decorative and informative. It was used to adorn a person or the home, and sometimes to signify rank or a clan.

Mention has been made of the decoration in architecture and on furniture. Mention has also been made of the artistry involved in gold and silver ornaments, the outfits of chiefs offering a startling example of it. The ancestral figures were decorative most of the time, and were put to a magical use only on those anniversaries when the ancestors were invoked. The ancestor figures were not meant to trap the spirits of ancestors in order to harness them. In any case, they did not look like the ancestors. They were only a focus for their presence when they were invoked.

The themes of the art with which we are concerned tended to be connected with origins and life, and included the gods, reproductive forces, usually mother and child, ancestors and forebears. There were masks for fertility rites, and symbolic designations of clans in the shape of plants and animals.

The problems which led to the selection of themes were theoretical ones, for the conservation of institutions had mapped out almost automatic remedies for practical ills. Since the society, from its spiritual orientation, could be loosely said to be sacred, the theoretical problems tended to bear on the nature of gods and other spirits, man's relationship to them, the symbolic designation of the spiritually interwoven clan, the provision of a *locus* for departed ancestral spirits, the provision of nature for man in agriculture and birth, and the exploration of disease.

As the Akans could not write, they expressed their philosophico-religious ideas through art, through the timeless, immemorial, silent, and elemental power so characteristic of African traditional art. Indeed this is the main reason why it was not life-like in a representational sense. Forms had to be distorted. In art, there was a moral-philosophical preoccupation which led it to portray forces of the world, and to portray a force it was essential that it should not be treated like something assimilated, and consequently like something overcome, as the rendering of it in life-like figures would have been. When the purpose of a work of art required it to be life-like, it was lifelike enough. The Ashanti wooden *maidens*, which epitomise the Ashanti ideal of female beauty, and which expectant mothers and children were encouraged to fondle in the hope that their children would be equally beautiful, were reasonably life-like. The life-like figurines of chiefs in Nigeria appear to have been archival in purpose. In the same way, commissioned portrait elsewhere easily serve the purpose of archives. When critics like Gombrich say that the African artists were incapable of realistic representation, they quite miss the point of African art. If they seek life-like representation, they should turn to secular art, the art which was produced for decorative purposes or the purposes of records, rather than moral art, the art whose inspiration is the intuition of a world force.

In examples of the mother suckling a child, the maternal expression of tenderness and solicitude is totally lacking in the mother's countenance. Instead, she tilts her head upwards, not downwards; she is erect and rigid, the unrelated seriousness on her face giving one the idea of occurring in a pattern and set-up of forces, already laid down for us. The Akans, like other African peoples, admitted no excuse for the abandonment of a child except as a religious obligation. The maternal care for a child was not a gift, not a matter of free personal relations, but a stipulation of ineluctable duty. Even the unnatural elongation of the mammary glands in such carvings sufficiently suggest primeval force, a non-private, non-individual, choiceless arrangement.

Traditional African art was not literary or descriptive, employing conventionalised devices for effects like a kind of code language. It was direct, magical, attempting a sort of plastic analogue of onomatopoeia, to evince and to evoke feelings which the subjects induced in one. It was a kind of para-ideography in wood, raffia, colour and stone. A similar effect is produced in African languages. Among the Zulus for example, the night from the depths of its darkness is almost supposed to be not blinding, but deafening. The expression for night and darkness is onomatopoeic of the particular sound that the night is supposed to utter. The name of night therefore seeks to promote the same feelings which night itself does. Among the Akans, too, there is a word, *munsum-munsum*, which evokes in one that sense of the sombre and the uncanny effluence which darkness and night in forest surroundings disengage around us. In sculpture, deformity was used on account of an already existing attitude to it. It was connected with evil and divine punishment. It was at least invested with a totally uncanny nature. The superlative achievement of African art probably lies in the control achieved over deformity and its associated feelings in their societies. Thus in the relevant works, there is near-vigour, but not vigour *à la* Japan, near-hideousness but not hideousness, near-distortion which is not complete, the complex of attributes which does not quite scarify, but leaves a ponderous aura of dark forces, of massive unreleased potency, of the unknown and the indeterminate, almost a hushed version of the ventriloquist ubiquity of the rattle-snake, the sense of mesmerised helplessness, still, cold, silent, enchantedly forlorn, and an aura of the numinous presence of primeval spirit. African art was testamental, except when it was secular.

It is, of course, dying out today. For example, the Ibibios of Nigeria carved skilful, reverent and sorrowful masks with which they covered the faces of their dead chiefs. They soon began to use 'fifth of November' caricatures. A number of reasons can be mentioned in explanation. First and foremost is its dislocation. The position of art in society has changed considerably in Africa with the loss of independence to Europe. It has lost its patronage. Furthermore, the poetic nature which produced the art is being undermined without balance by those attitudes which the impingement of science plus scepticism fosters. The pervasive sense of ultimacy about certain questions which forced one simply to utter a cry, is being lost in key positions in favour of the approach usually called scientific method. The art, which gave expression to that pervasive sense, now stands, like that sense, disgraced.

In the modern Europeanistic setting, art comes to be enjoyed for technical reasons, design, mixture of colours, or otherwise for its arbitrariness, as when a patch of paint is called 'the castle ruins.' Both types of reason equally represent the sloughing-off of art by society as a cement factor. Representation and photography in art are technical, not inspirational. Even the titillation under the skin which works of art deriving from the impressionistic tradition can produce belongs to representation. In Europe, testamental art perished with Goya.

6. INSTITUTIONS AND THEORY

In the treatment of the Akan civilisation in a paradigmatic way, a number of features have emerged. The civilisation operated an essentialist doctrine of man, according to which man had an irreducible essence, which was constant and unchanging. This is a point on which one should expect similarity, if there is a unity in African cultures. This similarity is in fact there. The irreducible elements into which man is separated are of course not given the same names, and are not surrounded by a dogma which is on all points unvarying. It is, however, significant enough for unity that the type of separation should be the same, and that the dogma surrounding the elements, dogma relating to their origins and their dynamic roles, should in salient features be the same.

The ethics flowing from the essentialist conception are again substantially the same, both in the kind of justification and argument that they allow, and even also in the enunciation of rules, which tend towards communalism. Here again, of course, certain differences occur, but these details can be explained by reference to differences in local conditions. Thus, in an area where there are no pigs, to point at the absence of rules mentioning pigs would admittedly be a testimony to one's observation, but hardly to one's sagacity. Rules touching the membership of a family, rules governing responsibilities, the explanation of the responsibilities, the nature of society, and the explanation of its organisation; these are central points over which the identity of African cultures is established. To mention that some societies in Africa are quasi-monarchic and others nomadic is to miss a real deal. Should a monarchic or quasi-monarchic society lose its territory, its organisation, but not its beliefs, is bound to change. Indeed, sometimes, in order to put exactly the same beliefs into practice with different resources, one has to devise different institutions, and organise things differently. The exaggeration of the importance of institutional differences is a perversity that arises from the conception of method as being concerned with the immediately overt, and from the conception of explanation of all societies as the apotheosis of its quite static and inertia-ridden institutional framework as its essence, as that in terms of which, rather than simply by reference to which, striking features of the society must be explained. The effect of this is to treat the institutions as though they were self mandated, and were only subject to an internal evolutionary principle. This, of course, is the wrong attitude to institutions. The approach becomes entirely insensitive to those silent forces which make even institutional changes easy or difficult, acceptable or unacceptable, legitimate or illegitimate. If one were to study the Church of England for example, it could never be sufficient to watch the behaviour of its members on Sundays when they go to church. True as it may be that people have gone to war for the right to genuflect, what they have fought for is not the simple anatomical posture that meets the eye. It presupposes a theology and a doctrine. To understand the Church of England, one has to take note of dogmatics. Ritual indeed enables one to express one's devotion in a satisfying way, but ritual is the result of concessions to realities of life, it represents a reaction between social facts and the religious mind. To suppose that ritual is the essence of religion is as quaint as regarding the signing of the register as the whole reality of the institution of marriage.

To understand a society as a dynamism, one has to look at the theory which underlies the institutions themselves. The explanation of the efficacy of an institution may sometimes be mechanistic, but the explanation of the choice of institutions, of their interrelation and subordination, cannot itself be mechanistic.

When one speaks of the unity of African cultures, one does not thereby imply any uniqueness. One does not necessarily wish to say that there is a certain minimal complex of significant elements which are common to African cultures and which are such that they have never been seen elsewhere before in the history of mankind. Such a claim would clearly be preposterous. After all, at the level of fundamentals there are only few alternatives which face mankind. A culture of man is either essentialist or not, lineages are either matrilinear or patrilinear or mixed. There are logical limits to versatility and creativity. Bearing in mind the fact that the world must have seen quite a few tribes in its time, one is not really surprised if at some time somewhere outside Africa, a people have arranged things in ways fundamentally identical to those in Africa. For the unity of African cultures, it is enough that the cultural complex should occur in sufficient areas of negro Africa. Unity does not imply uniqueness.

The similarity in the European domination of Africa, reacting with negro cultures similar among themselves, has led to urban cultures which are comparable. It has also led to substantially identical problems facing newly independent African countries. The question of what one does with political independence is a very genuine one. If a policy, deriving from the heritage of Africa, could be agreed pan-Africa-wise, then solutions validated within such a policy could be found and simply multiplied to the advantage of economy, effect, and natural unity. The variety of policies gives it today the aspect of multiple wounds. Agreement would draw the skin together, and give Africa a continental outlook.

Questions for Chapter 3
A Paradigm of African Society

1. TRUE or FALSE?

    a. According to Abraham, the Akans believe that all problems admitted of a metaphysical solution.
    b. According to Abraham, the Akans did not believe in religious worship.
    c. According to Abraham, the Akans expressed their philosophical ideas in art.
    d. According to Abraham, African cultures are similar and unique.

2. According to Abraham's account, the Akans believe that human being are not:

    (A) accidents.
    (B) spirits.
    (C) created.
    (D) God's messengers.

3. According to Abraham, the Akans conceived of God as:

    (A) the Sky-God.
    (B) the Shining One.
    (C) the only Great One.
    (D) None of the above.

4. Do you agree with Abraham that the Akan society is a paradigm of African society? Give sound arguments to support you answer.

5. 'According to Abraham, there is no African philosophy.'
Discuss.

Chapter 4

African and Western Philosophy: A Comparative Study

Kobina Oguah

Asɛm ba a, na abebu ba. —When there is a problem, there is a proverb. (Akan Proverb)
Asɛm mma a, abebu mma. —When there is no problem, there is no proverb. (Akan Proverb)

PROLOGUE

Kobina Oguah is a member of the Awutu group of Akans who are closely related to the Fantis. He was born in Ghana on May 1, 1945. He studied philosophy under Emmanuel Abraham and Kwasi Wiredu at the University of Ghana before proceeding to Oxford University for his Doctor of Philosophy (D. Phil.). He has taught at the University of Ghana and several universities in the United States. He taught at Fayetteville State University in North Carolina before leaving for Egypt as a visiting professor at the American University of Cairo where he died of cardiac arrest in December 1994.

Oguah argues for the existence of African philosophy. His reasons are that philosophy is universal and many analogous Western philosophical doctrines relating to metaphysics, epistemology, ethics and political philosophy exist independently in African proverbs, ritual songs, folktales and customs such as those of the Fantis. He argues for dualism, anti-egoism, rationalism and libertarian basicalism among the Fanti subgroup of Akans in West Africa.

Oguah, unlike Wiredu, agrees with Gyekye that the Akans tend to believe in dualism. Unlike Gyekye, however, he believes that Akans tend to use life after death rather than freewill to solve the problem of evil. While Danquah suggests that Akans tend to think of the knowledge of God as mediated by vision and inferred from sensory experience of some kind and Abraham suggests that it is intuitive, Oguah suggests that it is completely innate.

Here are some of Oguah's arguments: "As far as the east is from the west, so far is Africa removed from philosophy...Nevertheless, I shall make an attempt to show in this paper that this image of Africa is a prejudice; that philosophy is a universal discipline. My object is to compare African philosophy with western philosophy. Many of the doctrines of western philosophy can be seen expressed in African thought as well, not in documents but in the proverbs, ritual songs, folktales and customs of the people...[The] dualistic conception of man is found in Fanti thought as well. For the Fanti, a man is made up of two entities: *ɔkra* (soul) and *honam* (body). The *ɔkra* and the *honam* are, like Descartes' soul and body, logically distinct. For the two can exist independently of each other. Thus at death the *ɔkra* is separated from the *honam* but the separation does not mean the end of the *ɔkra*. The *ɔkra* continues to live as a *saman* (ghost) in *samanadze* (the place of the dead)...On the issue between rationalism and empiricism as to the origin of human knowledge, Fanti philosophy takes sides with rationalism. The Fanti believes in innate ideas. Thus there is the saying *Obi nnkyere abofra Nyame* (No one teaches a child about God). A child does not acquire knowledge of God from experience or teaching. He is born with that knowledge. It is not only the idea of God which is innately given to man. The Fantis believe that certain individuals are born with certain abilities, abilities which are not acquired from, though developed through, experience...There are usually representatives of the various language groups of the community on the council. It might be thought that because the councilors are not elected by popular vote Fanti society is undemocratic. This inference does not at all follow. The reason why the councilors are not elected is that there is no need for them to be elected. For all adult members of the society have a right to be present at the meetings of the council, participate in the eloquent debates, and to vote by exclaiming approval or disapproval...If a democratic government is defined, not as one elected by the people, but as one which does the will of the people, then the Fanti system of government is democratic."

African and Western Philosophy:
A Comparative Study

Kobina Oguah

The very concept of African philosophy is apt to cause scornful or, at least, sceptical laughter in certain quarters in the west. As far as the east is from the west, so far is Africa removed from philosophy. The west is the home of civilization and philosophy; Africa is the home of wild trees, wild animals, wild people and wild cultures.

Prejudice dies hard and western anti-African prejudice dies even harder. Nevertheless, I shall make an attempt to show in this paper that this image of Africa is a prejudice; that philosophy is a universal discipline. My object is to compare African philosophy with western philosophy. Many of the doctrines of western philosophy can be seen expressed in African thought as well, not in documents but in the proverbs, ritual songs, folktales and customs of the people. We shall also see, especially when we come to consider ethical and political problems, how African philosophy differs from western philosophy. In this paper, I shall consider one African language group, the Fantis of Ghana. The philosophical ideas of the Fantis are reflected in the philosophies of many other African societies.

1. METAPHYSICS
A. PERSONS

What is a person? To this question René Descartes, the father of modern western philosophy answers that a person consists of two logically distinct, though causally related, entities: a mind or soul and a body. This dualistic conception of man is found in Fanti thought as well. For the Fanti, a man is made up of two entities: *ɔkra* (soul) and *honam* (body). The *ɔkra* and the *honam* are, like Descartes' soul and body, logically distinct. For the two can exist independently of each other. Thus at death the *ɔkra* is separated from the *honam* but the separation does not mean the end of the *ɔkra*. The *ɔkra* continues to live as a *saman* (ghost) in *samanadze* (the place of the dead). Like Descartes' soul and body, the *ɔkra* and *honam* are, while they are together, causally related. Not only does the body act on the soul but also the soul acts on the body. What happens to the *ɔkra* takes effect in the *honam*. If the *ɔkra* of person A is attacked by evil forces, the effect of the spiritual attack appears in the body of A in the form of, perhaps, illness. To heal the body, it is not sufficient to apply physical remedies to the body. Unless the soul is healed the body will not respond to any physical treatment. The curing of the *ɔkra* is one by *eninsifo* (spiritual healers) who perform certain spiritual rites—the slaughtering of a sheep, incantations, etc.—to pacify the attacking spirit. It is after the spiritual healing rites that the physical treatment of the body begins. Physical events are said to have spiritual causes. Thus if a person suffers bodily injuries in an accident, if he is bitten by a snake, if he is struck down by lightning, if he drowns, the cause is attributed to some condition of the *ɔkra*; his soul has done something wrong (*ne kra afom*) his soul is 'weak' (*ne kra ye har*), his soul is grieving (*ne kra ridzi yow*), his soul requests something (*ne kra pe biribi*), etc. Finding the spiritual cause of physical events is the special office of the *akomfo* (seers). We thus see in Fanti philosophy a version of Cartesian dualism and body-soul interactionism. Man consists of a body and a soul which, though logically distinct, act on each other.

B. OTHER MINDS

The *ɔkra*, like the Cartesian soul, is not spatially identifiable. It does not exist in space. It is an immaterial substance. But if so a problem arises as to the existence of others' souls or minds. Descartes considers that he cannot doubt the existence of his own mind. He has to think in order to doubt. But there can be no thinking without a thinker or a mind. *Cogito, ergo sum*, he concludes. He thus has no doubt about the existence of his own mind. But what about the minds of other people? If I have no access to the minds of others how do I know that they have minds? According to the argument from analogy I can tell that others have minds from their external bodily behavior because in my own case I notice a certain correlation between similar bodily behavior and my mental states. When I feel internally happy I bare my teeth and laugh. When I feel depressed tears stream down my face. Therefore when tears stream down my neighbor's face I can be sure that he is depressed. When my neighbor bares his teeth and laughs I can be sure that he is happy. I therefore attribute consciousness to others on the basis of their overt behavior by analogy with my own case.

This argument, however, philosophical scepticism will not countenance for the following reasons. Firstly, it is an inductive argument and therefore suffers the fate of all such arguments: its conclusion is merely probable. But the sceptic has little patience with mere probability. Secondly, even if we accept inductive reasoning as valid this particular kind of inductive reasoning is especially poor. For the analogical argument arrives at the conclusion that the existence of other minds is not doubtful by examining merely one case. By examining myself alone and finding a correlation between certain mental and bodily states, I conclude that in the case of others also the same correlation holds. Reasoning from only one case to a conclusion about a multitude of cases is the worst kind of inductive reasoning which itself, even at its best, does not satisfy the sceptic. Thirdly, the fact that it is theoretically possible for a robot to imitate human bodily behavior in all its complexity shows that bodily behavior is no infallible criterion on the basis of which to ascribe consciousness to others. Hence arises one of the perennial problems of western philosophy, the problem of our knowledge of the existence of other people's minds.

But the problem of other minds is not confined to western philosophy. We find the same problem expressed in Fanti philosophy thus: *Obi nnyim obi ne tsirmu asem* (No one knows what goes on in the head of another).

C. PHILOSOPHICAL THEOLOGY

(a) *The ontological argument*. In the appellations of God in the Fanti language one can see the very same idea that leads Anselm to formulate the ontological argument for the existence of God. In Fanti thought God is considered as the Highest being conceivable. Thus God is likened to the elephant: *Oson kese a w'ekyir nnyi abowa* (Thou mighty elephant: there is no animal mightier than you). The elephant has no superior among the animals of the forest. It is the largest of them all. He is the Highest conceivable being. He is called *Bubur-a-oburadze-do* (He who is infinitely greater than all). From the conception of God as the Highest conceivable being Anselm argues that God must exist. If He did not exist necessarily He would not be the Highest conceivable being since we can conceive of a being who exists necessarily. If, therefore, God's existence is merely contingent He would not be the Highest being conceivable. This argument is, of course, unsound and the Fanti philosopher does not argue that way. But we see in Fanti philosophy at least that conception of God from which Anselm works out his proof.

(b) *The Cosmological argument.* One of the arguments for the existence of God in Fanti philosophical theology is the cosmological argument. God is described as *Boadze* (The creator of the world). A justification for regarding God as the creator of the world in western philosophy is the principle of universal causation, the principle that whatever exists must have a cause. The principle of universal causation is expressed in Fanti in the proverb *'se biribi annkeka mpapa a, nkye mpapa annye kredede'* (If nothing had touched the palm branch, the palm branch would not have emitted a sound.) If every event has a cause the world must also have a cause.

One of the objections to the cosmological argument is that if the principle of universal causation is true then God must also have a cause. It is, however, not only the western philosopher who has raised this objection. Many an African child has received a smack from the Sunday School teacher for asking *'Woana boo Nyame?'* (Who created God?) To this question Aristotle's followers answer that God has no creator: God is the 'unmoved mover.' Whether satisfactory or not this answer finds expression in Fanti philosophical theology as well. God is described as *Obianyewo* (The uncreated one), *Onnyiahyese-Onnyiewie*: (He who has no beginning or end), *Daadaa Nyankopon* (The God who has always been).

(c) *The teleological argument.* The Fanti mind is impressed by the enormous manifestations of order, art and design in the world. Even the maggots, which seem to be in utter disarray, have each a definite path which they follow (*Nsambaa nyakanyaka wonan hon akwan do*) . This order, this plan must have a cause because *Se biribi annkeka mpapa a nkye mpapa annye kredede* (If nothing had touched the palm branch, the palm branch would not have emitted a sound). Everything has a cause. The cause of the plan evident in the universe is *Opamfo Wawanyi* (The Wonderful Planner)—which is one of the appellations of God in Fanti. He is the wonderful planner who planned the universe. Thus we see in Fanti philosophical theology another of the arguments advanced by western theologians in proof of the existence of God, the teleological argument. We are not here concerned with its validity but only to show how it appears in Fanti philosophy.

(d) The problem of Evil. The Fanti recognizes the presence of evil, at least in the present world. Thus many lorries in Ghana carry the inscription '*Wiase ye yaw*' (The world is tragic). Given the fact of evil, how can it be said that the world was created by an omnibenevolent, omniscient and omnipotent God? This is what is called in western philosophical texts the problem of evil. We can also see in Fanti theology these very three attributes of God which generate this problem.

The Fanti believes in divine omnibenevolence. God is compared to a nursing mother: *Obaatan kese a wo do wonsusu* (Thou mighty nursing mother whose love is immeasurable). '*Nyame ye do*' (God is love) can be read on many lorries in Ghana. God is described as the Father of orphans and the Husband of widows (*Nganka hon Egya, ekunafo hon kun*). God stops the tears of orphans (*Oma ngyanka gyae su*). God does not discriminate (*Ompa mu nyi*): He feeds both the good and the evil; *onyen aboronoma, onyen nanka* (He feeds both the dove and the panther). He feeds both great and small. *Se oma oson edziban a ne wire mmfir mpatakowaa* (When He gives food to the elephant He does not forget the ant). God is called *Nyankopon* (The Mighty Friend).

But God is not only all-loving. He is also all-knowing. Divine omniscience is expressed in the appellation *Huntanhunli* (He who sees the hidden). God is able to count the footsteps of a deer on the driest rock (*Okan otwe n'anamon wo obotan sakoo do*). The deer is a light-footed animal. It hardly leaves traces of its footsteps even on ordinary ground. But God can, in His omniscience, trace and count the footsteps of a deer on the driest rock. In addition to being all-loving and all-knowing God is all-powerful. His omnipotence is expressed in Fanti thus: *Otumfo* (the Powerful); *Oso-kor-otsee-apem* (The one ear which hears and discriminates the voices of thousands at the same time); *Ehunabobrim* (All tremble when they see Him); *Mbonsamsuro* (The Terror of the devils); *Biribiara nnso Nyame ye* (Nothing is beyond the power of God).

(e) Immortality. The Fanti answer to the problem of evil may, perhaps, be seen in the doctrine of immortality. The Fantis believe that when a person dies the *ɔkra* continues to live. It departs to *somanadze* (the place of the dead) where it answers for its deed on earth. The righteous *ɔkra* may have seen a lot of suffering in this present world, but in the next world this injustice is righted. The righteous are rewarded with happiness in the life after death. The wicked are there punished with misery, and justice is done. The problem of evil arises only when we take the present world for all that there is. But if we see the picture in its entirety, if we see the universe as consisting not only of the present world but also of the next, there is no problem of evil. For the present injustices are only temporary. In the end justice will prevail. For the Fanti it is the end that matters: *'Ahyese nnhia de ewiei'* (The beginning is not as important as the end). That all will reap the consequences of their deeds is expressed in the thought *'Ibu dzea idua'* (you reap what you sow). The same idea is expressed in the saying *'Obi nhuhu na obi nkeka'* (No one prepares the food for another to eat it).

But if God is all-good, why does He allow evil at all in the present world? Why does He not make the universe uniformly good? Why does He not, for example, prevent the criminal from committing murder but instead allows him to do so and then punishes him in the after life? To this question western philosophical theologians have given various answers. Augustine's lay in the doctrine of free will. Man is a free agent. If God were, therefore, to interface in this, way He would be divesting man of his freedom to choose between good and evil, of his free will.

Fantis do not defend the fact of evil in the present world this way. But what I want us to note here is that the western doctrine of the freedom of the will is also a Fanti doctrine. We have already seen that the principle of universal causation—the principle of determinism—is accepted by Fantis. But there is another school in Fanti philosophy which believes in the doctrine that men are free agents. The doctrine of free will is expressed in the saying, *'Obra nyi woara abo'* (Life is as you make it). We are the authors of our destiny. We are responsible for our actions. No one is to blame for our actions but we ourselves. We are free beings.

2. EPISTEMOLOGY
A. RATIONALISM AND EMPIRICISM

On the issue between rationalism and empiricism as to the origin of human knowledge, Fanti philosophy takes sides with rationalism The Fanti believes in innate ideas. Thus there is the saying *'Obi nnkyere abofra Nyame'* (No one teaches a child about God). A child does not acquire knowledge of God from experience or teaching. He is born with that knowledge. It is not only the idea of God which is innately given to man. The Fantis believe that certain individuals are born with certain abilities, abilities which are not acquired from, though developed through, experience. Thus some herbalists are said to possess their knowledge of the use of herbs not from experience but innately. Some spiritual experts are supposed to possess their knowledge of spiritual matters innately.

B. EXTRA-SENSORY PERCEPTION

Some of these 'special' abilities are also supposed to be acquired through extra-sensory perception. There is a wide belief among Fantis in extra-sensory perception. *Akomfo* (seers), *Eninsifo* (healers) and *Abayifo* (witches) are widely believed to possess the faculty of extra-sensory perception. It is through this that they are able to perceive spirits and receive messages from them for communication to those who visit them for spiritual inquiries (*ebisa*). There is, however, an equally wide disbelief among Fantis in these supernatural phenomena. Many believe that these 'special' people are tricksters. Thus there is the sceptical saying '*Nananom mpow nyimpa na woyee*' (The mysteries surrounding the grove of the dead fathers were created by men). A brief word needs to be said about the origin of this saying. There was on the outskirts of Mankessim, one of the big towns in the Fanti areas of Ghana, a grove which for a long time served as a cemetery. As time went on it fell into disuse. Then a group of cunning people decided to use it as a means of gain. At night they would take their places in the grove, pretend to be the spirits of the dead fathers, make loud frightful noises, demand sacrifices in the form of money, sheep and fowls, and threaten to destroy the city if their demands were ignored. The money was to be deposited in the grove, and the sheep and fowls were not to be slaughtered but to be tied to some of the trees in the grove. The next morning the mayor of the town and his councilors would collect from the citizens the things that the 'Spirits of the fathers' demanded and take them to the grove. The night after, the tricksters would enter the grove and take everything away to a safe place for their use. The next day the mayor and his councilors would visit the grove to see if their sacrifices had been accepted; there was no money, sheep and fowls to be seen where they were left. This practice went on for a long time and reduced the citizens to considerable misery. A group of men became suspicious and decided to make investigations. One evening they went where the grove was and hid themselves near it. Then, when night fell, they saw to their great astonishment some thoroughly familiar faces, living citizens of Mankessim, entering the grove with the instruments with which they made the noise! Quietly the men who had gone to investigate returned to the town and announced their discovery. The whole town was alerted. At midnight the tricksters began their noise.

The mayor and the whole town rushed to the grove. Lo and behold! There were respectable citizens of Mankessim ruining the town through treachery! They were apprehended and punished and the mystery surrounding the grove of the dead fathers ended. This is how the saying *'Nananom mpow nyimpa na woyee'* (The mysteries surrounding the grove of the dead fathers were the work of ordinary human beings) began. It expresses a widespread Fanti scepticism with regard to anything mysterious or supernatural. The saying serves as a precept urging people to exercise a healthy scepticism about whatever appears mysterious, never to give up the search for a naturalistic explanation of such things, and not to yield readily to superstition. Extra-sensory perception is widely accepted but also widely denied among the Fantis.

3. ETHICS
A. THE REPUDIATION OF EGOISM
The Fanti system of ethics is essentially anti-egoistic. Egoism, the theory that each individual should seek his own good and not the good of his neighbor or his community, is frowned upon by the Fanti moralist. For the Fanti the good of the individual is a function of the good of society. The *summum bonum* of Fanti moral philosophy is the welfare of the society. For the individual cannot prosper unless the society prospers. A great emphasis is placed on social ethics as opposed to the ethics of the self, the kind of ethics which the west, with its maxim of 'Each one for himself and God for us all,' practices. Here the west may learn something from Africa. It is no exaggeration to say that the practice of competitive personal accumulation is one of the main factors that generate violence in western society. What you compete to gain you must compete to guard. For others will compete to take from you what you compete to take from them. Competition leads to suspicion and suspicion to violence and tragedy. One of the things that must strike the visitor who comes to the United States is the omnipresence of the police officer carrying a pistol. This potential death dealer is seen patrolling university premises, patrolling grocery stores, patrolling streets and highways. This show of militarism is, without doubt, ultimately attributable to the individualistic ethics practiced in the society. For if it is impressed on the individual not to seek his own good first but that of the community, there will be less of that savage competition which leads to violence and consequently there will be less need for this death dealer. The individual cannot expect to enjoy his wealth in safety surrounded by a world of need. If you do not ensure

that the world around you has something you cannot have everything. *Se amma wo nyenko eentwa akron a wo so irrentwa du* (If you do not make it possible for your neighbor to have nine you will not have ten). Each is his brother's keeper. Each has a right and an obligation to expect help from, and give help to, his neighbor. In this way the phenomenon of concentration of wealth in the hands of a few surrounded by poverty-stricken neighbors is avoided. The doctrine of the interdependence of human beings, the doctrine of social ethics is what accounts for many of the institutions that one comes across in Africa. Thus the extended family system whereby a man's obligation extends beyond his own wife and children to his other relations, is meant to ensure that there be no haves and have-nots.

The Fantis have a way of giving moral instructions to their children. This is often done through folk tales. There are many Fanti folk tales whose object is to impress upon the hearer this doctrine of social ethics. Thus many of the stories about the cunning egoist, Kewku Ananse (The Wednesday-born Spider), are meant as attacks on egoistic ethics. The stories themselves are often simple, but it is the theory behind the story that matters to the story teller. Thus the Fanti expert story teller adds at the end of his tale, in tones of thunderous conviction: Seek the good of the community, and you seek your own good. Seek your own good, and you seek your own destruction. Mutual aid is a moral obligation.

B. THEORY OF PUNISHMENT

Why should a person be punished for wrongdoing? To this question western philosophers have given various answers. According to one school the purpose of punishment is to deter others from committing the crime for which the offender is punished. According to another school, the retributivist school, punishment ensures that the offender is paid back in his own coin. An eye must be taken for an eye, and a tooth for a tooth. Both of these theories of punishment appear in the Fanti penal system; but there is a third theory which is more dominant in the system. For the Fanti punishment is not only a deterrent or a means of exacting restitution but also a means of reforming, 'purifying' the offender. The offender, in committing adultery, for example, not only wrongs his neighbor but also brings upon himself and his own a curse, *mbusu*. To punish him he is not only made to pay damages to the offended but also he is asked to bring a sheep to be slaughtered in the court, which consists of the chief and his councilors, the offended party, a traditional priest and the inquisitive citizen. The priest performs certain rituals with the blood of the sheep to remove the curse from the offender, thereby purifying him. This ritual practice serves as a psychological therapy, freeing the offender of the feeling of guilt. The western judge pronounces the offender guilty, but does not have a means for ridding the offender of the guilt-feeling, which modern psychiatry shows is responsible for many nervous conditions that psychiatrists have to treat. The ritual is not only psychologically therapeutic but also its very solemnity is often enough to reform the offender.

4. POLITICAL PHILOSOPHY
A. SOCIALISM

Fanti political philosophy rejects both socialism and capitalism. The German Jew, Karl Marx, the chief priest of the socialist faith, sees society as a battleground where the forces of the rich and those of the poor are eternally pitched against each other. The rich, by their wealth, dominate the politics of the community and arrange all other matters to suit themselves, and oppress the poor. Marx therefore urges the poor to seize political power. How? By voting? Marx was scornful of the ballot box as a means of effecting social change. In his day the majority of the poor did not have voting rights. But even if the working classes could vote, the rich had the means for ensuring their success at elections; they had the money to bribe their way to success. But if, *per impossible*, elections could be fair, the poor could not afford the money needed for a thorough election campaign. For Marx the poor could come into power only through force, only through revolution. But—

"The same arts that did gain A power, must it maintain."

Having come into power the poor are urged to establish a dictatorship of the proletariat. Why? The reason is that if they do not, the overthrown classes will attempt to return to power through the very means by which the working class came to power. Thus having once come into power the proletariat finds itself in an eternal contract with force. Force must be used to destroy the might of their former oppressors lest they should return to power. As time goes on, however, not only the former rich oppressors but also some members of the proletariat who dare to dissent from the decisions of the new leaders become victims of the new dictatorship. Fanti philosophy, with its doctrine of the citizen as *odehye* (free-born), repudiates the concept of government by the sword, which is what socialism is both in theory and in practice. For the Fanti, the citizen is born free (*Amamba ye adehye mba*) and he cannot, whether rich or poor, be maltreated without just cause. Dictatorship, whether it be that of the proletariat or of the rich classes, is not countenanced in Fanti political philosophy.

Though the chief is not elected by popular vote he has to govern in accordance with the popular will. For the people retain the right to destool their chief at any time. When he is appointed to lead the community he becomes a leader for life but only insofar as he remains an *ohen pa* (a good chief). The moment he begins to exhibit dictatorial tendencies the people initiate a destoolment suit against him. What shames the Fanti ruler most is to hear the expression '*Woetu no egua do*' (He has been removed from the stool). Thus the fact that the Fanti ruler holds his appointment for life does not mean that he is licensed to dictate for life.

For the Fanti chief's rule is not an autocracy but a consultative system of government. He has to consult his councilors on all decisions affecting the society. Indeed, while in council he does not speak. It is his first minister (*Okyeame* or State Linguist) who does all his speaking. If there is a major disagreement between him and his councilors on any decision of his, the decision cannot be put into effect.

His council usually consists of the elders of the society. For the Fantis tend to equate maturity with age and experience, as the saying '*Opanyin ne tu wo kotokorba*' shows. (This does not admit of literal translation. What it means is that an old man s word cannot be safely set at nought). The elders are not appointed as councilors because of their wealth but because of their maturity. Thus rich and poor both find themselves on the council. There are usually representatives of the various language groups of the community on the council. It might be thought that because the councilors are not elected by popular vote Fanti society is undemocratic. The inference does not at all follow. The reason why the councilors are not elected is that there is no need for them to be elected. For all adult members of the society have a right to be present at the meetings of the council, participate in the eloquent debates, and to vote by exclaiming approval or disapproval. In practice only the inquisitive few attend the meetings of the councilors. But when there is a controversial issue hundreds of citizens turn up at the meetings to ensure that the will of the people prevails. If a democratic government is defined, not as one elected by the people but, as one which does the will of the people, then the Fanti system of government is democratic.

Traditional Fanti libertarianism is inconsonant with socialism. The socialist conceives of society as a parallelogram of antagonistic forces. The socialist ruler therefore sees himself as perennially fighting the 'enemy.' But 'enemy' is a variable which takes for its value, at the initial stages of the revolution, the rich, and, later, the poor. Thus the Fanti saying comes true: 'Abaa no a wodze boo Takyi no, wodze bobo Baah so' (The very rod which was used to beat Mr. Takyi will eventually be used to beat Mr. Baah, the beater's own ally). Eventually not only the rich but also the poor, who dare to refuse to dot the i's and cross the t's of the regent, become objects of official persecution; they too are denied employment, imprisoned without trial, tortured to make confessions, murdered, and have their houses burned down. Fantis value human life too much to allow the politician to make it his plaything.

B. CAPITALISM

But neither is Fanti society capitalistic. Behind the western capitalist philosophy is the doctrine of *laissez-faire*, Adam Smith's doctrine of free individual enterprise. It is interesting to note, in reading western political philosophers, Hobbes, Locke, Rousseau, etc., that the function of government is seen as being primarily legal: government exists not to create wealth for society but to provide legal protection for the citizens. The greatness of Karl Marx as a political philosopher lies in part in his widening of the function of government to cover the economic. For the capitalist the economic activities in the state are the prerogative of the individual. The individual should be free to undertake economic enterprises. The state should interfere as little as possible with the individual s economic ventures. Now, since the individual's aim is to make a success of his venture, he employs every means to ensure success. One of the means he uses to maximize his profits is to pay his employees as little as is convenient. This system eventually leads to the maximization of the gap between the rich and the poor. But wealth offends the eye of the poor and absolute wealth offends absolutely; and so friction is begotten.

C. LIBERTARIAN BASICALISM

Fanti political philosophy rejects the doctrine of *laissez-faire*. The purpose of government, for the Fanti, is not only to give legal protection to society but also to ensure, as far as possible, that all have and none is in need. Government is both the legal and economic custodian of society. For unless there is economic justice, legal justice becomes a chronic problem. *Se amma wo nyenko eentwa akron a wo so irrentwa du* (If you do not make it possible for your neighbor to have nine, you will not have ten either). People can have true legal freedom to enjoy their property only if their neighbors are not hungry. *At least the basic necessities of life must be provided freely for all in a free society.* For the sake of a label we might call this doctrine Libertarian Basicalism. This is the political philosophy of the Fantis, as also of many other African societies.

The world today is on the brink of self-destruction because of idealogical conflicts, because of wrong philosophies, capitalism and socialism. The capitalist cries: Wealth for the wealthy, poverty for the poor! The socialist cries: A pint of blood for a loaf of bread! The world is asked to choose between the scylla of capitalism and the charybdis of socialism. But might there not be a third? The Fanti political philosopher answers: Yes, Libertarian Basicalism.

Questions for Chapter 4
A Comparative Study of African and Western Philosophy

1. TRUE or FALSE?

   a. Oguah really believes that Africa is as far from philosophy as the east is from the west.
   b. According to Oguah, the Fanti conception of a person is Cartesian.
   c. According to Oguah, the Fantis are empiricists.
   d. On Oguah's account, the Fantis prefer capitalism to socialism.

2. Which of these arguments, according to Oguah, is not used by the Fantis?

   (A) The Ontological Argument.
   (B) The Cosmological Argument.
   (C) The Teleological Argument.
   (D) None of the above.

3. Do the Fantis (Akans) succeed in solving the problem of evil? Give reasons for your answer.

4. Evaluate Oguah's account of the differences between African and Western philosophies.

Chapter 5

Ethnophilosophy and its Critics: A Trialogue

Kwame Anthony Appiah, Kobina Oguah and Kwasi Wiredu

Ti nyinaa sɛ, na emu asɛm nyɛpɛ —**All heads are alike, but not all their contents are alike. (Akan Proverb)**

PROLOGUE

In this chapter, Kwame Anthony Appiah (see his biographical sketch in the Prologue of Chapter 1) applies his ideas about philosophy expressed earlier in Chapter 1 to Kobina Oguah's comparison of Western and African Philosophies (See Chapter 4). Appiah suggests that Oguah's account of Akan (Fanti) metaphysics (dualism) is uncritical and, hence, produces ethnophilosophy rather than real philosophy:

> ...it seems to me that the imputation of philosophical doctrines as specific as Cartesian dualism to a whole people in virtue of their possession of a notion that has some of the characteristics of a Cartesian mind is intrinsically not very plausible. Were Descartes' peasant contemporaries dualists, because they used such words as *penser?* Oguah offers evidence on these issues in the form of proverbs, and this is part of an established tradition in African ethnophilosophy.

Oguah, whose biographical sketch appears at the beginning of Chapter 4, suggests that such arguments are ethnocentric:

> ...The general effect of his [Appiah's] criticism is that the philosophical

certification of African Thought is questionable because the system is uncritical. It is important, however, to note the following: Philosophy is both expository and critical. Ethnophilosophy is of considerable explanatory value in the field of philosophy known as the HISTORY OF PHILOSOPHY...To consider Jewish, Islamic or Christian concepts of a person as dualistic and to deny that the African doctrine is dualistic...is to apply dual standards...The significance of Kwasi Wiredu's discovery that Akans do not have a 'substance' conception of mind is only matched by the dearth of proof...Akan anthropological data...make his attribution improbable.

In reply, Wiredu (whose biographical sketch appears at the beginning of Chapter 8) writes: "...the reason for saying that the afterlife is conceived by the traditional Akans in quasi-material terms is not just that they would, for example, stuff a coffin with money and clothing. The important reason here is that they *explain* that these will be needed during the journey to the land of the ancestors."

Ethnophilosophy and its Critics

Kwame Anthony Appiah

...What we must be careful of is simply projecting Western ideas, along with these Western-derived methods, into the indigenous conceptual framework and Oguah seems to me not to have successfully negotiated this problem. I want to consider this issue in the context of his interesting discussion of Fanti philosophy of mind, but for reasons that will become clear, I shall begin by saying a little about the philosophical psychology of the Asante people, whose culture and language belong to the same Akan culture area as the Fanti.

According to most traditional Asante people, a person consists of a body (*nipadua*) made from the blood of the mother (the *mogya*); an individual spirit, the *sunsum*, which is the main bearer of one's personality; and third entity the *ɔkra*...

Since Asante-Twi and Fanti-Twi are largely mutually intelligible, it is reasonable, I think to consider Oguah's account in the light of these Asante conceptions.[1] Oguah asserts that the Fanti conceptual scheme is dualist—in fact, Cartesian. But at least three caveats need to be entered about this claim. First, since Fanti is an Akan language and the word *ɔkra*, which Oguah translates as "soul" is, of course, the same as the word for what, in Asante, I identified not with the mind but with the life force, we might wonder why there is no mention, in Oguah, of the *sunsum*...Even if, therefore, there is, for the Fanti, no *sunsum*, we are not free to infer that this is a fact about unadulterated Fanti traditions; it might be the result of Christianization.

Second,... the Fanti, for example, according to Oguah's own account, hold that "what happens to the *ɔkra* takes effect in the *honam*"[2] — that is body. And Oguah offers no evidence that they find this idea at all problematic. But if that is so, their dualism must be at least in some respects different from Descartes's since, for a Cartesian, the relation of mind and body is felt as problematic.

Excerpted from *In My Father's House: Africa in the Philosophy of Culture* by Kwame Anthony Appiah (**98-100**), © **1992 by Kwame Anthony Appiah.** Reprinted by permission of the author and Oxford University Press, Inc. World rights excluding the U. S. and Canada with permission of Brandt & Brandt Literary Agents, Inc.

More than this, there is as Kwame Gyekye—another distinguished
Twi-speaking philosopher—has pointed out, a good deal of evidence
that the Akan regard the psychic component of the person as having
many rather physical-sounding properties. So that even if there were
not these problems with the general notion of the Fanti as Cartesian
interactionists, Oguah's insistence that the "ɔkra, like the Cartesian soul
is not spatially identifiable"[3] looks to me like a projection of Western
ideas. For if, as I suspect, my Fanti step-grandmother would have
agreed that the ɔkra leaves the body at death,[4] then there is no doubt
that at least sometimes—namely, as it leaves the body—it its thought
of as having a spatial location; even if, most of the time, it would be
thought strange to ask where it was since the answer, for a living
person, is obvious—in the body; and for a dead person is likely to be
regarded as speculative at best.

But, third, it seems to me that the imputation of philosophical
doctrines as specific as Cartesian dualism to a whole people in virtue
of the possession of a notion that has some of the characteristics of a
Cartesian mind is intrinsically not very plausible...

I do not myself believe that any of Ghana's Akan peoples are dualist.
But I do not think that it makes sense to say they are monists either:
like most Westerners—all Westerners, in fact, without a philosophical
training—most simply do not have a view about the issue at all.[5] For,
as I have argued already, the examination and systematization of
concepts may require us to face questions that, prior to reflection,
simply have not been addressed. What the Fanti have is a
concept—ɔkra—ripe for philosophical work. What is needed is someone
who does for this concept the sort of work that Descartes did for the
concept of the mind, and, in doing this, like Descartes, this Fanti
philosopher will be covering new territory...

NOTES

1. Indeed the literature on Akan ideas does not often distinguish among the various Twi-speaking Akan cultures; that it is potentially different schemes that are being compared is thus an issue that has not usually been raised.
2. Ben Oguah, "African and Western Philosophy: a Comparative Study" in Wright, *African Philosophy: An Introduction*, 170; reprinted as Chapter 4 in this volume.
3. *Ibid.*, 177; compare Gyekye, "Akan Language and the Materialism Thesis."
4. But my stepgrandmother was a very active Methodist and would probably have taken me to be asking only about the Christian soul: about which she would, however, probably have believed the same.
5. I say "most" because Kwasi Wiredu is a monist and Kwame Gyekye a dualist: but each of them is the product, of course, of an extensive Western training.

Ethnophilosophy and its Critics—a Rejoinder

Kobina Oguah

There are at least two criticisms in Chapter Five of Kwame Anthony Appiah's book, *In My Father's House: Africa in the Philosophy of Culture.1992.* (New York: Oxford University Press, reprinted above), that need to be addressed. The first concerns African Philosophy in general and the second, the Akan conception of a person.

1. DECERTIFYING AFRICAN PHILOSOPHY

The general effect of Appiah's criticism is that the philosophical certification of African Thought is questionable because the system is uncritical. It is important, however, to note the following: Philosophy is both expository and critical. Ethnophilosophy is of considerable explanatory value in the field of philosophy known as the HISTORY OF PHILOSOPHY. A study of ancient Egyptian accounts of the origin of the universe, for example, explains the otherwise strange views of such Pre-Socratic philosophers as Thales, Anaximander, Anaximenes, or Heraclitus.

African nationalists who are philosophers merely believe that the views of Aristotle, Vico, Hegel, Hume, Marx, Russell etc., on Africa's contribution to the history of Philosophy are politically motivated. We merely seek to demonstrate that the views of these Western philosophers (such as Hume, Hegel and Russell) are not based on fact. Hume, for example, said in his *Essays* (London: George Routledge & Sons Ltd., footnote on pp. 152 and 153) in a section on "National Characters:" "I am apt to suspect the Negroes to be naturally inferior to the Whites. There scarcely ever was a civilized nation of that complexion, nor ever any individual, eminent either in action or speculation...In Jamaica, indeed they talk of one Negro as a man of parts and learning; but it is likely that he is admired for slender accomplishments, LIKE A PARROT WHO SPEAKS A FEW WORDS PLAINLY." Hegel writes in his introduction to *The Philosophy of History:* "This distinction between himself as an individual and the universality of his essential being, the African in uniform, undeveloped oneness of his existence has yet not attained; so that the Knowledge of an absolute Being, and Other and a Higher than his individual self, is entirely wanting. The Negro, as already observed, exhibits the natural man in his completely wild and untamed state. We must lay aside all thought of reverence and morality if we would rightly comprehend him; there is nothing harmonious with humanity to be found in this type of character."

In his introduction to *A History of Western Philosophy*, Russell writes that "Philosophy, as distinct from theology, began in Greece in the sixth century B.C." He adds (on the first page of the first chapter) that "Philosophy begins with Thales..." What evidence Russell and other commentators have for claiming Thales to be the first philosopher or more philosophical than African predecessors, for example, remains shrouded in racial mystery. Not a single fragment of Thales' "writings" is extant. For the most part, our knowledge of his teachings derives from Aristotle's confessed rationalization. (See Artistole: On the Heavens, ii. 13. 294a, 13-35). Thales is credited with having said that water was the basic substance of the universe. Yet in Ancient Egyptian cosmologies, developed in such educational capitals as Heliopolis, Memphis, Thebes and Hermapolis some two thousand years before Thales, water (*Nun*) featured prominently as the source and basic essence of life. It is interesting to note, by way of parenthesis, how close the Ancient Egyptian word for water is to words used in southern Ghana today in reference to water. The Ga people call it *Nu*. The Awutu verb for "to drink" is *nu* and the Twi equivalent *num*.

2. PERSONS

On the Akan conception of a person, Safro Kwame seems to be in agreement with Appiah and Wiredu in opposition to my dualistic interpretation of Akan metaphysics. In his 1992 correspondence with Gyekye, for instance, Kwame argues as follows:

> I believe Appiah raises important questions about the attempt to characterize traditional African beliefs and thought. For instance, if the premises of Western philosophy exist in African societies as Oguah for example sometimes suggests, does that mean that the corresponding Western conclusions also exist in African societies? It does not seem to follow, unless the premises in question entail the conclusion in question. But even if the premises e.g. for dualism entail the conclusion, in this particular example, that the mind and body are made of different substances, it would not follow that the people in those African societies who endorse the same premises reach the same conclusions unless they apprehend that relationship of entailment or—at least—inferability. As far as I can see, the belief in life after death, which Westerners share with

Africans and Easterners too, is neither necessary nor sufficient for a belief in dualism. The reason is that one can believe that the life hereafter is either a physical one involving spatial location and subsistence by means of foods, drinks, and clothes or one that requires a mind and, therefore, a brain. It seems to me that both disjuncts are consistent with Akan beliefs and practices and constitute (logically) possible—even if (empirically) false—interpretations of Akan beliefs and thought.

For a fair discussion of the Akan conception of a person, Safro Kwame must give PRECISE illustrations of what he means by "premises," "entailment," and "conclusion" before agreeing with Appiah and Wiredu that the traditional Akans were not dualistic. For instance, what are the "premises for dualism"? What counts as awareness of an entailment or inferablility relationship? Isn't Christian Theology, for example, dualistic? To consider Jewish, Islamic or Christian concepts of a person as dualistic and deny that the African doctrine is dualistic because African traditions lack awareness of these logical relationships is to apply dual standards.

Kwasi Wiredu supports the view that the Akan conception of a person is not dualistic. One of his reasons is that Akans, for example, do not have a 'substance' conception of mind. According to his account, Akans do not think of a person as a composition of logically distinct mental and physical substances but, rather, as a basic, fundamental, primary 'something' to which mental and physical properties are ascribed. A person is, according to his characterization of Akan thinking, neither mental nor physical nor a composition of the two but, rather, that to which mental and physical predicates are ascribed. The significance of Kwasi Wiredu's discovery that Akans do not have a 'substance' conception of mind is only matched by the dearth of proof. In the absence of proof he should, at least, provide a definition of 'substance' which makes the doctrine intuitively tolerable. Akan anthropological data regarding beliefs about birth and reincarnation, naming, marriage, healing, death, destiny, divination, witchcraft, etc., make his attribution improbable.

Another reason which he and others give for denying the Akan system to be dualistic is the claim that Akan rituals and practices appear to conceive of life after death in quasi-physical terms. (See Kwasi Wiredu's "The Akan Concept of Mind" in *Ibadan Journal of Humanistic Studies,* No. 3, 1985, and "An African Conception of Nature," 26th Annual Boston Colloquium for the Philosophy of Science,

Boston University, February 1986.) But does the fact that Christians in the West lay flowers on the graves of their loved ones, maintain perpetual flames at such sites, dedicate books and buildings to them, etc., mean that these Christians believe that the dead relatives continue to live a physical existence?

It must be realized that food, drinks, clothes and money at grave sites in Africa are mere symbols—symbols of the continuing love and affection of the living for the departed. African traditionalists are, of course, aware that the dead do not eat, drink or dress physically. A Ga *wulomo* (priest) who pours his drink liberally to the ancestors at a libation ceremony is quickly reminded by salivating onlookers: *Buulu, kaafite da lɛ!* ("Fool, don't waste the drink!"). Nor does a Fanti who leaves an offering of money or food when he comes across a *Nyamedua* ('Tree of God') believe that Nyankopɔn ('The Mighty Friend' or God) is possibly a physical being! The general African practice of offering physical sacrifices makes the system no more possibly physicalistic than the Jewish faith with its elaborate system of sin offerings, originating, most likely, from ancient African religion. (See Leviticus). The Catholic cross, holy water, alter, incense, Bible, rosary, communion wine, etc., do not make Catholicism physicalistic. (It was disconcerting when my daughter discovered that her Sunday School dollar offering went to the deacons not to God!)

Appiah's main argument for the view that Akans are not dualists is that they seem to believe in three 'entities': *honam, ɔkra* and *sunsum.* See, for example, Chapter Five (page 99) of *In My Father's House,* where he writes that "There is, of course, no reason why the Fanti should have precisely that tripartite system we find among the Asante (and other Akan peoples)." If he is attributing 'tripartitism' to the Akans, exactly what does it mean? The distinction between *ɔkra* and *sunsum* is one of those esoteric distinctions without a difference—rather like 'soul' and 'spirit' in Western Systems. It is important that Appiah's insistence on critical analysis should not ignore African anthropological facts.

Ethnophilosophy and its Critics—a Reply to Oguah

Kwasi Wiredu

With regard to Oguah's comments on my account of the Akan concept of a person, I wish to make a couple of disclaimers. He says that, according to my characterization of Akan thinking, a person is 'neither mental nor physical nor a composition of the two but, rather, that to which mental and physical predicates are ascribed.' In itself, this is an extremely interesting view of the nature of persons, which in contemporary Western philosophy has been exquisitely argued by Strawson. If the Akans traditionally held such a view, it would be gratifying to me to 'discover' it. In the event I have to decline that honor, for I don't think that is the case; and, moreover, in the paper of mine that Oguah cites, I do not suggest that it is.

Oguah is right, however, in noting that I make the claim that the Akans do not entertain a 'substance' conception of mind. As to this, he demands that I 'should, at least, provide a definition of 'substance' which makes the doctrine intuitively tolerable.' Fair enough. But I would like to refer him, if I may, to pages 164-166 of the article (i.e. "The Concept of Mind with Particular Reference to the Language and Thought of the Akans" in Floistad, *Contemporary Philosophy, Vol V: African Philosophy*—a version of which is reprinted in chapter 8 of this anthology). I regard that portion of the article as its most fundamental part, as far as my own doctrinal input is concerned—remember, that article is partly an interpretation of the Akan traditional conception of the mind and partly an articulation, in a preliminary sort of way, of my own views about the mind. Now, in the passage in question I try to explain why mind cannot be any sort of entity at all; and in the course of that project I also explain what I understand by an entity. The point now is that when I said that the Akans do not traditionally hold a 'substance' view of mind, all I meant, as is customary in the terminology of contemporary Anglo-American philosophy of mind, was that they do not hold that mind is any kind of entity.

Another disclaimer: Although Oguah correctly observes that I suggest that the Akans in certain 'rituals' and practices 'appear to conceive of life after death in quasi-physical terms,' he seems to think that I implied by this that they believe that their dead relatives 'continue to live a physical existence.' I did not. To be conceived in quasi-physical, or, as I have tended to express it, in quasi-material terms, is to be thought of on the basic model of material entities but not with all the essential properties of that class of things. In my understanding ghosts (*asaman*), for example, are of this status. They are supposed to be perceivable as of a certain color, shape and, by some Ashanti accounts, smell (the smell of *aprekese*). Yet, they are not supposed to be touchable. Nor, in their dynamics, are they supposed to be at all delayed by the laws of impenetrability, being able to appear at and disappear from places at will. Note, incidentally, that in this conception of ghosts the Akans do not differ in any basic way from, say, Western Christians, although, perhaps, Christian ghosts may lack some of the olfactory richness of their Ashanti colleagues.

But to return to the Akan case: Oguah objects to the suggestion that the rituals in question warrant a quasi-physical interpretation. But the reason for saying that the afterlife is conceived by the traditional Akans in quasi-material terms is not just that they would, for example, stuff a coffin with money and clothing. The important reason here is that they *explain* that these will be needed during the journey to the land of the ancestors. By contrast, when Christians lay flowers on graves, they are explicitly symbolic, which is why that ritual does not invite a quasi-material interpretation. It is not, however, as if orthodox Christian eschatology is innocent of quasi-material conceptions. All descriptions of heaven known to me are unambiguously quasi-material. The Akans don't regale us with stories of the beatitudes of heaven, but, to my knowledge, all the descriptions they give of the world of the ancestors are quasi-material. The same has often been noted with respect to the thought of many other peoples, even if not in so many words.

Still, the Akan conception of a person is quite a complex topic, and I accept Oguah's demand for proofs of my interpretations as a reasonable request. I consider my publications on the subject so far as only a beginning and hope that in the continuing investigations the give-and-take of this dialogue, which I appreciate, and further ones, which I would welcome, will prove helpful.

Questions for Chapter 5
Ethnophilosophy and its Critics

1. According to Appiah, most Akans:

   (A) are dualists.
   (B) are monists.
   (C) Cartesians.
   (D) do not have a view on dualism.
   (E) are all of the above.
   (F) are none of the above.

2. According to Oguah, Appiah's criticisms:

   (A) do not apply to African Philosophy.
   (B) decertifies all philosophical systems.
   (C) suggest that philosophy is expository, but not critical.
   (D) are such that he (Oguah) can't protest too much against them.
   (E) are all of the above.
   (F) are none of the above.

3. State and evaluate Appiah's three caveats about Oguah's claim that the Fantis (Akans) are dualists.

4. What is ethnophilosophy and of what value is it?

5. State and evaluate the arguments by Oguah and Wiredu on the Fanti/Akan conception of a person.

Chapter 6

The Akan Meaning of God

Joseph Boakye Danquah

Obi nkyerε abofra Nyame. —**No one teaches a child God. (Akan proverb)**

PROLOGUE

Joseph Boakye Danquah was a philosopher by training and a lawyer by profession. Although Kibi in the Akim region was his hometown, he was born on 21st December 1895 at Bepong in the Kwahu region in the land of the Akans of Ghana. He, together with Kwame Nkrumah and others, led Ghana's independence movement. When Nkrumah became president of Ghana, Danquah became the leader of the opposition party. He was arrested by Nkrumah's government on 8th January 1964 and detained at Nsawam prison until his death on 4th February 1965.

Both Danquah and Abraham acknowledge that the Akans conceive of God as a male who, like boys born on Saturday, is called Kwame. They both reject the view that *Nyame*, the one and only God of the Akans, is a sky-God. That view, Danquah argues, identifies God with his abode and relies on foreigners and lay-people for the true interpretation of a technical term. Danquah, unlike Abraham, thinks that the Akans conceive of God, *Nyame*, as the Shining One. Some of the reasons given for this conception are that the Akan words *Onyam* and *Nyam* mean glory, bright or shining and a popular Akan proverb suggests that no one needs to point God out to a child.

Here are a few of Danquah's arguments in his own words: "The

Akan designate the Supreme Being by three distinctive names, *Onyame, Onyankopon* and *Odomankoma. Onyame,* we shall show presently, corresponds to the basic idea of Deity as commonly understood in Christian theology...I think, the designation of the Akan *Nyame* by the term "Sky" God is meaningless, soley upon the evidence that He had left the earth and gone to live in the sky...The other evidence obtainable from Christaller unmistakably shows, to my mind, that *Onyame* or *Nyame* is derived from the word *onyam* which means glory, dignity, majesty, grace, etc...as in the phrase, *ohye ne ho nyam,* "he glorifies himself;" *"mehye m'anim nyam wo Farao so,"* "I will be honored upon Pharaoh," or "I shall be glorified in Pharaoh"...Obviously, from the above evidence, we are driven to one only conclusion, namely, to say with Christaller that the word *onyame* as meaning heaven or sky was "probably called so from its splendor or brightness"...The point of this argument may best be seen in the Maxim: "No one points out the *onyame* (i.e. the luminous place) to a child," or, as Rattray comments, "little children who lie sparwling on their backs looking up to the sky do not need to have it pointed out to them." The obvious reason for the maxim is that the thing, heaven or sky, yields its own significance and meaning: Where it is brightest. The native and attributive power of *Nyame,* God, is that he is a shining living being elevated above, beyond the ordinary reach of man, but manifest to them through His light which is visible even to a child. The fact that He is not identified with the sun, nor with the moon or stars, although associated with the firmament above, and the mind and intelligence is attributed to him, gives him a personality that must be something divorced from the impersonal sky or the firmament...Our conclusion in the present section must be as follows. That *onyame* was made the substantive name of a power, living and personal, by the subjunction of the usual pronominal prefix 'O-' to *nyame,* and the addition of the suffix '-e' to the final 'm' in *nyam* to give the verbal balance for a proper name. Hence *O-nyam-e* is from *Nyam,* shining, glory or bright, and there are still people who pronounce *Nyame, Nyam,* in poetry and elsewhere. The Fantis always say *Onyam,* and the view is held that the final *e* in *Onyame* is probably an Ashanti and Akim refinement of dialect in much the same way as the Fantis say *ohin* (king) and the Ashanti and Akim say *Ohene* (king). In a word, the Akan root name for Deity is *Nyam,* the Shining One."

The Akan Meaning of God

J. B. Danquah

I. *ONYAME*, THE AKAN DEITY
1. IN WHAT SENSE A "SKY"-GOD

The most used name of God in Akanland is *Onyame*, often pronounced *Nyame*, and modern anthropologists say He is a "sky" God. I feel convinced from internal evidence that the appellation is misleading and does little credit to *Nyame* Himself.

The Akan designate the Supreme Being by three distinctive names, *Onyame*, *Onyankopon* and *Odomankoma*. *Onyame*, we shall show presently, corresponds to the basic idea of Deity as commonly understood in Christian theology. Next is *Onyankopon*, who is more appropriately described as Supreme Being or Supreme Deity in the sense of a personal religious God. The third, *Odomankoma*, corresponds to a conception of the Godhead as the Interminable or Infinite Being.

Common to each of these is the appellation of *Boadee (Booadee)*, Creator, and specifically to *Odomankoma* is that of *Borebore*, Excavator, Hewer, Carver, Creator, Originator, Inventor, Architect. Each of the three names of God is recognized as possessing certain qualities characteristic of its function. One of the best known of such qualities is that of *Onyankopon* who is called *Kwaame*, or *Kwaamen*, that is, "He whose day (of birth, or of worship) is Saturday." It is for this reason, namely, that the day of birth of *Onyankopon* is known, that under this name He is made the object of religious adoration to a far greater extent than either *Onyame* or *Odomankoma*.

Now, until anthropologists left Europe to study "native" races the idea of a "sky"-God was not commonly associated with the Supreme Deity. He was, to them, either the God of Heaven or the Celestial Godhead, or in Milton, plain Celestial. But, for one reason or other, it has become the fashion to designate the high-gods of "native" races as "sky" Gods, and one's admiration cannot but be stirred by the studied insistence to dissociate the Akan *Onyame* from "heaven," keeping him pinned, as far as bearable, to the rather funny idea of "sky."

Reprinted by permission of **Frank Cass & Company Limited, England,** from *The Akan Doctrine of God: A Fragment of Gold Coast Ethics and Religion* by **J. B. Danquah, (30-57) © 1968.**

There was, of course, some justification for this linguistic acrobatic to jump one godhead over the other in precedence within the firmament. According to Rattray, he was told that *Onyame* was "some power usually considered non-anthropomorphic which has its abode in the sky"; that *Onyame* was derived from *onya*, to get, and *mee*, to be full, satiated; that "long, long ago *Onyame* lived on earth, or at least was very near to us, and not then high up in the sky, and that it was much later that 'he took himself away up in the sky.'"[1]

In other words, *Onyame* was not, or of, the sky. Originally he was some one staying on the earth, or near the earth, who later acquired new quarters in the sky, like some of the Greek gods did. Before the Akan God acquired this new domicile his name or nature was, according to Rattray's guides, that of giving satiation or satisfaction. (It should be noted that I do not subscribe to the interpretation of the word *Onyame* to be derived from *onya*, to get, and *mee*, to be full, satiated. *Onya* does not mean "to get" it means "he gets." *Nya* is the infinitive form, "to get." For the purpose of argument, however, it seems convenient to work with Rattray's own premises.)

I believe it ought to have struck Rattray that if indeed the Akan had wished to look upon *Onyame* as "sky"-God, they would have changed his name as soon as he changed his domicile from the earth to the sky. But apparently they did not think the change of domicile made any difference to the nature of *Nyame* for whether he lived on earth or in the sky, he was known to the Akan as *Onyame*, and remained to them as such.

It follows that, to the Akan mind, the fact that *Onyame*, for some reason unstated, was elevated to the sky, did not thereby cause his native quality to be altered. The Akan people appear to have looked at the matter this way: If a hunter, living in a mud hut with his family, subsequently changed the form of his dwelling and went to live in a grass house, or a glass house, he would not thereby have exchanged his trade to acquire a new name or characteristic. He would still remain to his fellow-men the hunter, or the ex-hunter, who now lives in a grass house or glass house. But no one would think of calling him grass or glass hunter, for it would be meaningless in the context.

So, too, I think, the designation of the Akan *Nyame* by the term "Sky" God is meaningless, solely upon the evidence that He had left the earth and gone to live in the sky.

Indeed, if Rattray and the other anthropologists were looking about for a proprietary character to distinguish the Akan *Onyame* from the other types of Akan gods, they could not have done better, with the information at their disposal, than to have called him the "Satiation or Satisfaction God," following the supposed etymology of the name given Rattray by the "natives."

But this was not to be. From now on, and to the very last, the Akan *Onyame* (as also *Onyankopon*), became to the anthropologists not "God of Satisfaction," or "Repletion," but "Sky" God. And thus was the mental horizon of European students of the Akan religion definitely "set" for them by the limitations they had chosen to impose on the workings of their own minds. The fixed firmament, possibly only the near-side of it, became for these students the limit of the horizon the Akan could be supposed to have reached in their search for Godhead. Is it any wonder, then, if students of Akan thought were progressively hindered in their effort to *understand* what the *Akan* were *thinking* about most of the time when they talked about God-*Onyame*? What these anthropologists and scientists did was, of course, to create confusion for themselves and others, for first they caused a misunderstanding and then called it learning, which is not a bad parody of the aggressor's conception of a new order: to make a solitude and call it peace.

It would not matter much to the Akan were such learned misunderstanding to be confined to field anthropologists, but, as in this case, the "Sky" God idea became so widespread that even the great Marett, of Oxford, after critically reading Rattray's, *Religion and Art in Ashanti*, and writing a treatise upon it, and after acknowledging that the Akan conception of Supreme Being was that of a *living* God, maintained, nevertheless, in addition, that to the Ashanti or Akan, God was a "Sky" God: Whereas, in truth and in fact, a God cannot be a "living" God if He lives in the sky.

2. SOME FALSE MEANINGS OF *NYAME*

A similar fusion of incompatible ideas would seem to have led Dr. M. J. Field in her *Religion and Medicine of the Ga People* (p. 61), published in 1937, to follow Rattray's style and describe *Nyonmo*, the Supreme Being of the Ga people, as "certainly...a sky-god" because in the Ga language "the word *Nyonmo* means rain. The only way of saying that it is raining is to say that *Nyonmo* is falling." In the major part of her book the Ga *Nyonmo* therefore remained sky-god and rarely a rain-God. Which, one must think, is a peculiar way of interpreting a people one is supposed to know to others who are not supposed to know them.

Probably Dr. Field is better justified in her interpretation than the

anthropologists of the Twi or Akan people. For she, at least gives the
Ga word for rain, which looks like being the same as the word for the
Supreme Being, or what she elsewhere calls "Nature." The Akan
anthropologists do not quite do the same thing.

All the same, Dr. Field is not less wrong than any others in calling a
Gold Coast God a "sky" God, even on the evidence of the similarity of
the names for rain and for God. Mr. E. A. Ammah, of Accra, a poet of
the Ga race and an authority on the language, has explained to me
personally that the term *Nyon* in *Nyonmo* does not mean rain. *Nyon* is
found in other compounds where it appears to mean bright, light, shine,
day, or the firmament. *Mo* is the Ga suffix for person acting or doing.
Thus *Nyonmo* (God) possibly means "The Master of Light" or "The
Actor of Light," etc. Other words in the Ga language using *Nyon* in the
sense of light or brightness are *nyon-tsele*, "moon", *nyonten*, midnight.
Mr. Ammah adds that the Ga word for rain is best written without the
middle "*n*" or "*ng*," *nyomo* and not *nyonmo*, the first "*o*," of course,
being the broad "*o*," as "*oa*" in *broad*, and not the "*o*" in "*told*." For the
benefit of the research student it may be useful to add that the "*tsele*"
in *nyontsele* means "brightening up," *tse* often means neat. (*Ehentse*, he
is neat, holy, or attractive); also the "*ten*" or "*teng*" in *nyonten* means
"the middle of." So that *nyontsele* primitively meant, probably, "Nyon
is brightening up," and *nyonten* also meant "The middle period of
Nyon," whatever *Nyon* may mean. In any case, there is here evidence
which points to the conclusion that the "Nyon" in *Nyonmo* belongs to
a certain fundamental general idea covering all the elemental changes
in the firmament, and not alone concerned with rain. If we may venture
an opinion, it would be that the *Nyon* in these words refers to the
firmament as a place associated with the "Shining One."

As regards the Akan *Onyame*, it may be useful to note first that the
principal syllables are or are nearly the same as in the Ga, and the
primitive consonants are much the same, NYNM. Students of other
African languages, east and west, would discover other similarities in
the different tribal names of God. Some of the East African tribes,
according to Edwin Smith, call God *Nyambi* or *Nzambi*, and we are
taught in philology that b, m and n, as also y and z, often assimilate.
Moreover, Father Williams, S. J., in his *Hebrewisms of West Africa*, has
suggested that the M in the Akan *Nyame* is the old W in the Hebrew
Jahweh, and Dr. Field has further suggested a certain similarity between
the Ga *Nyonmo* and the Hebrew Jahveh; Captain Rattray also, we recall,
made the same suggestion concerning the Ashanti *Nyame*, that He is the

Jehovah (Jahweh) of the Israelites. Dr. Williams' view, in fact, is that the Hebrew Tetragrammaton is no other than these African names of God: JHWH, NZMB, NYNM. But this is probably a problem best left to the philologists.

As regards *Onyame*, we may note, in the second place, that Rattray and others were ignorantly following the "man in the street" interpretation when they said that *Nyame* meant the "sky" God. There is no doubt that in poetry and other language the sky is often referred to as the *onyame*, but the Akan name for sky, as such, is not *onyame* or *nyame*, but *ewie* or *ewim*, which is clearly so stated in Christaller's *Dictionary*, 2nd edition, p. 576. The word *ewim* is obviously from *owia mu*, "in, or, at the place of the sun," *owia* being the ordinary word for sun. Literally, *ewim* means "Where the sun reigns." There is another word, *ewie*, which means "the overhanging firmament," and it or *ewim* usually means the air, atmosphere, heaven (Christaller).

Ordinarily, the Akan word for the upper part or parts, or any space above, is *osoro*, which, at p. 472 of Christaller, is given to mean the upper world, what is above, upper regions, sky, heaven. Throughout his edition of the great Twi Bible never does Christaller use the word *onyame* as meaning heaven or sky. At all times he translated heaven by the word *osoro*, e.g., the angels are called *osoro-abofo*, messengers of heaven.

As already noted, the word *onyame* is used in poetry and the maxims metaphorically to mean the upper parts, heaven, even the clouds, as of rain, but not to such an extent as to lead a scientific investigator to identify the God-idea with the sky-idea exclusively. The whole effort is a sad story. It is well known that for nearly 2,000 years at least, and for 4,000 years at least, among the Europeans and the Hebrews respectively, the idea of a heavenly or celestial God, located at a certain distance in the sky, has been a fixed one among these nations. And they always called this God the heavenly God, the Celestial God, or the God of Heaven. How anthropologists hailing from these countries came to locate another class of gods, skyscape, or sky-ward "high-gods" in Africa, and among "native" races generally, must be merely a curious geographical and psychological study.

Part of this sad story must be ascribed to the fact that the Akan had chosen to leave the study of their thought to foreign nationals who were imperfectly acquainted with the language and ethos of the Akan. A little knowledge of the Akan language made each of such men an authority on the Akan. The same sad story might be written of an Akan who, taking up a study of native European languages and cultures, came to discover that the word God for the Supreme Being was a Teutonic word derived from Guth or Gud or Goth or Ghen, which, in its turn, is derived from a Sanscrit root, *gheu*, to invoke, to pour, the latter being the sense in which the word was used by the ancient Teutonic races in sacrificial offerings. Now, if any Akan anthropologist in Europe was, for this reason, to call the Teutonic God a "Pouring God," would not research students pick a quarrel with him for mistaking the root of a word for its present usage or meaning? Indeed, if we are to pay due compliments to one another's gods, we should call them by none but their proper names.

As regards the suggestion by Rattray that the Akan God or Supreme Being is conceived to be a Satiation God or God of Fulness, looking at the form of the name (*Onya-me, mee*), it is perhaps, enough to point out that the highest authority Rattray discloses for that derivation is that it was "given by natives."

Now, of course, no scientific enquirer would be satisfied with the merely popular or "man in the street" interpretation of a highly technical theological term like *Nyame* of God. Doing that could never bring us exact knowledge. Like the popular belief that the English word God is associated with "good" must be this explanation of the similar Akan word given to Rattray by "natives." Unless we are told who the natives are—their ability or opportunity for giving a correct interpretation—it must be obvious that the evidence may be quite worthless.

As to "satiation" there can be no doubt that any one who "gets God" (*onya me*) would be full or satisfied, in the same way as any one with whom God abides (in the phrase "God be with you," corrupted into "goodbye") would be good, or expected to have God with him. But both interpretations are ignorant popular etymologies, and *Onyame* no more originates from "Obtain-and-be-satisfied" than God is from "Good."

3. THE TRUE MEANING OF *NYAME*

The question has been seriously put to me in discussions with Mr. K. B. Ateko and Dr. J. W. de Graft Johnson that if Dr. Williams is right in suggesting that the Hebrew tetragrammaton is the same, discoverable in several of the African tribal names of God, then what is the explanation for peoples so distantly separated having a similar name for one idea? And, further, does the etymology or derivation of the Hebrew Jahveh or Jahweh, agree with the etymologies in the several African names for God? In other words, does, e.g., the Akan group of consonants NYM stand for a meaning similar to the Hebrew group JHVH?

These are difficult questions. The first is mainly historical, namely, whether the African tribes have at any time had such connection with the Hebrews, in Egypt or elsewhere, as to have led the one to borrow an important word from the other. It is well known that Moses had not a name for God when he met the angel of the Lord on Mount Horeb. He had married Zipporah, daughter of Jethro, a Midian priest, and had been staying with the family for some period until "in the process of time, the king of Egypt died." At a loss for a true name for Adonai who had sent him to go to the Israelites in Egypt, Moses may well have adopted from his father-in-law the name for God that Jethro was in the habit of using as a priest. At any rate we are told in Exodus iii. 14 that God told Moses His name was I AM, that is *Jahveh*, in Hebrew.

Now, the Akan word for I am is *Eye me*, or *Meme Me*, and it is quite impossible for us to say here whether, like the Hebrews the Akan people turned *EYEME* into *NYAME*, or that the Ga people turned *MIDZI-ME* into *NYONMO*. It is enough to say that in most of the tribes in which *NYNM* or *NZMB* appear in the name of God, *ye* or *dzi* is the indicative of the verb "to be," *am*, and that the personal pronoun (nominative) is *me* or *mi*. Where the English would say, "I am what I am," the Akan would say, "*Me ne nea me ne*," or "*Me ye nea me ye*."

But, as aforesaid, these are very difficult and complicated issues, requiring considerable research, for which the present writer is not well equipped without a knowledge of Hebrew, little only of African languages, and much less access to the original books and other sources. Meanwhile, by going back to Christaller, our sure and certain guide, we may hope to arrive at a certain fundamental meaning of the word *Nyame*, by appealing mostly to the best form of evidence, internal evidence. It is just possible that in all the languages in which the *NYM*, or *NYMB* or *NZNM* formula is found for the name of the Supreme Being, the root meaning is I AM, as in the Hebrew *JHWH*, but I have not enough evidence to be certain.

The other evidence obtainable from Christaller unmistakably shows, to my mind, that *Onyame* or *Nyame* is derived from the word *onyam* which means glory, dignity, majesty, grace, etc., as in the phrase, "*ohye ne ho nyam*," he glorifies himself; "*mehye m'anim nyam wo Farao so*," "I will be honoured upon Pharaoh" (A.V.), or "I shall be glorified in Pharao" (Douay Version), of Exodus xiv. 4. Another example is, "*n'anim ye nyam*," "he is honourable, illustrious, dignified, respectable."

It is from the same source that we obtain the Akan word *anuonyam* (Fanti, *anyim-nyam*), literally, "splendour of the face," glory, splendour, brilliancy, excellency, celebrity, honour, dignity; or the phrase *hye anuonyam*, to glorify, to honour. An *onuonyamfo* is an illustrious or distinguished person.

In fact, all such words eventually derive from the verb *nyam* to move quickly or rapidly, to wave, to brandish, flourish, as in the phrase *onyam gya*, he waves a firebrand. It means also to wink or squint, and *nyama*, to beckon, to move to and fro, would seem to be connected with the same root.

The reduplicative of *nyam* is *anyinnyam*, connected with *nyinam*, to glimpse, to appear by glimpses, to flash, to glitter, gleam, giving the noun *anyinam*, lightning.

Obviously, from the above evidence, we are driven to one only conclusion, namely, to say with Christaller that the word *onyame* as meaning heaven or sky was "probably called so from its splendour or brightness."

Christaller went on to add that this derivation was similar to the use of "the root div- in Sanscritic languages," such as the name *deva* in ancient Indian mythology which "denotes the shining powers of the upper world, the radiant dwellers in the sky" (Carpenter, *Comparative Religion*, 210). The evil spirits were called in India *asuras*, a word which in Iran (Persia) was, conversely or perversely, made the name of God the Lord (*Ahura*). As already remarked, among the Indo-Iranian peoples the opposition of light and darkness, good and evil, was central for the understanding of their religious doctrine. This opposition led to the Iranian philosopher, Zoroaster, elevating the conception of the *Ahura* and degrading the Indian *deva, dæva*, or *daivas* to the rank of malicious powers and devils. And this unfortunate confusion all English-speaking peoples have inherited in the use of both "divine" and "devil," which are derived from the same root, *div-*, the "devil" meaning simply the little god, or the little of "that which shines," *div-*.

Here, it may be said, we have veered round to the point where we had left the "sky" God school, namely, that the Akan God is so described because of a certain connection between his nature and the brightness of the sky or heaven. Obviously. But there is a certain distinction, and it is a distinction with a great amount of difference.

It is legitimate to infer from the evidence Christaller affords, that the name *Onyame* as meaning Heaven or Sky arose because the thing so named (the high expanse or firmament) is the bright or shining place, the place of the sun and lightning, the glorified or illuminated place. This is not the same as saying *Onyame* is called Sky God because he lives there, or has gone to live there. The Akan, it must be urged, should be credited as having, from the very beginning, conceived the idea that if there is to be a God, then He must have qualities and powers which are illustrious, glorious, luminous, shining and bright, and the *association* but not identification, of Heaven or the Firmament with that idea is a natural and highly instructive one.

The point of this argument may best be seen in the Maxim 227: "*No one points out the onyame* (i.e., the luminous place) *to a child*," or, as Rattray comments, "little children who lie sprawling on their backs looking up to the sky do not need to have it pointed out to them" (*Ashanti Proverbs*, p. 24). The obvious reason for the maxim is that the thing, heaven or sky, yields its own significance and meaning: Where it is brightest. The native and attributive power of *Nyame*, God, is that he is a shining living being elevated above, beyond the ordinary reach of man, but manifest to them through His light which is visible even to a child. The fact that He is not identified with the sun, nor with the moon or stars, although associated with the firmament above, and that mind or intelligence is attributed to him, gives him a personality that must be something divorced from the impersonal sky or the firmament.

To Him is attributed also the providence of rain, sunshine and growth, and indeed, of life generally. Now, once such a beginning is made by any intelligent race, the idea of the Bright One being the source or creator of life, or of Being, or of all things, could not be long in coming to the apprehension of the race. Says Christaller, "according to the notion of the natives," *Onyame* or God is "the Creator of all things," and "God never ceases to create things."

Further, Christaller suggests that originally the word *Onyame* had no plural, but that in recent use the name had come to mean a "god of polytheists, with a newly introduced plural, *a-nyame*." "The heathen Negroes are," he goes on, "at least to a great extent, rather monotheists, as they apply the term for God only to the Supreme Being."

Now, the remarkable thing is that these words were first published by Christaller as far back as 1881 and are retained in the 1933 edition of his classic dictionary. Yet European anthropologists of the present century, in reckless or more probably ignorant disregard for what this great pioneer had discovered and established before them concerning the thought or mind of the Akan perpetually go on creating a spate of literature about the Akan most of it based upon a misunderstanding, but put forth to the world with a great show of profound learning as result of having "lived with *the natives*" for a tour or couple of tours.

In consequence, among Europeans, the popular idea of Akan "religion" is as part of West Africa's "fetish" cult. Actually, Akan religious doctrine knows only one God. Everything else found in the land, in the form of religion, is nothing else but superstition, and one may even make a study of the many ramifications or "systems" of such superstitions—just as many have made a study of witchcraft among the European nations—but, in justice to the Akan, the cults of the private man desirous for short cuts to satisfy the natural craving for some religion, should not be ascribed to the Akan as their racial or national conception of God. To some extent, it must be admitted, the Akan themselves are to blame for having no native literature, their own religious doctrine being embodied in certain traditional forms and sayings which, of course, are not easily comprehensible to students of anthropology, armed, as most of them are, with the belief that everything in Darkest Africa is dark, and without the "Christian" light. But at least Christaller should have been a warning, and it is much to be regretted that so much misunderstanding has been suffered to pass under the umbrella of learning, or "anthropology."

Be that as it may, our conclusion in the present section must be as follows. That *onyame* was made the substantive name of a power, living and personal, by the subjunction of the usual pronominal prefix O- to *nyam*, and the addition of the suffix -*e* to the final *m* in *nyam* to give the verbal balance for a proper name. Hence O-nyam-e is from *Nyam*, shining, glory or bright, and there are still people who pronounce *Nyame*, *Nyam'*, in poetry and elsewhere. The Fantis always say *Onyam*, and the view is held that the final *e* in *Onyame* is probably an Ashanti and Akim refinement of dialect, in much the same way as the Fantis say *ohin* (king) and the Ashanti and Akim say *Ohene* (king). In a word, the Akan root name for Deity is *Nyam*, the Shining One.

4. THE UTILITARIAN NATURE OF *NYAME*

The nature of *Nyame* is that he is the Shining Power, but that does not explain his functions. We gather the sum and substance of these from his appellations or strong names. He is called *Amowia*, the Giver of Light or Sun, *Amosu*, the Giver of Rain, and *Amaomee*, the Giver of Repletion, that is to say, Sufficiency of Good.

Thus to *Onyame* are ascribed many of the utilitarian or pragmatic qualities in Deity or Providence which man appreciates as making essential provision for the primary economies of life, making the day-to-day life possible for each of us.

Onyame is, in this sense, pre-eminently the useful God, a God suited to the pragmatists because He works, He gives to life a hum and a song. In the most material and matter of fact sense He opens up for man an appetite for life, makes life worth living for him.

For the purpose of comparative religion and psychology, we would discover, upon inquiry, that the Akan *Nyame* corresponds to the appetitive nature of man which the Greek philosopher, Plato, found to be the first element in man's being, what he called *To epithumetikon*. Modern psychology would discover in the nature of God, *Onyame*, the feeling or affective nature, in the realm of being, the ontologists would say *Onyame* corresponds to that which is known or experienced; in the physical realm, *Onyame* would correspond to the *phusis* or framework or ground plan, what the Akan call the *nipadua*, man's stem. In previous books we spoke of an Akan conception of a fundament spirit or power called *E-su*, which is at the root of the universe of being, and *Onyame* would correspond to that idea in the religious sense, he being the irreducible minimum of the Deity idea.

In contrast to this quality would be that of *Nyankopon*, the Greater Supreme Being, whose comparative nature would correspond to *Sunsum*, the personality behind Deity, *sunsum* being derived from *e-su*.

In brief, in so far as the Akan system may be said to have developed in line with other theological ideas, *Onyame* would be the foundation of Akan Deism. He would be the darling of the busy man of action, the materialist who wants to get things done for particular uses.

But this utilitarian quality is carried higher in the Maxims having particular reference to *Nyame*, excluding *Nyankopon* or *Odomankoma*. Indeed, it would be dangerous to draw a sharp and fast line between the functions of the three Akan conceptions of the Godhead, but distinctions are just discernible. We have already noticed one of these in Maxim 227: "*No one points out the Nyame to a child,*" which, on the surface, looks like a simple reference to the wide expanse, but can be seen to bear the deeper meaning. The higher metaphorical significance is noticeable also in Maxim 1653: "*When the fowl drinks water it shows it to Nyame,*" suggesting that even the lowest of our domestic animals are conscious of the utilitarian providence of *Nyame*.

In the remaining Maxims, however, the references to *Nyame's* functions and powers in relation to man and other created beings show a much deeper significance than the merely utilitarian. Consider Maxim

2538: "*There is no by-pass to Nyame's destiny*," meaning, it is not given to man to subvert the order of nature. In this, and in the following five Maxims, we pass from the consideration of *Nyame* in relation to the traditional "sky" idea to a higher order of his nature:

> 234: "No one teaches smithery to a smith's son;
>   if he knows it, it is *Onyame* who taught him."
> 2436: "All men are *Onyame's* offspring; no one is the offspring of Earth."
> 2777: "Says the Hawk: All *Onyame* did is good."
> 2787: "The earth is wide but *Onyame* is chief."
> 2855: "The order *Onyame* has settled living man cannot subvert."

These maxims refer to qualities which many other races have also attributed to God: 234 identifies *Onyame* with mind or nature, 2436 makes *Nyame* the Father of all men; 2777 shows *Nyame* as Creator and as one whose nature must be good; 277 shows *Nyame's* supremacy over the totality or sum of creation, and 2855 shows the orderly nature of *Nyame*, his supremacy over men, and his interest in the final destiny of man, his religious relation to *Nyame*.

In fine, the most common name for Deity in civil conversation among the Akan is *Nyame*, especially in all cases where the reference to divinity is not specific as to a particular exercise of His power, or where it is not necessary to look upon him as a Person, but as a universal immanent Power only. I feel that, in this sense, it may be justifiable to render the Akan word *Nyame* or *Onyame* by the English word Deity or Godhead, reserving, as aforesaid, the name *Nyankopon* for the reference to divinity as a personal God.

This conclusion is further supported by the form of the three main strong names or honorifics specifically assigned to *Nyame* in contradistinction to those of *Nyankopon* and *Odomankoma*; namely, *Amowia, Amos* and *Amaomee*. In all three cases the particle *A*, and not *O*, begins each name, the idea having become so abstract that the appropriate pronoun would be It and not He, where *Onyame* is concerned. We may exemplify this by reference to two words in the language, *Owia*, the Sun, and *Awia*, Sunshine, or sun's time. "*The sun is shining*" is expressed thus: *Owia (no) abo*, but "*It is sunshine*," i.e., it is day time, is expressed thus: *Awia abo*. Here *Owia*, because of the *O* prefix, suggests a personification of the entity implied, where *A* in *Awia* connotes for the Akan mind an abstraction (It) and not a person (He). It is the same with the use of *Amowia, Amos* and *Amaomee* in relation to the definiteness or otherwise of *Nyame's* individuality. He is Dieity or pervasive divinity, not God or the religiously inclined personality. It is wrong to speak of Him as "The Sky God," and it is correct to consider His nature as that behind or beneath things, the ultimate irreducible Godhead, the blue print of Akan Divinity.

II. *ONYANKOPON KWAAME*, OR THE GOD OF SATURDAY
1. THE "GREATER" *NYAME*

Rattray was one of the first to recognize that the Akan have a particular name for the God of religion, who is called "He of Saturday," *Nyankopon Kwaame*. Any Akan male born on Saturday is called *Kwaame* or *Kwaamen* (female, *Ama* or *Aba*). Saturday is recognized by the person born on that day as particularly appropriate for soul worshipping or "washing." Those born on other days of the week observe the equivalent ceremonies for their souls as the Saturday-born do for Saturdays. The God of religion is therefore called "He of Saturday," either because he is supposed to have been born on Saturday or that Saturday is the appropriate day for his worship. On every fortieth Saturday, called *Dapaa* or *Dapaada*, Open or Free Day, special ceremonies are performed in respect of Saturday's God. There are nine *Dapaa* days in the Akan calendar.

Onyankopon, like *Onyame*, may be written or pronounced without the *O*, -*Nyankopon*. The obvious meaning of the word is: "Alone the Greater *Nyame*," for -*pon* is an Akan suffix for great, and -*ko* is from *okoro, biako*, single, alone, one.

There are several variants of the name of the Saturday God. Christaller's view is that *Onyankopon* or *Nyankopon* is the settled form, it being also one of the Akim forms, a dialect which, he holds, is the purest Akan, being "dainty and affected," Ashanti being "broad and hard" and not as "soft and delicate" as the Akim. My own view is that it is because of a prevalent poetic strain in the Akim tribes (the Akim Abuakwas, Akim Kotokus, Akim Soaduros and Ashanti Akims) that the dainty and affected forms of the Akan language are so noticeable among them.

These other ways of writing or pronouncing *Nyankopon* are: *Onyankompon, Onyankoropon, Onyankorompon, Onyankoropono, Onyankorompono*, and, again, the same words without the prenominal *O-*. The Afutu (Winneba) tribes speak of *Onyankome* and the Ga (Accra) people speak of *Nyankomli*.

In Akan mythology and folk tales the name *Ananse* or *Ananse Kokuroko*, Gigantic Ananse, often replaces the use of *Nyankopon*.

Ananse (spider?) is the ubiquitous hero of the Akan mythos, noted for his great skill and ingenuity, and for bringing knowledge and science to man. It is to *Ananse Kokuroko* that reference is made in the following mythical ditty as the middle or second Person of the Trinity through or by Whom creation came or was brought into being. The first of the three is *'Te (Ote), i.e.,* Hearing, signifying speech or word, a reference to *Onyame*, an idea similar to the Greek *Logos* (Word). *Ote*, in the sense used in the ditty (Hearing), may probably be rendered better as "Understanding." The ditty below is played on the *Ntumpan* or Talking Drums, and also sung on the Speaking Horns (*Asese-ben*):

> *Hena ko se,*
> *Hena ko se,*
> *Hena ko se,*
> *Hena na oko see 'Te,*
> *Ma 'Te ko see Ananse,*
> *Ma Ananse ko see Odomankoma,*
> *Ma Odomankoma*
> *Boo Adee?*

Meaning:

> Who gave word,
> Who gave word,
> Who gave word?
> Who gave word to Hearing,
> For Hearing to have told *Ananse*,
> For Ananse to have told *Odomankoma*,
> For *Odomankoma* To have made the Thing?

That is to say, how did the idea occur to God to create the Universe, the Thing? The process must have involved first a "hearing" or a taking of notice, i.e., understanding; then a knowledge or cognition involving experience; and then an insight or apprehension of the entire idea or concept. Not at all an easy matter as an exercise in epistemology. Of the three Persons in the Trinity of Godhead who first thought of creation? Or, in simple human terms, how did *thinking* come about?

These are some of the problems that a delving into the significance of Akan thought are likely to present to us. We need not go into this particular problem of the origin of thought at the present juncture, but there will be plenty of work to do when the time arrives.

We consider here the significance of the name *Nyankopon*. Apart from recognizing that *Nyankopon* is "He of Saturday," it did not seem to appear to Rattray that *Nyankopon* was given qualities that could not be confused with those of *Onyame*. He called both of them the "Supreme Being" or "sky-God" without distinction. An attempt was made by one eminent Gold Coast writer, Joseph Ephraim Casely Hayford (Ekra Agyeman) in his "Gold Coast Native Institutions" to give a derivation of *Nyankopon*. He said it was derived from the beautiful idea of "Great Friend," taking *Nyanko* in the name to be the equivalent of the Fanti *nyanko (nyonko)*, friend.

I believe Casely Hayford was wrong in this effort, and it is much to be regretted that a whole generation of College boys, at Achimota and elsewhere, has been taught to believe that *Nyankopon* means, by etymology, "The Only Great Friend."

To begin with, *nyanko*, or *nyonko*, does not mean friend in the usual acceptation of the term. It means neighbour or the other fellow. A friend is a person joined to another in intimacy and mutual benevolence apart from sexual or family love. A fellow is a comrade or associate, a neighbour, the dweller next door. It seems to me most unlikely that the Akan *Nyame* or Shining One should suddenly take on the form of "the other fellow," or the near neighbour, ceasing thereby to be the dear and near God, Creator and Father. Finally, if *nyanko* in *Nyankopon* means "friend" or fellow, what does the *nyan* or *Nyam* in *Onyame* signify? Casely Hayford's explanation does not help at all. In the Akan language, as aforesaid, *m* assimilates to *n* in compounds, and it is the same *Nyam* in *Onyame* that becomes *Nyan* in the compound *Nyankopon*.

My own view is as already stated: *Nyankopon* is correctly and most obviously derived from *Onyame* and *koro*, from *biako*, one; and from *-pon*, great, such that the entire name means, by etymology, "The Only Great *Onyame*," "The Only Great Shining One," or "He who alone is of the Greatest Brightness." *Nyankopon* is the only Great *Nyam*, the Greater God.

1. "*Ashanti Proverbs*," pp. **18, 19** and **20**.

Questions for Chapter 6
The Akan Meaning of God

1. TRUE or FALSE?

   a. Danquah claims that the most popular Akan word for God is *Nyame*.
   b. According to Danquah, the Akans have several ancestral and divine altars and shrines.
   c. On Danquah's account, Akans describe God as the Excavator.
   d. Danquah claims that Akans strongly believe that God must be worshipped only on Saturday.

2. Danquah believes that *Nyame* means:

   (A) sky God.
   (B) the Shining One.
   (C) the Only Great One.
   (D) the High or Almighty God of the Akans.

3. Compare Danquah's interpretation of the Akan proverb *Obi nnkyere abofra Nyame* (No one teaches a child God or points God out to a child) with Abraham's and Oguah's.
   Whose interpretation is the best?

4. Compare Danquah's account of the Akan meaning of God with Abraham's.
   Which account is preferable and why?

Chapter 7

On the Absence of Sensation in the Human Mind

Antonius Gvilielmus Amo

Ntɛtea na obu ne bɛ se: Me kosɛɛ wɔ me tirim. —**The Ant has a saying to the effect that my grievances are in my head.**
(Akan proverb)

PROLOGUE

Anthony William Amo or Antonius Gvilielmus Amo Afer—as he called himself—was an Akan from the Axim area of Ghana who, probably, as a result of slavery found himself in the German court of Wolfenbuttel via Amsterdam in 1707. He studied and became a professor of philosophy, medicine and physiology at the Universities of Halle, Witenberg and Jena where we are told that "intellectual backwardness, racial prejudice and nationalistic arrogance drove Amo back to the land of his fathers in 1747."

In his inaugural philosophical dissertation, he disputes René Descartes' claim that the mind has sensations by showing that that leads to the contradictory claim that the mind or soul is and, at the same time, is not (a) divisible, (b) an organ of the body and (c) the faculty of thinking. Hence, he attempts to provide an indirect proof of the thesis that sensations do not belong to the human mind.

Here are some of his arguments:

"Man has sensation of material objects not as regards his mind but as regards his organic and living body. These statements are here asserted and are defended against Descartes and his expressed opinion in his *Correspondence*, part 1, letter XXIX, where the passage reads: "For since there are two factors in the human soul on which depends the whole cognition which we can have concerning its nature, of which one is the part that thinks and the other which united to the body moves it and feels with it"...But he openly contradicts himself, *loc.cit. part 1, espistoloa 99*, in the preceding programmatic investigation where he lays it down that the nature of the soul consists solely in the faculty of thinking;   and yet thinking is an activity of the mind, not the passion...But he stands in contradiction to himself with the words: "To receive sensible forms is the function of an organ.   To judge it when received is the function of the soul." To receive the sensible forms is to feel; but this is appropriate to organs, and in consequence to body, for organs are appropriate not to mind but to body. Again he himself distinguishes between feeling and judging, attributing the former to organs and the latter to minds...Whatever lives and depends on nourishment grows; whatever is of this nature is in the end resolved into its basic principles; whatever comes to be resolved into its basic principles is a complex; every complex has its constituent parts; whatever this is true of is a divisible body. If therefore the human mind feels, it follows that it is a divisible body. No spirit has sensation of material objects. Since the human mind is spirit, it has no sensation of material objects."

On the Aπαθεια of the Human Mind

Antonius Gvilielmus Amo

1. CONTAINS APPLICATIONS OF OUR GENERAL CONCLUSIONS WHICH WE HAVE BROUGHT OUT AT LENGTH IN WHAT HAS GONE BEFORE

1.1 THE STATE OF THE ARGUMENT

Man has sensation of material objects not as regards his mind but as regards his organic and living body. These statements are here asserted and are defended against DESCARTES and his expressed opinion in his *Correspondence*, part I, letter XXIX, where the passage reads: "*For since there are two factors in the human soul on which depends the whole cognition which we can have concerning its nature, of which one is the part that thinks and the other that which united to the body moves it and feels with it.*"[1]

To this statement we give the following warning and dissent: that the mind acts with the body with which it is in mutual union, we concede; but that it suffers with the body, we deny.

NOTE. Among living things, to suffer and to feel are synonymous. But among things destitute of life, to feel is to admit in oneself changes coming from elsewhere as far as quantity and quality are concerned. In other words it is for them to be modified and determined from outside.

First Caution. But he openly contradicts himself, *loc. cit.* part I, *Epistola* 99, in the preceding programmatic investigation where he lays it down that the nature of the soul consists solely in the faculty of thinking;[2] and yet thinking is an activity of the mind, not a passion.

Against SENERTIUS in his *Natural Science* bk. VIII ch. 1 on the subject of the rational soul[3] where he writes: "*Even if indeed the human soul is strengthened by means of the faculties which we have so far attributed to it regarding the vegetable and the sensitive soul nevertheless the two, etc.*" Again bk. VII ch. 1 p. 562[4] on the sensitive soul: "*For to feel is the work of the soul.*"

Second Caution. But he stands in contradiction to himself p. 563[5]

Reprinted by permission of the Faculty of Philosophy, Martin Luther University from *Antonius Gvilielmus Amo Afer of Axim in Ghana: Translation of his Works*, by Anton Wilhelm Amo, (73-76) © 1968 Halle (Saale, Germany): Martin Luther University, Halle-Wittenberg.

with the words: "*To receive sensible forms is the function of an organ. To judge it when received is the function of the soul.*" To receive the sensible forms is to feel; but this is appropriate to organs, and in consequence to body, for organs are appropriate not to mind but to body. Again he himself distinguishes between feeling and judging, attributing the former to organs and the latter to minds.

Also contrary to what Johannes CLERICUS has in the fourth book on the *Physiology of Plants and Animals* ch. X on sensible and mobile animals § 2.[6]

Third Caution. He contradicts himself further § 3 subsequently[7] where he says that three things are to be distinguished: (1) the action of an object on an organ, (2) the passion of the organ, (3) says he: "*When an organ is affected, the mind is upset, and the mind feels the sensation of its body being affected.*" Now if the mind should really have this feeling he should have expressed it in this way: "*and the mind feels its body to be affected, it feels, or rather it understands itself not to have been affected.*" But he confuses the act of understanding with the business of feeling: it is the same as if he should have said: "*and the mind understands its body to have been affected.*"

Likewise, contrary to what George Daniel COSCHWIZ says in his *Organism and Mechanism* S.I.C. VIII, thesis 3.[8] And against several others.

The Aristotelians agree with us. In bk. II of "*de generatione et corruptione*" ch. 9 p. 49:[9] "*It is the characteristic of matter to suffer and be moved, etc.*" Contrary to John Frederich TEICHMEYER in his "Elements of Natural and Experimental Philosophy," ch. III on the principles of physics p. 18,[10] where he has these words: "*We understand by sensation, etc.*"

Also John Christopher STURM in the "*Hypotheses of Physics,*" bk. I or the General Part, section I, chapter II in the 5th Epilogue.[11] Again p. III. 232 and what follows thereafter.[12]

2. SPECIAL PART
2.1 1ST NEGATIVE THESIS
The human mind is not affected by sensible things.

EXPOSITION. The thesis means the same as if you said: The human mind is not affected by sensible things however much they are immediately present to the body in which the mind is. But it has knowledge of the sensations arising in the body and employs them when possessed in its operations. See the *Essay on Physics* chapter III, p

107.[13]

NOTE. When man is considered logically, mind, operation of mind, idea and immediate sensation must not be confused; mind and its operation are immaterial. For as is the nature of a substance so is the nature of the property of the substance, and yet that mind is immaterial, has been shown in what we have already said and therefore its property too is immaterial. Idea is a composite entity; for there is an idea when the mind makes present to itself a sensation pre-existing in the body, and thereby brings the feeling before the mind...

First Proof of Thesis. Whatever feels, lives; whatever lives, depends on nourishment; whatever lives and depends on nourishment grows; whatever is of this nature is in the end resolved into its basic principles; whatever comes to be resolved into its basic principles is a complex; every complex has its constituent parts; whatever this is true of is a divisible body. If therefore the human mind feels, it follows that it is a divisible body.

Second Proof of Thesis. No spirit has sensation of material objects. Since the human mind is spirit, it has no sensation of material objects.

The major premise has been proved under the first exposition with notes and applications supplied. The minor premise is incapable of contradiction.

NOTE I. To live and to have sensation are two inseparable predicates. The proof is in the following inversion: everything which lives necessarily feels; and everything which feels necessarily lives. The result is that the presence of one feature imports of necessity the presence of the other.

NOTE II. To live and to exist are not synonyms. Whatever lives exists, but not everything that exists lives, for both spirit and stones exist, but can hardly be said to live. For spirit exists and operates with knowledge; matter exists and suffers the action of another agent. On the other hand both men and animals exist, act, live and feel.

Third Proof of Thesis. "*Fear not,*" our Saviour says, "*those who killing the body yet cannot kill the soul.*" Matthew X 28. From that we gather that whatever is killed or can be killed, necessarily lives. (For to be killed is to be deprived of life by violence from some other quarter.) If therefore the body is slain or can be slain, it follows that it lives; and if it lives, feels; and if it feels, it follows that it enjoys the faculty of sensation. For living and feeling are always and right from the beginning conjoined in the same subject.

NOTE. There is agreement between us and the whole assembly of medical men and others whose opinion is that sensation occurs in fluid of the kind in the nerves, and this nervous fluid was by the ancients called animal spirits. See the illustrious DE BERGER in his *Physiology*, bk. 1, On human nature, ch. XXI on secretion and motion of the nervous fluid, p. 277.[14] See also the most distinguished Dean, my own Chairman, in his compendious second edition of the *Experimental Physics*. C.V.Q. XXV.[15] *Essays on Nature* part one, ch. VIII, Of Sensations § 5, p. 102;[16] SENERTIUS in his *Epitome of Natural Science*, bk. XV ch. 2 p. 671.[17]

EXAMPLE. Exceptionally appropriate here is the solemn pronouncement of FREDERICK the WISE, Elector, of the most glorious memory, most beneficent founder of our University which flourishes here, Wittenberg. In his last breath of life he was asked how he felt. He answered that his body was in mortal pain but his mind was at peace: *"who on his death-bed was asked how he felt, and made answer: The spirit is restful, but the body is in gross pain."* —See BRUCKNER in *"The Hall of Fame"* on the life of Frederick the Wise,...[18]

2.2 THESIS II.

And there is no faculty of sensation in the mind.

PROOF. Anything to which circulation of blood is appropriate is that also to which the principle of life is. Whatever the latter pertains to, to that also does the faculty of sense. Yet circulation of the blood, and the principle of life pertain to the body. See the illustrious DE BERGER ch. 5 to the end of p. 112. In the same book also p. 56.[19] Let me refer you in addition to my worthy President in the work mentioned, to Christian VATER C.V.Q. XII[20] in *Physiology*, s. IV ch. II, on life and nutrition, thesis 1 towards the end.[21] Likewise the Bible clearly marks the distinction between the soul and the breath, Job XII, v. 10 where the seventy men say: *"If in his hands are the souls of the living things and the breath of all have life and the spirit of everything that has flesh."* The expression ἡ ψυχή indicates the principle of life of animals, Genisis 1 verse 24, also ch. IX verse 4. *"Flesh in the blood, which is the life thereof, shall ye not eat." "Except meat"* etc. *"Eat not of flesh which yet lives in its blood,"* and in the same place DR. LUTHER rendered τὴν ψυχήν as the life of man.[22] Likewise Proverbs 4.[23] *"Keep thy heart with all diligence, for out of it proceeds life."* But the heart with its cycle of blood means the body. Further turn to Leviticus ch.

XVII:[24] *"For all life is blood."* But blood here is traced back to body. Add the *Essays on Nature,* part 1, chapter VIII on sensations pp. 102, 103.[25] Since these things are so, it follows that the principle of life with the faculty of sense is not appropriate to mind. Rather, they belong to the body.

2.3 THESIS III.
Hence sensation and the faculty of sense belong to the body.

PROOF. Sensation and the faculty of sense belong either to the mind or to the body, not both. That they do not pertain to the mind has been shown by our broad conclusions. Therefore, they belong to the body. I refer you to the proofs of Theses I and II.

FINAL NOTE. To conclude this dissertation: for the refutation of contrary opinions to my position see this chapter on the form of the question. In the same way we must not confuse the things which belong to the mind and the body respectively. Whatever is subject to sensation and the faculty of sensation and involves the concept of matter is entirely to be attributed to body. THAT IS ALL.

NOTES

The following notes refer to editions which can be presumed to have been at Amo's disposal. They are based on the books available in the libraries at Halle and Wittenberg Universities. In the usual fashion of the times, Amo's references are often defective and quotations are not always given exactly, word for word. Since this is a regular feature, no special mark has been used to denote this. In addition, no reference is made to printing errors in Amo's works.

1. DESCARTES, *Epistolae*, part 1, no. 29, 59.
2. *ibid.*, no. 99, 319ff.
3. SENNERT, *op. cit.*, VIII, 1, 629.
4. *ibid.*, VII, 1, 540.
5. *ibid.*, VII, 1, 540.
6. Jean LECLERC: Physicae liber quartus: De Plantis et Animalibus X, 2 in: *Opera Philosophica*, vol. 4, Leipzig 1710, 134.
7. *ibid.*, X, 3, 134.
8. Georg Daniel COSCHWITZ (d. 1729), professor of medicine at the University of Halle. —*Organismus et Mechanisms in Homine Vivo Obvius et Stabilitus seu Hominis Vivi Consideratio Physiologica*, Leipzig 1741, i, 8. 3, 196ff.
9. ARISTOTLE—De Generatione et Corruptione II, 9; in: Opera Omnia, Graece et Latine, pub. *Guillaume DU VAL*, vol. 1, Paris 1654, 739.
10. Hetmann Fredirich TEICHMEYER (1685-1746), professor of physics and medicine at the University of Jena. —*Elementa Philosophiae Naturalis Experimentalis*, Jena 1717, III, 8.
11. Johann Christoff STURM (1635-1703) professor of mathematics and physics at the University of Altdorf. —*Physica Electiva sive Hypothetiea*, vol. I, Nuremberg 1697, I, 1, 2, epilogue 5, 65.
12. *ibid.*, I, 1, appendix III, 231ff.
13. *Essais de physique, loc. cit.*
14. v. BERGER, *Op. cit.*, I, 21, 277.
15. Martin Gotthelf LOESCHER: *Physica Experimentalis Compendiosa*, Wittenberg 1715, III, 5, 20, 150. (The second edition of 1717, cited by Amo, is not available.)
16. *Essais de physique, loc. cit.*
17. SENNERT, *op. cit.*, VIII, 2, 641ff.
18. Siegmund von BIRKEN (BETULIUS) (1626-1681), German author: *Chur- und fürstlicher sächsischer Helden-Saal*, 2nd edn., Nuremberg 1678, 532.
19. v. BERGER, *op. cit.*, I, 5, 112 and 56.
20. LOESCHER, *op. cit.*, III, 5, 5, 140.

21. VATER, *op. cit.*, IV, 2, 303.
22. *Gen.* 9, 5.
23. *Prov.* 4, 23.
24. *Lev.* 17, 11 and 14.
25. *Essais de physique, loc. cit.*

Questions for Chapter 7
On the Absence of Sensation in the Human Mind

1. TRUE or FALSE?

    a. Amo denies that the human mind is a spirit.
    b. Amo believes that Descartes is not a dualist.
    c. In effect, Amo's main aim is to show that Descartes' premises are false.
    d. Amo claims to be a materialist.

2. Amo denies that:

    (A) people have sensations.
    (B) Descartes believes that people have sensations.
    (C) the body has sensations.
    (D) the mind has feelings.

3. Amo denies:

    (A) that whatever lives feels.
    (B) that whatever feels lives.
    (C) that mind is different from the body.
    (D) none of the above.

4. Identify and evaluate all of Amo's arguments.

5. Do you agree that if Amo's arguments derived from physiology, (medicine) and religion (the Bible) are sound, then there is probably no life after death?

Chapter 8

The Concept of Mind with Particular Reference to the Language and Thought of the Akans

Kwasi Wiredu

Eti nyε bor ɔfere na w ɔapae mu ahu mu as εm. —The head is not a pawpaw to split in order to perceive its thoughts. (Akan proverb)

PROLOGUE

Kwasi Wiredu is an Akan from the Kwahu region of Ghana and a classmate of Abraham's both at the University of Ghana and Oxford University. He was for many years the chairperson of the Philosophy Department at the University of Ghana, Legon, before taking up appointments at the University of California at Los Angeles, the University of Ibadan in Nigeria and, currently, the University of South Florida. Unlike Oguah and Gyekye, he argues that since the Akans do not consider the mind to be a substance and, hence, exclude it from the list of the things that make up a person, it is a mistake to take the mind to be an additional entity to the body as Oguah and Gyekye suggest. From his point of view, it is also a mistake to identify the mind with the brain or part of the body as suggested by the mind-body identity theory and some forms of idealism.

Here is a portion of Wiredu's argument for what may be termed quasi-physicalism or, as Wiredu prefers, quasi-materialism which is neither a form of traditional monism nor a form of traditional dualism:

"An interesting contrast between the two languages in this connection is that, whereas in English the notion of the identity of mind and brain can appear to make sense, no such appearance is possible in Akan. Mind (*adwene*) being conceived of in an exclusively nonsubstance way in Akan, the slightest temptation to suggest such an identity would betray a radical mixing-up of categories, specifically, of the categories of concept and object at one level and of the categories of potential and actuality at another. This is because, as might be inferred from earlier remarks, particularly, about the relationship between the words *adwene* (mind) and *dwen* (to think) mind is from the Akan point of view, a logical construction out of actual and potential thoughts. To adapt a phrase of John Stuart Mill, mind, at any rate in its aspect of potentiality, is the relatively permanent possibility of thought. Now neither a thought (i.e., a combination of concepts) nor the mere possibility of thought could, as a matter of logical impossibility, be any kind of object. A concept is, by definition, a non-object, and, as will be pointed out more at length below, an object is, by definition, a non-concept. Therefore, since the brain is a species of object, it is evident that to identify the mind with the brain would be to commit the multiple error of confusing not only a class of concepts but also their possibility with an object—a particularly full-blooded example of what Ryle called a category mistake...A particularly problematic case is that of the *ɔkra*. This Akan term is often translated into English as 'soul.' This is quite definitely wrong. The soul is supposed in Western philosophy to be a purely immaterial entity that somehow inhabits the body. The *ɔkra*, by contrast, is quasi-physical. It is not, of course, supposed to be straightfowardly physical as it is believed not to be fully subject to spatial constraints. Nor is it perceivable to the naked eye. Nevertheless, in some ways it seems to be credited with para-physical properties...The chief point to be emphasized here is that the Akans most certainly do not regard mind as one of the entities that go to constitute a person. And the reason is simple: Mind is not conceived as an entity. The same reason accounts, of course, for the absence of any mention of *adwene* in the Akan enumeration of the components of a person. Another important point that emerges from the foregoing is that in Akan thought whether a person is in essence a spiritual being or not has nothing to do with his having a mind...Finally, how does the Akan concept of mind stand vis-a-vis the monism-dualism opposition of Western psychology? Dualism asserts that mind and matter are entities that are real and irreducible. Monism standardly asserts either that mind is the only irreducible reality or that matter is the only irreducible reality. Insofar as both types of theories presuppose that mind is an entity they are unacceptable from an Akan point of view."

The Concept of Mind

Kwasi Wiredu

1. INTRODUCTION

I wish in this chapter to discuss some issues in the philosophy of mind with particular reference to the traditional thought of the Akans of Ghana. One reason for restricting myself to just one small ethnic group on the vast continent of Africa is that I wish to keep the discussion within reasonable anthropological bounds. There is too much easy generalizing about African traditional philosophy. It seems to me that at present there are not enough philosophically analytical studies of the traditional thought of the various peoples of Africa to support any very responsible or illuminating generalisations. The times, then, seem to call for ethnically specific studies. My own hope is that such inquiries would disclose a variety of philosophies, similar in some important respects, but distinct, nevertheless. It would be exceedingly useful, for example, to know from a philosophical elucidation of Yoruba or Mende or Luo or Banyarwandan conceptions of mind, as distinct from unanalytical narratives about their beliefs on the subject, how the thought of other African peoples compares with that of Akans on the same matter. At present, references to the concept of mind in discussions of traditional African philosophies (at least in English) are either nonexistent or utterly perfunctory.

Another reason for narrowing down my concerns in this discussion to the Akans relates to language. Language and culture are important in all philosophy, but in philosophy of the sort to be considered below they are especially so. We are to discuss a folk philosophy, a body of originally unwritten ideas preserved in the oral traditions, customs, and usages of a people. For this purpose a close acquaintance with the language of the people concerned is of the greatest relevance. Being born and bred an Akan, I may perhaps be excused the temptation to think that I might be able to elicit some points of a philosophical significance regarding the topic in hand from an intuitive understanding of Akan life and language.

Reprinted by permission of the author and publisher, Faculty of Arts, University of Ibadan, Nigeria, from *Ibadan Journal of Humanistic Studies* No. 3, October 1983.

Two things ought to be made clear from the outset, however. The first is that in talking of Akan traditional thought I do not mean to imply that there is a monolithic corpus of ideas entertained by all traditional Akans. On the contrary, one not infrequently encounters variations in belief among the branches of the Akan tribe and sometimes even among the inhabitants of a single village. Furthermore, if one talks with the real philosophers among our traditional elders, i.e., those among them who are willing and able to think rationally and critically about fundamental aspects of nature and human experience, one is soon impressed with their capacity to dissent from received conceptions and to break new ground. Accordingly, when one speaks of the Akan view of one thing or the other, all that one is, as a rule, entitled to claim is that the view in question is the most usual one in the folk thought of Akanland. The second remark is a disclaimer. I do not mean to attribute wholesale the conclusions I reach in my interpretations of the Akan language to the traditional Akans, and I hope it will be sufficiently clear where a suggestion is the result of my own critical or reconstructive reflection on Akan data.

After these preliminaries let us consider the question of language in more specific terms. In discussing Akan traditional conceptions in the medium of the English language there are obviously issues of translation that have to be faced. One major issue is whether there is any exact equivalent in Akan of the English word 'mind.' To answer this question we need, of course, to know the meaning or meanings of that word itself in English. But it turns out that to formulate its meaning is not as straightforward as one might have thought. We are at this stage looking for the ordinary meaning of the word, that is to say, the meaning the word has in ordinary, as distinct from technical, philosophical discourse. Yet it quickly becomes apparent that the ordinary usage of such a philosophically sensitive word as 'mind' is apt to become entangled in philosophical tradition. The nearest to a safe expedient in the circumstance seems to me to be to have recourse to an unpretentious dictionary. I found the following entries under 'Mind' in *The Random House Dictionary*: '1. The part of a human being that reasons, understands, perceives, etc. 2. The faculty of reasoning or understanding. 3. A person considered in relation to his intellectual powers. 4. Reason or sanity. 5. Opinion or intentions. 6. Psychic or spiritual being. 7. Remembrance or recollection. 8. Attention or thoughts.'

With the exception of the sixth item this seems to be as near as one can get to a philosophically neutral lexical definition. The exception is, however, very much worth noting. A native English-speaking philosopher who does not, as some do not, believe that there is any such thing as 'a psychic or spiritual being' cannot, surely, be accused of not knowing the ordinary semantics of the word 'mind.' Actually, the dictionary itself, by ranking it sixth, suggests that the item in question does not give the primary meaning of the word. In this it seems rather less tendentious than some of the more celebrated dictionaries. *The Shorter Oxford Dictionary*, for example, gives the following as one of the word's principal sets of meanings: '(a) The seat of consciousness, thought, volition feelings; also the incorporeal subject of psychical faculties; the soul as distinct from the body. (b) Used of God. (c) Mental or psychical being opposed to matter. (d) A person regarded abstractly as the embodiment of mental qualities etc.' This is heavily loaded with metaphysics. Indeed, two philosophers are quoted into the bargain: In illustration of usage, Locke and Mill are quoted respectively as follows: 'No proposition can be in the mind which it was never conscious of' and 'Mind is the mysterious something which feels and thinks.' The entanglement with philosophical tradition is obvious.

Let us, then, return to our unassuming dictionary. According to its first entry, it will be recalled, mind is the part of the human being which reasons, understands, perceives, etc. Though this is to a large extent philosophically neutral, it is not completely so. It does not prejudice the issue between those philosophers who hold that what does the thinking is the brain and those who credit the thinking function to some immaterial entity. But it prejudges the issue as to whether mind is an entity of any sort at all. Here again it is relevant to note that there are native English-speaking philosophers who deny that mind is an entity. For example, Gilbert Ryle, the celebrated author of *The Concept of Mind*, took such a view. And yet no one would have the temerity to suggest that Ryle, whose mastery of the English language was beyond the remotest doubt, did not understand the English word 'mind.' On the other hand, one cannot deny that the notion of mind as the part of a human being that reasons, understands, perceives, etc., is a very common, perhaps the most common, acceptation of 'mind' in the English language: which proves, incidentally, that a commonsense notion is not necessarily innocent of all philosophical preconceptions. Let us call the assumption that mind is an entity of some sort the substance[1] view of mind. Then we can see, on surveying our dictionary's entries under 'Mind,' that they fall into two broad classes, one representing a substance view of mind and the other a nonsubstance variety. The first and sixth items in the lexical inventory belong to the former while the rest belong to the latter class.

It ought to be clear from the foregoing that the ordinary meaning of 'mind' in the English language reflects elements of both the technical and folk philosophies of the people to whom it belongs. It is clear also that in that language each of the substance and nonsubstance views of mind provides an adequate basis for the semantics of 'mind.'

There is a further distinction to be made at this stage of our discussion. The second entry under 'Mind,' according to which mind is 'the faculty of reasoning or understanding,' contrasts in a very significant way with the fifth, seventh, and eight, which define mind, respectively, as 'opinion or intentions,' 'remembrance and recollection,' and 'attention[2] and thoughts.' According to our dictionary,[3] a faculty is an ability, a power, a capability. The faculty of reasoning or understanding is, thus, simply the ability to reason or understand, and this is, of course, not an entity but a disposition. Turning to the other side of the contrast, we find that though the items mentioned, viz., opinion, intentions, thoughts, etc., are not entities, they are not dispositions either. They consist of ideas or concepts. A thought is an idea or concept or a combination thereof. The following distinction, then, suggests itself. Within the broad category of the nonsubstance view of mind, we may distinguish between a dispositional and an ideational sense of 'mind.' These two senses, unlike the substance and nonsubstance pair, are not contradictories. A disposition is a potentiality, and its actual exercise may take the form of a conceptualization. Therefore, far from being contradictories, the disposition and its ideational actualization may be thought of as complementary phases of mind. Nevertheless, it is important to distinguish them clearly for reasons which will emerge in due course.

2. THE AKAN CONCEPTION OF MIND

The preceding remarks permit us now to begin to answer the question whether there is any exact equivalent in Akan of the English word 'mind.' A simple yes or no answer is not available. It matters little, I think, whether we answer: 'Yes, with a qualification' or 'No, with a qualification.' In either case it is the qualification that is crucial for our purposes here. The only conceivable translation of 'mind' into Akan is 'adwene.' However, while the word 'mind,' as we have seen, is susceptible of either a substance or a nonsubstance interpretation, 'adwene' is susceptible of only a nonsubstance one. The same word, 'adwene,' also translates the English word 'thought;' and 'adwene' is simply the noun form of the verb 'dwen,' which means 'to think.'[4] In the English language, in which 'mind' does not have the same sort of relationship with 'thought,' it is natural, though not unavoidable, to think of mind as that which produces thought. In Akan there is little temptation to think in this way.

It might be insisted that the Akans ought to have a conception of what it is that thinks. If there is thinking, it might be argued, there must be something that does the thinking. The Akan answer would be simple: What does the thinking is the person, *onipa*. Our interlocutor is unlikely to be satisfied with this. He might urge the following consideration to try to show that the answer is inadequate. Although it is correct—so might go the reasoning—to say in the case of thinking, as in regard to any human activity, that it is the person who does what is done, it might still be necessary to indicate which part or aspect of a person is actually involved in the execution of a particular type of activity. Thus it is true that walking is done by a person, but it is appropriate to note that a person walks with his legs rather than, say, his tongue. So the question remains open as to the part or aspect of a person that is most directly involved in the thinking process. Alternatively, it might he suggested that even if it be accepted without any qualms that the agent of thought is the person, it may still be that a person, as a thinking being, is something more rarefied than the moving object that is visibly encountered in the external world.

As regards the first point, it should be noted that what it shows is only that some part or aspect of a person may be the *instrument* of thought: it does not show that any such part could appropriately be called the *agent* of thought. As to the instrument or mechanism of thought, it is clear from the speech of the Akans that they believe that it is the brain, *amene*, that has this status. They know that thinking cannot go on in a human being without the brain, that certain injuries to the brain will impair thought and that generally there is a correlation between brain activity and thinking. This is responsible, by the way, for the figure of speech by which, wishing to intimate that a fellow is thoughtless, an Akan might say that he has no *adwene* in his head. And while on figures of speech, it might be of interest to note one parity and a couple of disparities of usage between Akan and English. Locating thought figuratively in the head is admissible in both languages, for in English too one can speak of a thought entering one's head. On the other hand, in English one cannot speak of the 'mind' in a person's head, while it is no breach of linguistic propriety in Akan to decry a person's mental habits by remarking that the *adwene* inside his head is no good. Furthermore, though it is accredited idiom in English to mention brain while meaning mind, as when it is said that somebody has good brains, it would be absurdly unidiomatic to say with the same purport in Akan that somebody has a good *amene*. One only talks of a good *adwene* in such a context.

These points of linguistic usage do not teach us much philosophy of mind beyond the fact that the speakers of both English and Akan recognize the instrumentality of the brain in thinking. This recognition does not, of course, necessarily imply the identity of mind and brain. In fact an interesting contrast between the two languages in this connection is that, whereas in English the notion of the identity of mind and brain can appear to make sense, no such appearance is possible in Akan. Mind (*adwene*) being conceived of in an exclusively nonsubstance way in Akan, the slightest temptation to suggest such an identity would betray a radical mixing-up of categories, specifically, of the categories of concept and object at one level and of the categories of potentiality and actuality at another. This is because, as might be inferred from earlier remarks, particularly, about the relationship between the words *adwene* (mind) and *dwen* (to think), mind is, from the Akan point of view, a logical construction out of actual and potential thoughts. To adapt a phrase of John Stuart Mill, mind, at any rate in its aspect of potentiality, is the relatively permanent possibility of thought.[5] Now, neither a thought (i.e., a combination of concepts) nor the mere possibility of thought could, as a matter of logical impossibility, be any kind of object.[6] A concept is, by definition, a non-object, and, as will be pointed out more at length below, an object is, by definition, a non-concept. Therefore, since the brain is a species of object, it is evident that to identify the mind with the brain would be to commit the multiple error of confusing not only a class of concepts but also their possibility with an object—a particularly full-blooded example of what Ryle calls a category mistake.

Using a terminology introduced earlier on, we may now characterize the Akan concept of mind as both ideational and dispositional. That it is ideational is immediately clear from the fact that mind is, as we have seen, conceived in one aspect as consisting of thoughts. On this conception, mind is not that which thinks, but the thought which is thought when there is thinking. What distinguishes mind in this sense from a fortuitous aggregation of isolated thoughts is the unity arising from possession by an individual. On this showing, thoughts are not in the mind but of the mind; that is to say, thoughts are what mind is made of; and if we talk, as we often do in both Akan and English, of thoughts in our minds, we must, in Akan at least, mean the 'in' genetively rather than locatively.

That the Akan conception of mind is also dispositional would be clear on a little reflection. When, for example, an Akan says of a person in deep slumber that 'he has a good mind' (*owo adwene paa*) he does not mean that any sequence of brilliant thoughts is taking place in him at the material time; what he means is that the person concerned has the capacity for thoughts of that quality. In other words, a certain kind of disposition is being attributed to the individual. This dispositional attribution implies that if and when the circumstances are ripe, he will display suitably impressive thinking. But its whole meaning cannot be thus hypothetical. The potentiality must have a categorical basis; there must be a present condition in the make-up of the person which accounts for it. If, as we have suggested already, the brain (*amene*) is recognized in Akan thought as the instrument of thought, then this categorical basis can be nothing other than the condition of the brain.

This last remark touches, of course, on the problem of the relation between the mind and the brain, which is one of the principal problems of the philosophy of mind. It is perhaps necessary to stress that the suggestion is not that the brian is identical with the mind but only that the brain is the basis of the mind. This in itself is not a particularly controversial thesis. It is recognized on all hands, even among the most 'spiritual' of idealists, that the brain is a necessary condition for human thinking. The question is whether it is also a sufficient condition. In Western philosophy the contention of idealists and dualists has been that it is not. Their view is that it is necessary to postulate an immaterial entity which works on, or alongside, the brain to produce thoughts. This entity is said to be the mind. If this were true, it would presumably be taken to bear out the view, noted in the second paragraph of the present section, that, although the agent of human thought is a person yet, as a thinking being, a person may be in essence a spirit or something of that sort. I will argue below that this is a conceptually faulty hypothesis. But what I want immediately to point out is that it is a hypothesis which does not have a place in Akan thought on account of its nonsubstance conception of mind.

3. THE ƆKRA AND SOUL

A cursory look at the Akan account of the constituents of a human
person might give a contrary impression, but a careful analysis will
dissipate it. As is well known, the Akans traditionally believe that a
person is made of *nipadua* (body), *ɔkra* (a life giving entity), and
sunsum (that which gives a person's personality its force).[7] Frequently
mentioned also are the *mogya* and the *ntoro*. A person's *mogya*
(literally, blood) is supposed to derive from his mother and is taken as
the basis of his clan identity while his *ntoro* is said to be something
inherited from his father and is similarly taken as the basis of
membership of a patrilineal group. According to some accounts, there
is a close relation between *sunsum* and *ntoro*. (Thus Busia says 'A
man's *sunsum* is a child of his *ntoro*.') The doctrine of *mogya* and
notoro is, presumably, bound up with some kind of rudimentary
genetics.

Considerable caution is needed in striking correspondence between
these concepts and Western concepts for analysing human personality.
A particularly problematic case is that of the *ɔkra*. This Akan term is
often translated into English as 'soul.' This is quite definitely wrong.[9]
The soul is supposed in Western philosophy to be a purely immaterial
entity that somehow inhabits the body. The *ɔkra*, by contrast, is quasi-
physical. It is not, of course, supposed to be straightforwardly physical
as it is believed not to be fully subject to spatial constraints. Nor is it
perceivable to the naked eye. Nevertheless, in some ways it seems to be
credited with para-physical properties. For example, highly developed
medicine men are claimed to be able to enter into communication with
an *ɔkra*, and those that have eyes with medicinally heightened
perception are said to be capable of seeing such things. Further, a
particular *ɔkra* may be allergic to a particular kind of food though the
same nutrition may leave other *akra* (plural of *ɔkra*) unaffected. A
person who helps himself to food obnoxious to his *ɔkra* could become
very seriously ill. When offended in this or other ways, the *ɔkra* may
need to be pacified with offerings of appropriate food and drinks. In my
opinion, the way in which traditional Akans approach such procedures
suggest that they take them more seriously than as just symbolic
gestures. There is also the fact that the *ɔkra* is sometimes said to be a
person's double, conceived in his material image complete with a head,
hands, legs, and all.[10] Conceived in this way, the *ɔkra* is described as
a person's companion. 'In this role it is a separate entity from the

person and it may fail to guide and protect him; hence the expression
Ne kra apa n'akyi, his soul (sic) or *ɔkra* has failed to guide him' (Asare
Opoku).[11] It is, of course, a nice problem, which we cannot stop here
to ponder, how the *ɔkra* can be both the 'principle' in a person which
makes him a living being and a separate entity which can go its own
way if so moved.[12] The point is simply that it is evident from this
account that *ɔkra* and 'soul' are two nonidentical concepts.

But by far the most significant difference between the *ɔkra* and the
soul is that while the *ɔkra* is very distinctly, indeed categorically,
different from *adwene* (mind), the soul seems to be regarded as being
the same as the mind. It will be recalled that one of the entries quoted
above from *The Shorter Oxford English Dictionary* under 'Mind' was
'The soul as distinct from the body.' In English philosophical texts one
frequently meets the expression 'mind or soul' where the 'or' means
'in other words.' The analogue of such a usage in Akan would be the
veriest babble. The *ɔkra* is a living entity; *adwene* is an individual's
capacity for thinking and/or the outcome of the exercise of that
capacity. One might conceivably talk of the *adwene* of an *ɔkra* but, on
pain of incoherence, not of the *adwene* as the *ɔkra*. Actually, from the
way the Akans talk of the *ɔkra*, it has to have an *adwene*. For example,
it is believed that before a person comes to be born into this world, his
or her soul meets God to take leave of him, whereupon it is given its
'message' of destiny.[13] If so, it must have the capacity to understand a
message or transmit one. In fact, in some accounts, the *ɔkra* is supposed
to propose its own destiny to God for approval.[14] In any case, if the
ɔkra can feel offended, then it must, almost tautologically, have the
faculty of apprehension and feeling, i.e., mind. It is therefore
inadvisable to translate *ɔkra* as 'soul.' We will have to make do with
some such phrase as 'that whose presence in the body means life and
whose absence means death and which also receives the individual's
destiny from God.'

The *sunsum* also calls for a similarly circuitous translation. It is
probably best to render it as 'that which is responsible for the total
effect communicated by an individual's personality' without trying to
appropriate to it any more simple English term. It is, if anything, more
obvious here than in the case of the *ɔkra* that the *sunsum* is different
from the soul or the mind, whatever the relation between these latter
concepts is supposed to be in English discourse. The incoherent
suggestion that in dreams the *sunsum* actually leaves the body and

engages in various activities is sometimes attributed to the Akans.[15] On this supposition, the *sunsum*, too, far from being identical with the mind, would have to be a possessor of mind.

This is not the place to enter upon a full analysis and evaluation of the Akan conception of a person. The chief point to be emphasized here is that the Akans most certainly do not regard mind as one of the entities that go to constitute a person. And the reason is simple: Mind is not conceived as an entity. The same reason accounts, of course, for the absence of any mention of *adwene* in the Akan enumeration of the components of a person. Another important point that emerges from the foregoing is that in Akan thought whether a person is in essence a spiritual being or not has nothing to do with his having a mind.

There is a prior question of what is meant by the word 'spiritual' in the metaphysical sense. It is hard to come by any but the most negative definitions in Western Philosophical literature. The spiritual seems to be just what is not physical. What this conveys is, for my part, very far from a determinate idea, and I cannot see that there is anything in Akan language corresponding to it. Certainly, it cannot be said that the *ɔkra* and the *sunsum* are conceived of as spiritual in this sense. As pointed out earlier on, the *ɔkra* seems to be thought of as having some quasi-physical properties. Particularly in its role as guardian, its conception is redolent with material analogies.[16]   As for the *sunsum*, it is not altogether clear that it is unambiguously conceived of as a kind of entity. But even if we assume that it is thought of in this way, it still cannot be called 'spiritual' in the present sense; for, apart from anything else, the *sunsum* is believed by the Akans to perish at death,[17] whereas spiritual beings are supposed to be immortal by nature.

Let us, however suppose for the sake of argument that the *ɔkra* and *sunsum* are conceived of as spiritual entities. Even so, in terms of Akan conceptions this would have no relevance to the metaphysical problem of body and mind. In truth there is no such problem in Akan thought. The metaphysical problem of the relation between the body and the mind as it exists in Western philosophy is the problem of how a material entity can have any interaction with an immaterial one. Since the Akans do not regard mind as an entity, this question does not arise. In Western philosophy the reason why a nonmaterial substance is invoked in this connection is that it is felt that it is unintelligible how thinking can occur except on the intervention of a nonmaterial entity. The underlying reasoning seems to be this: Thought is immaterial;

therefore, only an immaterial entity can produce it.

The fundamental mistake in this reasoning is that it construes thought as a kind of entity. It seems to be assumed that thought is a rarefied entity which can only have affinities with an immaterial entity. But to think in this way is to trifle with what I believe is the most basic ontological distinction in the whole gamut of human thinking, namely, the distinction between concept and object. I have alluded previously to this issue and will now attempt some clarification. In a certain sense, we do talk of every item of discourse as an *object*, an *entity*, a *thing*, these words being used synonymously. But there is undoubtedly also a narrower usage. Suppose, in the Lewis Carroll mode, that you were to say that nothing passed you by as you raced along and someone were to comment that in that case *Nothing* reached first and that therefore he won the race. Obviously the hypothetical observer would be misconstruing *nothing* as an object or entity. We know, of course, that we can use and mention 'nothing' without having to suppose that nothing is an object. In this narrower sense of object one distinguishes between objects and abstractions, and there is no difficulty in seeing that *nothing* is an abstraction rather than an object or entity.

The distinction just mentioned is perhaps more familiarly known as the distinction between the abstract and the 'concrete.' The term 'concrete,' however, can be misleading, and it is more instructive in this context to express the distinction as being between the general and the particular or, in somewhat more technical language, between universals and particulars. Consider now the notion of generality. What is general is what can be instantiated, i.e., what can have an instance. Of course, what can be instantiated may itself be an instance of something more general, so that we can speak of degrees of generality. For example, kindness has instances in particular kind acts, but it is itself an instance of a moral attribute. Generality, however, comes to an absolute stop and we enter the territory of a new category when we come to items which can only be instances. A table, for example, is an instance of tableness, if we may flirt a little with a Platonistic phraseology, but it is not itself instantiable by anything. It would be uncommonly absurd to talk of one table being an instance of another one. True, one table can resemble another, but that is a different matter not to be confused with the relation of instantiation. This characteristic of being capable of being an instance but incapable of being instantiated is the mark of particulars, in other words, of objects, entities; while the characteristic of being instantiable is the mark of the conceptual. Thus an uninstantiable referent is necessarily nonconceptual. It follows that the definition of an object or entity given two sentences back can be reformulated as follows: An object (or entity) is that which can only be a nonconceptual referent.[18]

If, therefore, an object is nonconceptual by definition, then to treat a thought, i.e., a conceptual unit, as if it is a species of object, is to court a contradiction.[19] And yet this is exactly what is done when it is suggested that intelligibility is gained by postulating an immaterial entity to account for the phenomenon of thinking on the grounds that thought is something immaterial. In reality the category difference, the ontological disparity, between thoughts and entities *is the same whether the entities concerned are supposed to be material or nonmaterial.* More specifically, a spiritual entity is as nonconceptual as a material entity. Hence the question of how any sort of entity can give rise to a thought is not placed in any better light by invoking the idea of a spiritual substance. On the contrary, that expedient is in the nature of a mystification because, as far as the metaphysical concept of spirit goes, we know nothing of such entities, assuming even that the notion is coherent. We are merely invited to envisage the involvement of a nonmaterial entity in the process of thinking. But the bare, negative, notion of a nonmaterial entity gives us no positive basis whatever to suppose that it has anything to do with thinking. It is thus clear that it is unavailing to argue: 'Spirit is nonmaterial. Thought is nonmaterial. Therefore, spirit is better adapted to bringing about thought than body.' It is equally worthless to argue: 'Since the body is material and thought is nonmaterial, the body cannot give rise to thought.' One might just as well argue: 'Since a thought is a conceptual unit and a spiritual entity is nonconceptual, a spiritual entity cannot give rise to thought.'

As a matter of fact, the brain is in a very much more favourable position with respect to its relation with thinking than any supposed spirit. It is a well-established empirical fact that brain states and processes are correlated with thought processes. Modern science does not as yet know everything about how brain processes are related to thought processes, but it is enough that some correlations are known and generally acknowledged. The point now is that it is a needless leap in the dark to interpose the activity of a nonmaterial entity between the brain process and the thought and christen it with the name *Mind.* Suppose, for example, that a brain injury should cause a person to lose the power of judicious reasoning as some such injuries are known to do. Is it not a gratuitous hypothesis to suggest that when the physical injury occurs a spiritual entity, which in any case is supposed not to be vulnerable to physical mishaps, first has to work itself into a state corresponding to stupidity before our poor patient starts manifesting behavior of suitable obtusity? And, presumably this spirit will elect to remain unsober until, if the patient is lucky, the brain is brought into an improved physical condition, upon which it would promptly occasion the return of sanity. It seems to me a strong point in favour of the Akan conception of mind that it is logically inhospitable to this kind of thesis together with all the variations wrought upon it in classical Western philosophy—interactionism, psycho-physical parallelism, occasionalism, pre-established harmony.

4. THE PROBLEM OF MIND

What, then, is the real problem of mind? one might ask. The question has a false presupposition. There is not just one problem of mind; there are a number of them.

(1) There is the metaphysical problem, noted awhile ago, of how mind, conceived as a nonmaterial entity, is related to the body, a material entity. In Western philosophy this problem is encountered in its acutest form in Descartes, though it is already acute enough in Plato. I have tried to show that it is founded on a mistake, and I am not at all averse to calling it a pseudo-problem,[20] which I think I can do with an easy Akan conscience.

(2) There is also the question of how the concept of mind is related to the concept of thought. This problem is rarely explicitly formulated in Western philosophy. It does, indeed, seem that philosophers in this tradition have been so exercised by the problem of Body and Mind that they have had little thought to spare for the problem of Mind and thought. Nevertheless, it is a very genuine conceptual problem, especially for languages like English in which, unlike the situation in Akan, the word for mind is not a form of the word for thought; and I am inclined to suggest substituting for 'Body and Mind' the more discriminating phrase 'Body, Mind and Thought' or better, 'Body, Thought and Mind' in all contexts in which attention is sought to be directed to the entirety of the problem of mind. The assumption, which I have criticised above, that a spiritual entity is intrinsically akin to thought may be construed as an implicit attempt to solve the Thought-Mind component of the cluster of problems about mind. In sum, my suggestion has been that the following straightforward answer can be extracted from Akan language and thought: Thought is *adwene*

considered episodically; mind is *adwene* considered as the relatively permanent possibility of thought.[21]

(3) The question naturally arises: 'What is the basis of this permanent possibility of thought?' As explained already, no serious philosophy of mind can evade this problem. It concerns the relation between what we called in Part I of this essay the ideational and dispositional senses of 'mind,' for we are here considering the thoughts and mental possibilities of individual human beings, which is a matter of their dispositions. If, as I have suggested above, the answer implicit in Akan speech is that the brain is the basis of this permanent possibility of thought, then one merit of distinguishing clearly between these two senses of 'mind' is that it forces us to confront the question of the relation between the physiological and the mental aspects of our being. However, as far as I know, the correlation between brain processes and thinking was not explored in any detail in Akan thought. Actually, this is a scientific problem. A lot is already known in neurophysiology about how various types of thought processes are related to processes in the brain or, more strictly, the central nervous system.[22] Infinitely more remains to be learnt, but what is known already begins to dispel some of the mystery of mind. Thus, the more the science of neurophysiology and related sciences advance, the less mysterious will mind become.

(4) But given all that can be learnt about the correlation between thought and brain process, there still remains a conceptual problem of how the *category* of brain process is related to the *category* of thought. It needs to be emphasised that this is quite distinct from the correlation problem commented on in the last paragraph. The empirically and scientifically established correlations may exist because brain processes and thought processes are the same phenomena viewed from different perspectives or because thought processes are events that follow upon, or in some way correspond to, brain processes but are distinct from them or because thought processes are an aspect of brain processes. These are philosophical rather than scientific alternatives. Scientific accounts of such correlations, as far as they go, help to provide explanations of mental facts; philosophical accounts of the categories involved in the correlations provide, not an explanation of behaviour, but a clarification of the very concept of a human being.

The first hypothesis has been canvassed in various versions in recent Anglo-American philosophy by proponents of the 'Mind-Brain Identity Theory.'[23] The second is a blanket alternative covering the theories of psycho-physical correspondence mentioned at the end of the last section plus classical epiphenomenalism, the theory that thought is a by-product of physical processes.[24] Both types of theory commit the category mistake of confounding concept with object. A thought cannot be the same as a brain process, for a brain process belongs to the category of object, while thought belongs to that of concept. Neither can it be a process distinct from brain process, for in that case, it would have impossibly to belong to the objectual category.

The hypothesis which seems most plausible to me is the third, namely, that thought is an aspect of brain process. It is not my purpose here to expound in full that characterisation of thought. I avow it here only because my inclination to it has been aided by reflection on the Akan concept of mind and perhaps by less conscious factors arising from an Akan upbringing. Still, I ought to explain that this view is not identical with the view known in Western philosophy as the 'Double Aspect' theory which was advanced by Spinoza in the seventeenth century and has been argued in a modified and very sophisticated form by Strawson in this part of the present century.[25] According to the Double Aspect theory, physical and mental attributes are aspects of one and the same reality. But it seems to me deeply erroneous to talk of the physical and mental as if they are categorically comparable. The phrase 'the physical' alludes to *physical* objects, but 'the mental' cannot allude to mental objects, since, as I have tried to explain above, the notion of a mental *object* is self-contradictory. In my view the mental presupposes the physical, in the human context at least, but not vice versa.[26] It is conceivable, in the abstract, that some nonphysical entities, if there are any such entities, also have thought as a dimension of their being. But the notion of a nonphysical entity is so obscure that this must remain a more or less dormant possibility. What seems to me to be of overriding importance is to realise that there is no good reason to think that a physical entity cannot have thought as an aspect of itself. No argument seems available for that assumption save the fallacious one, discussed earlier on, based on the supposed immateriality of thought. The truth is that thought, not being an entity, is neither material nor immaterial, physical nor nonphysical.

One great problem for the view that thought is an aspect of brain process is to elucidate the concept of aspect. Not that this word is especially perplexing normally, but it is necessary to explain how this way of conceptualising the relation between thought and brain process can remove the intellectual discomforts of our thought about thought. An important part of this task is to counteract invalid preconceptions about mind and thought. I have tried to do a certain amount of this. The more positive task of clarification, however, must await another occasion.

5. DUALISM, IDEALISM AND MATERIALISM

Now some concluding comparisons. A principal strength of the Akan concept of mind, in my view, is its nonsubstance character. This is not, of course, peculiar to the Akan view. In Western philosophy some philosophers have advocated nonsubstance theories—for example, Gilbert Ryle in *The Concept of Mind*. But the Akan view has an associated virtue which, as far as I know, is lacking in the principal philosophies of mind of the West. I am referring here to the fact that in Akan thinking the question of mind is quite distinct from that of the *soul* or, more generically, of *spirit*. I have already suggested that there does not seem to be anything in Akan thought corresponding exactly to the concepts of soul and spirit conceived as purely immaterial entities. However, it is noticeable that even in Western thought, particularly outside technical philosophical circles, souls (and spirits generally) are sometimes conceived on a quasi-material model. Given some such conception, the question of the existence of spirits begins to be meaningful in the context of Akan thought. Then, my point is that, in contrast to the situation in Akan thought, Western philosophies of mind frequently conflate the issues of mind and spirit. And this is true not only in substance theories of the mind, but also in nonsubstance ones. Thus, for example, when Ryle criticises the substance view of mind well known in Western philosophy, which I believe he does very successfully, he supposes himself *ipso facto* to have debunked the idea of a thinking soul. But this, quite definitely, is a *non sequitur*. That mind is not an entity is abstractly compatible with there being nonmaterial or quasi-material entities having the capacity to think. Only, it will have to be noted that the mind of any supposed nonmaterial entity too cannot be an entity.

The philosophy of mind is an enterprise in conceptual elucidation, but any theory of souls or spirits can only be an empirical theory. If a determinate and coherent definition of spirit can be given, the question whether such things actually exist can only be answered by empirical research. The 'if,' though, is quite a tremendous one, for insisting on satisfying it might well result in the evaporation of alleged spirits. Still, in spite of any such philosophical exorcism of spirits, it must remain conceivable that, for instance, some of the familiar parapsychological reports of remarkable quasi-material goings-on might add up to some kind of coherent conception of spirit. I will return to the question of parapsychology, but before then let me discuss a further contrast between the Akan concept of ɔkra and the concept of the soul, a contrast which is very closely related to that noted in the immediately preceding paragraph. The ɔkra is postulated in thought to account for the fact of life and of destiny but not of thought. The soul, on the other hand, seems in much Western philosophy to be intended to account not just for life, but also for thought. Indeed, in Cartesian philosophy, the sole purpose of introducing the soul is to account for the phenomenon of thinking. In Descartes the soul is a pure thinking substance. As Bernard Williams has pointed out, for Descartes, 'since the body is a mechanical system, the soul is not (as in the opinion of the ancients) the principle of life: Live bodies differ from dead ones as stopped watches differ from working ones: the body does not die because the soul leaves it, but the converse (*Passions of the Soul 1, 5 and 6*).'[27] Thus, when we come to Descartes, the difference between the ɔkra and the soul becomes radical and complete. When Descartes says that the soul is a thinking substance (*res cogitans*) he does not merely mean that it is a substance which has the capacity to think; he means that it is a substance whose whole *essence* is thought. Any reader who has followed our discussion thus far will be hard put to it to envisage a more incoherent conception than this. The incoherence is due, of course, to the conflation of the concepts of soul and thought.

The concept of ɔkra is free from the particular incoherence just mentioned. But unfortunately it shares with the pre-Cartesian notion of the soul as the principle of life a certain quite serious defect. The trouble is that the manner of its postulation leads to an infinite regress which renders it logically futile. The idea seems to be that since there is life, there must be a principle of life. In one interpretation this is a tautology. If the principle of a process is that which makes it happen, in the sense of the particular way in which the elements concerned are constituted, it is a logical truth that life must have its principle. On the other hand, in the case of the ɔkra and the particular concept of soul under discussion, that which is responsible for the phenomenon of life in the human person is presented as itself a living entity. In this case the rationale for postulating the ɔkra becomes something like this: 'A living being must have an entity as the principle of its life.' But if so, then, by parity of reasoning, the ɔkra too must have an entity as its own principle of life, and this second-degree ɔkra must similarly have a third-degree ɔkra, and so on ad infinitum.[28] However, if to avoid this logical difficulty one were moved to reject the principle that a living being has to have an entity as its principle of life, that would remove the reason for postulating the ɔkra in the first place. Thus, while it is tautologically true that, if there is life, there must be a principle of life, it is logically disastrous to construe that principle of life as itself an entity. In general, to convert something abstract, such as a principle, into an object or entity is to commit the error of hypostasis.[29]

The Akan concept of ɔkra, then, seems to be born out of hypostasis. Nevertheless, by comparison with the conflation of the concepts of mind and soul prevalent in Western philosophy, the Akan separation of the ɔkra from adwene suggests a more analytical awareness of the stratification of human personality. This impression is strengthened by another feature of the Akan concept of mind. In Akan thought, mind (adwene) is purely intellectual. This implies, in particular, that it is non-sensative, if one may be excused such an expression. In other words, sensations are not within the province of mind (adwene);[30] so that in terms of the Akan concept of mind sensations[31] are not mental, if 'mental' means 'of the mind.' This is in very marked contrast with Western views of mind. In the Western tradition an essay such as J. J. C. Smart's 'Sensations as Brain Processes'[32] can be recognised as a contribution to the theory of mind. In the context of Akan thought the essay may still merit recognition, but only as a contribution to the elucidation of an aspect of human personality other than mind. Since there can be sensation without the capacity for thought, as in the more lowly animals, it seems philosophically judicious to keep the distinction between the two types of phenomena always clearly in mind. In spite of the fact that both sensations and thoughts are forms of consciousness, it is important to recognise that there is a categorical disparity between them. For example, sensations can be located in space (portions of the skin, for instance) in a way which is inapplicable to thoughts without loss of sense. Moreover, sensations are, so to speak, dumb existences incapable of referring to anything beyond themselves, whereas this referential capacity is the very defining characteristic of thought. The categorical separation, therefore, between mind and sensation seems to me apt.

To return to the virtue, claimed earlier on for Akan thought, of separating the concepts of mind and 'spirit,' I would like, very briefly to call attention to some confusions which its absence from certain theories has generated. Take idealism, for example. The proponents of this theory seem to want to say indifferently that everything is ultimately mind or spirit. But in terms of the analysis given in this discussion quite different claims emerge depending on whether the thesis is taken with respect to mind or to spirit. Taken with respect to mind, it amounts, in view of all that has been said above, to the deepest incoherence. The trouble, however, if this is any consolation, is one which philosophy can diagnose and cure. On the other hand, taken with respect to spirit, the issue becomes empirical. To say that everything is spirit, even if only ultimately, is to advance a wild empirical claim which any slight empirical reflection must discourage. In either case, then, the Akan concept of mind gives scant comfort to idealism.

What of materialism? Here again we meet ambiguities deriving from the mind-spirit admixture of Western philosophy. Materialists are prone to frame their thesis as being indifferently about mind or spirit.[33] Yet, as in the case of idealism, different issues arise depending on whether what we have in mind is mind or spirit. Suppose materialism is interpreted as claiming that mind is ultimately a form of matter. Then, on the basis of our analysis, the verdict must be that the theory thrives, equally ultimately, on the category mistake, already explained, of confusing concept with object. But here too there is the same consolation, if such it be, that philosophical therapy can be effectual. Suppose, however, that the thesis is about spirits. Then, since historically, in Western philosophy at any rate, materialists have tended to be hardheadedly scientific in orientation, they might be presumed to deny the existence of any such entities. Insofar as the Akans traditionally believe in entities such as the *ɔkra* and sundry 'unseen' forces which seem to have affinities with some of the less rarefied apparitions frequently alleged in Western 'spiritualism,' the Akans would seem to be in conflict with the materialists. In this my own sympathies would be with the materialists, albeit undogmatically with the materialist, but not necessarily with materialism, for the nonexistence of spirits is an empirical hypothesis not logically entailed by the thesis of philosophical materialism. And this is a point worth emphasising. Materialism asserts that everything is ultimately a form of matter. From this what follows logically is not that there are no such things as spirits, but only that, if there are spirits, they must ultimately be forms of matter. This is of course, on the supposition that some coherent and determinate definition of spirit is available. If 'spirit' is defined merely as a nonmaterial entity, one need not be a materialist to protest, as I have in fact already done above, that no determinate conception is thereby offered.

The foregoing discussion of the concepts of mind and spirit has an important implication for the question of the bearing of parapsychology on the problem of the nature of mind. It is sometimes suggested that the results of parapsychological investigations could settle some issues in the philosophy of mind. Thus one author says 'The unchallengeable establishment of the reality of paranormal phenomena would demolish both Central State Materialism and the new Epiphenomenalism. And we cannot yet say with a clear mind either that this has been or will be established, nor that it will not.'[34] I applaud the open-mindedness of the second sentence but must demur at the prediction in the first. Let us suppose, for the sake of argument, that it is established, for example, that on the death of an individual something is let loose which is able to think in the manner of the deceased and even communicate with a paranormal elite among mankind. Assume further that although normally unperceivable to the naked eye, it can occasionally manifest itself ('materialize') in a human image uniquely reminiscent of the late individual, appearing at, and disappearing from, different places untrammeled by spatiotemporal limitations. This would, presumably, prove that there is a spirit associated with the departed individual which has a mind closely related to that individual's mind. But there is nothing in this hypothesis to prove that while the individual lived, his thoughts were not an aspect of his brain processes or their epiphenomenal concomitants or that they were not actually identical with his brain states. Furthermore, there would be nothing in it to show that this roving spirit is not itself endowed with a suitably ethereal brain. Indeed, in the given hypothesis, this would appear to be the most reasonable supposition; for if it can have phantom hands and legs on trunk capped with a phantom head, why may it not have a phantom brain to match?[35] Possibly this is the logic behind that version of the concept of the *ɔkra* among the Akans according to which a person's *ɔkra* is his double. (The soul too is sometimes conceived in this way.) It may very well be, in fact, that the notion of soul or spirit is logically parasitical on material analogies. Be that as it may, it must be apparent now that while it is conceivable that parapsychology might disclose the existence and activities of spirits, it cannot be expected to prove anything about the nature of mind.

Finally, how does the Akan concept of mind stand vis-a-vis the monism-dualism opposition of Western psychology? Dualism asserts that mind and matter are entities that are real and irreducible. Monism standardly asserts either that mind is the only irreducible reality or that matter is the only irreducible reality.[36] Insofar as both types of theory presuppose that mind is an entity they are unacceptable from an Akan point of view. If, on the other hand, the issue is construed to be about the real existence of spirits alongside matter, then Akan traditional thought might take on a dualistic countenance. But any such 'dualism' would, strictly, not be a fundamental ontological dualism and would, in any case, not appertain to the philosophy of mind.

Conceptual comparisons across cultures in philosophy do not, of themselves, determine doctrinal validity either way. Validity can only accrue to independent considerations. I have tried to adduce considerations of this sort, however, compressedly, whenever I have sought to urge the theoretical superiority of an Akan conception. Such comparative analyses seem to me to suggest that contemporary African philosophers can profitably cast their philosophical nets in their own indigenous conceptual waters. The enterprise seems to me, moreover, to be urgent at this particular juncture in our history.

NOTES

1. The term 'substance' is apt to recall a history of metaphysical speculation in Western philosophy which I do not wish to invoke by the adoption of this terminology. I understand by 'the substance view of mind' simply the view according to which mind is an entity of some sort.
2. Attention is, actually, partly dispositional and partly ideational. The same is true of intentions.
3. It should be noted that since two paragraphs ago the reference has been *The Random House Dictionary*.
4. We do in Akan have another word 'susuw' for the verb 'to think.' Literally, 'susuw' means 'to measure;' its use to mean 'to think' is a trifle figurative. 'Dwen' is relatively more literal as a rendition of the verb 'to think' though it too is probably connected etymologically with 'adwini' which means 'design' In English there is, of course, the verb 'to mind', but it does not have the same scope of meaning as 'to think.'
5. 'Matter,' said Mill, 'is the permanent possibility of sensation.' Mill was inclined to define mind analogously as the permanent possibility of feeling. But he fell, by his own admission, into irresolvable difficulties because he wanted also to conceive of mind as the 'Ego' which is aware of itself. See A. J. Ayer and Raymond Winch (eds.), *British Empirical Philosophers* (Routledge and Kegan Paul, 1965), 545-555 (on Matter) and 555-560 (on Mind).
6. To assume the contrary would be analogous to a mistake familiar in Western philosophy in the doctrine of phenomenalism which, following Mill, construes unperceived objects as mere possibilities of sensation without a thought of the basis of the possibilities.
7. See, for example, K. A. Busia, 'The Ashanti,' in Daryll Forde, *African Worlds* (Oxford, 1954); W. E. Abraham, *The Mind of Africa* (Windenfeld and Nicolson, 1967), Chap. 2; Kwame Gyekye, 'The Akan Concept of a Person,' *International Philosophical Quarterly*, Vol. XVIII, No. 3 (September 1978): Kofi Asare Opoku, *West African Traditional Religion* (Singapor: FEP International Private Ltd., 1978).
8. Busia, *op. cit.*, 198.
9. Matters are not improved by calling the *ɔkra* the 'life-soul' and the *sunsum* the 'personality-soul' as for example by Debrunner, *Witchcraft in Ghana* (Accra: Presbyterian Book Dept. Ltd., 2nd ed., 1961), 9, 14.
10. See, for example, H. Debrunner, *op. cit.*, 9.
11. Asare Opoku, *op. cit.*, 96.
12. Compare E. Bolaji Idowu, *Olodumare, God in Yoruba Belief* (London: Longman, 1962), 172: 'The idea of the ori is further complicated when

it is conceived as a semi-split entity in consequence of which it is at the same time the essence of the personality and the person's guardian or protector.' It would be interesting to compare and contrast the *ɔkra* with the 'ori' in detail.

13. One folk song says 'I saw God and took leave of him before coming' (*'Mihuu nyame na mekraa no ansa na meba'*).

14. Asare Opoku, *op. cit.*, 100. Compare, here again Idowu, *op. cit.*, 173f.

15. Abraham, *op. cit.*, 60; Kwame Gyekye, *op. cit.*, 282; Asare Opoku, *op. cit.*, 96f. Frederick Engels, by the way, has the following comment on a somewhat similar belief reported among a far distant people. 'Among savages and lower barbarians the idea is still universal that the human forms which appear in dreams are souls which have temporarily left their bodies; the real man is, therefore, held responsible for acts committed by his dream apparition against the dreamer. Thus Imthurn found this belief current, for example, among the Indians of Guiana in 1884.' Engels, *Ludwig Feuerbach and the End of Classical German Philosophy in Karl Marx and Frederick Engels: Selected Works*, Vol. 11 (Moscow: Foreign Languages Pub. House, 1951), 334, fn.

16. The North African philosopher Tertullian held that the soul was an ethereal kind of body. This probably is as near as one can get to the concept of the *ɔkra* in Western philosophy. See, for example, extracts from Tertullian in Anthony Flew, *Body, Mind and Death* (London: Collier Macmillan, 1964). Some Western mystical sources, such as those that frequently receive expression in the journal Prediction, also speaks, apart from the physical body, of 'the Astral body' and 'the Etheric body' (the soul) and, on top of all these, of 'the spiritual self.'

17. 'A man's *sunsum*... is not divine, but perishes with the man'; Busia, *op. cit.*, 197.

18. This definition coincides with the one I proposed in J.E. Wiredu, 'Logic and Ontology IV: Meanings, Referents and Objects,' *Second Order, An African Journal of Philosophy*, Vol. IV, No. I (January 1975). An object was there defined as 'what can be a non-conceptual referent of a symbol' (40).

19. I have pointed out further infelicities besetting this practice in Kwasi Wiredu, 'A Philosophical Perspective on the Concept of Human Communication,' *International Social Science Journal*, Vol. XXXII, No. 2 (1980), esp. 200f.

20. Herbert Feigl seems, in the title of his article 'Mind-Body, Not a Pseudoproblem,' to assume that there is a single problem, though in his actual discussion he shows a sensitivity to the multiplicity of problems in this area of thought. See Feigl in Sidney Hook, *Dimensions of Mind* (New York: Collier Books, 1961).

21. Mill, as noted earlier on, maintained a view of the relation between

thought and mind that was basically similar to this, though with failing steadfastness. (See note 5 above.) Making due allowances for his psychologistic empiricism and certain conceptual difficulties in his tradition, as, for example, the apparent identification of *mind* and *self*, Hume's theory of mind would seem to be of the same orientation. (See Hume's *A Treatise of Human Nature*, Book I, Part IV, Sec. 6. Flew, *op. cit.*, has a convenient section on Hume containing this reference together with an extract from an appendix to the *Treatise* and Hume's essay 'Of the Immortality of the Soul.' Ryle and Dewey, each in his own way, might be cited as entertaining conceptions of the relation between *thought* and *mind* not very dissimilar to the Akan one stated in the text. See Gilbert Ryle, *The Concept of Mind* (Hutchinson's University Library, 1949), or, more briefly, the extracts from this book plus a symposium contribution by Ryle in Flew, *op. cit.* For Dewey, see, for example, his paper *Body and Mind* in John Dewey, *Philosophy and Civilisation* (New York: Capricorn Books, 1963, 1st ed., 1931).

22. For a recent interesting philosophical exploitation of this fact, see Ted Honderich, 'One Determinism' in Ted Honderich and Myles Burnyeat, *Philosophy As It Is* (Penguin Books, 1979).

23. See, for example, C.V. Borst (ed.), *The Mind/Brain Identity Theory* (Macmillan, 1970); David M. Rosenthal, *Materialism and the Mind-Body Problem* (Prentice-Hall, 1971) (with some overlapping with the previous work). For an influential criticism of the identity theory, see Saul Kripke, 'Identity and Necessity,' in Honderich and Burnyeat, *op. cit.* Ted Honderich in the same volume gives a powerful but marvelously simple critique of the identity thesis in footnote 8, on page 275.

24. See selection from Thomas Huxley in Flew, *op. cit.* or in Paul Edwards and Arthur Pap (eds.), *A Modern Introduction to Philosophy*, 3rd ed. (Free Press, 1973). A discussion of epiphenomenalism not as strongly committed as Huxley's, but showing some good will towards it, is found in C.D. Broad, *The Mind and its Place in Nature* (London: Kegan Paul, 1925). For a recent critical analysis, see Jerome Shaffer, *Philosophy of Mind* (Prentice Hall, 1968); also, Keith Campbell, *Body and Mind* (Macmillan, 1970).

25. P.F. Strawson, *Individuals* (London: Methuen, 1959). Spinoza expounded his views of mind in his *Ethics*. Useful extracts from the Ethics are available in Flew, *op. cit.* and G. N. A. Vesey (ed.), *Body and Mind* (London: Allen and Unwin, 1964).

26. In this respect, my view might perhaps be called a logical ephiphenomealism as opposed to classical epiphenomalism of Western philosophy, which is causal. But the Akan affiliations of my view make it more extensively different from classical epiphenomalism than this

logical-causal contrast might suggest.

27. Bernard Williams, 'Descartes' in Paul Edwards, *The Encyclopedia of Philosophy* (London: Macmillan, 1967), Vol. 2, 353.

28. Postulating the *ɔkra* to account in like manner for the fact of destiny also faces the same infinite regress, for the *ɔkra* will itself have a destiny. It should be noted also that any theory that infers a soul on the ground that any thinking being must have an entity in it which is responsible for the thinking is beset by a similar infinite regress.

29. If the *sunsum* (that which is responsible for the force of personality) is considered as an object. it is easy to show that it can only be thanks to hypostasis.

30. I have always wondered whether Anthony William Amo, the Ghanaian philosopher who taught philosophy in the Universities of Halle, Wittenberg, and Jena in Germany in the eighteenth century was not perhaps unconsciously manifesting an Akan predisposition in his view, which he stoutly maintained against Cartesianism, that the mind is incapable of feeling sensation. This thesis was advanced in his *On the Apatheia of the Human Mind*. See the translation of his extant works published by the Martin Luther University of Halle-Wittenberg (Halle a.d. Saale, 1968), under the title *Antonius Gviliemus Amo Afer of Axim in Ghana*. Amo was carried away from his homeland at the age of four or so, but he seems to have retained such strong memories of his origins that it is perhaps not altogether outlandish to speculate on a residual tinge of Akan culture in his consciousness in spite of his upbringing in European culture and, in particular, of the Cartesian influence which led him to adopt a substance view of mind.

31. By 'sensations' here I mean only 'such things as pains, tickles, feelings of nausea, suffocation, thirst and the like'. See Gilbert Ryle, 'Sensations.' in H.D. Lewis (ed.), *Contemporary British Philosophy* (London: Allen and Unwin, 1956). Ryle disentangles various other uses of 'sensation.'

32. *Philosophical Review*, LXVIII, 1959. Reprinted in Borst, *op. cit.* and Rosenthal, *op. cit.* The point made in our text is subject, however, to the qualification that Smart sometimes uses 'sensation' broadly to refer to ideational phenomena.

33. Thus Engles, for example, speaks in terms of 'the question of the relation of *thinking* to being, the relation of *spirit* to nature the paramount question of the whole of philosophy....' Engles, op. cit., 334, my italics.

34. Keith Campbell, *op. cit.*, 124. See also, for example, D.M. Armstrong, *A Materialist Theory of Mind* (London: Routledge and Kegan Paul, 1968), 364.

35. F.H. Bradley from a different philosophical outlook argues forcefully

in his essay on 'The Evidences of Spiritualism' against the view that 'Spiritualism, if true, demonstrates mind without brain...' See Flew, *op. cit.*, 212ff.

36. There is also a nonstandard form of monism known as neutral monism. This is 'the view of William James and the American new realists, according to which the "stuff" of the world is neither mental nor material, but a "neutral stuff" out of which both are constructed.' This view was endorsed and developed by Bertrand Russell in his *Analysis of Mind* (London: Allen and Unwin, 1921) from which this formulation is quoted (6). See, however, *My Philosophical Development* (London: Allen and Unwin, 1959), Ch. XII, for Russell's second thoughts.

Questions for Chapter 8
The Akan Concept of Mind

1. TRUE or FALSE?

a. According to Wiredu, the Akans believe in spirits.
b. According to Wiredu, the Akans believe that people have immaterial souls.
c. On Wiredu's account, the Akan conception of mind is dispositional not ideational.
d. According to Wiredu, there are not enough philosophical studies of African traditional thought to support generalizations.

2. According to Wiredu, the Akans are:

(A) idealist.
(B) dualists.
(C) identity theorists.
(D) none of the above.

3. Compare Wiredu's account of mind with Oguah's and Amo's. Which of them best captures the Akan conception of mind?

4. From your point of view, what is the bearing of Wiredu's account on the acceptability or otherwise of the following conceptions of a person?

(a) idealism
(b) dualism
(c) the identity theory
(d) functionalism

Chapter 9

The Concept of a Person

Kwame Gyekye

Nnipa nyinaa yɛ Onyame mma: obiara nyɛ asase ba. —**Everyone is a child of God: none is a child of the earth. (Akan proverb)**

PROLOGUE

Kwame Gyekye, like Danquah, is an Akan from the Akim region of Ghana. He was educated at the University of Ghana and Harvard University. He was a colleague of Wiredu's and, at present, the chairperson of the Philosophy Department at the University of Ghana at Legon. He disputes Wiredu's characterization of the Akan conception of a person in terms of physical and quasi-material entities. He prefers to characterize it as dualistic because of the Akan belief in (a) life after death, (b) non-physical personality traits like courage, (c) consciousness as experiencing something non-physical, and (d) dreaming as making a non-physical journey. In his opinion, these beliefs support the thesis that there are physical as well as non-physical components of a person that are responsible for these activities.

Part of Gyekye's argument is as stated below in his own words: "I understand the term "quasi-physical" to mean "seemingly physical," "almost physical." Such description of the ɔkra (soul) in Akan thought runs counter to the belief of most Akan people in disembodied survival or life after death. For a crucial aspect of Akan metaphysics is the existence of the world of spirits (*asamando*), a world inhabited by the departed souls of the ancestors. The conception or interpretation of the ɔkra as a quasi-physical object having paraphysical properties would mean the total or "near total" (whatever that might mean) extinction of the ɔkra (soul) upon the death of the person. And if this were the case, it would be senseless to talk of departed souls continuing to exist in the world of spirits *(asamado)*...Experience is the awareness of something. Since a purely material thing, such as wood or a dead body, cannot experience anything, it follows that the *sunsum, qua* subject of experience, cannot be material...The explanation given by most Akans of the phenomenon of dreaming also indicates, it seems to me, that *sunsum* must be immaterial...The fact that dreaming occurs only in sleep makes it a unique sort of mental activity and its subject, namely *sunsum,* a different sort of subject. A purely physical object cannot be in two places at the same time: A body lying in bed cannot at the same time be on top of a mountain. Whatever is on the top of the mountain, then, must be something nonphysical, nonbodily and yet somehow connected to a physical thing—in this case, the body. This argument constitutes a *reductio ad adsurdum* of the view that *sunsum* can be a physical object."

The Concept of a Person

Kwame Gyekye

What is a person? Is a person just the bag of flesh and bones that we see with our eyes, or is there something additional to the body that we do not see? A conception[1] of the nature of a human being in Akan philosophy is the subject of this chapter.

1. ƆKRA (SOUL)

We are given to understand from a number of often quoted, though mistaken, anthropological accounts that the Akan people consider a human being to be constituted of three elements: ɔkra, sunsum, and honam (or nipadua: body).

The ɔkra is said to be that which constitutes the innermost self, the essence, of the individual person. ɔkra is the individual's life, for which reason it is usually referred to as ɔkrateasefo, that is, the living soul, a seeming tautology that yet is significant. The expression is intended to emphasize that ɔkra is identical with life. The ɔkra is the embodiment and transmitter of the individual's destiny (fate: nkrabea). It is explained as a spark of the Supreme Being (Onyame) in man. It is thus described as divine and as having an antemundane existence with the Supreme Being. The presence of this divine essence in a human being may have been the basis of the Akan proverb, "All men are the children of God; no one is a child of the earth" (nnipa nyinaa yɛ Onyame mma, obiara nnyɛ asase ba). So conceived, the ɔkra can be considered as the equivalent of the concept of the soul in other metaphysical systems. Hence, it is correct to translate ɔkra into English as soul.

Wiredu, however, thinks that this translation "is quite definitely wrong."[2] He, for his part, would translate the ɔkra as "*that whose presence in the body means life and whose absence means death* and which also receives the individual's destiny from God."[3] Surely the (here) italicized part of the quotation accurately captures the Akan conception of the soul—ɔkrateasefo, the living soul—whose departure means death. This is indeed the primary definition of the soul in practically all metaphysical systems. I do not think, however, that the concept of destiny is an essential feature of the Akan definition of the soul, even though the concept of the soul is an essential feature of the Akan conception of destiny.

Wiredu's reason for thinking that it is wrong to translate ɔkra as soul is mainly that whereas "the soul is supposed in Western philosophy to be a purely immaterial entity that somehow inhabits the body, the ɔkra, by contrast, is quasi-physical."[4] He adds, however, that "It is not of course supposed to be straightforwardly physical as it is believed not to be fully subject to spatial constraints. Nor is it perceivable to the naked eye. Nevertheless, in some ways it seems to be credited with paraphysical properties."[5] Wiredu's characterizations of the ɔkra as "quasi-physical" and having "paraphysical" properties are completely wrong. He acknowledges that "highly developed medicine men" or people with extrasensory (or medicinally heightened) perception in Akan communities are said to be capable of seeing and communicating with the ɔkra. It must be noted, however, that these phenomena do not take place in the ordinary spatial world; otherwise anyone would be able to see or communicate with the ɔkra (soul). This must mean that what those with special abilities see or communicate with is something nonspatial. Thus, the fact that the ɔkra can be seen by such people does not make it physical or quasi-physical (whatever that expression means), since this act or mode of seeing is not at the physical or spatial level.

I understand the term "quasi-physical" to mean "seemingly physical," "almost physical." Such description of the ɔkra (soul) in Akan thought runs counter to the belief of most Akan people in disembodied survival or life after death. For a crucial aspect of Akan metaphysics is the existence of the world of spirits (asamando), a world inhabited by the departed souls of the ancestors. The conception or interpretation of the ɔkra as a quasi-physical object having paraphysical properties would mean the total or "near total" (whatever that might mean) extinction of the ɔkra (soul) upon the death of the person. And if this were the case, it would be senseless to talk of departed souls continuing to exist in the world of spirits (asamando).

In attempting further to distinguish the Akan ɔkra from the Western soul, Wiredu writes:

> The ɔkra is postulated in Akan thought to account for the fact of life and of destiny *but not of thought*. The soul, on the other hand, seems in much

Western philosophy to be intended to account, not just for life *but also for thought*. Indeed, in Cartesian philosophy, the sole purpose of introducing the soul is to account for the phenomenon of *thinking*.[6]

Wiredu, I believe, is here taking "thought" in the ratiocinative or cognitive sense, its normal meaning in English. But his position is undercut by his reference to the concept of *thought* in Cartesian philosophy. For it is agreed by scholars of Descartes that by *thought* (or thinking: *cogitatio*) Descartes means much more than what is normally connoted by the English word. Thus, Bernard Williams writes:

> It is an important point that in Descartes' usage the Latin verb *cogitare* and the French verb *penser* and the related nouns *cogitatio* and *pensée*, have a wider significance than the English *think* and *thought*. In English such terms are specially connected with ratiocinative or cognitive processes. For Descartes, however, *cogitatio* or *pensée* is any sort of conscious state or activity whatsoever; it can as well be a sensation (at least, in its purely psychological aspect) or an act of will, as judgment or belief or intellectual questioning.[7]

Thus, what Descartes means by mind or thought is *consciousness*. Despite his reference to Descartes, I think Wiredu uses "thought" in the narrow sense, that is, of ratiocination or cognition. "Thought" in the narrow sense is of course a function or an act of consciousness. Any living human being must have consciousness. This being the case, consciousness, which is equivalent to the soul or mind in Descartes, can be a translation of *ɔkra*. On this showing, it cannot be true, as Wiredu thinks, that "when we come to Descartes, the difference between the *ɔkra* and the soul becomes radical and complete."[8] My analysis, if correct, implies the opposite. I argue below that thought (*adwen*) in the narrow sense is in Akan philosophy an activity of the *sunsum*, which I interpret as a part of the soul (*ɔkra*). Having raised some objections to Wiredu's interpretation of what he calls the Akan concept of mind, I return to my own analysis of the Akan concept of the person.

The conception of the *ɔkra* as constituting the individual's life, the life force, is linked very closely with another concept, *honhom*. *Honhom* means "breath;" it is the noun form of *home*, to breathe. When a person is dead, it is said "His breath is gone" (*ne honhom kɔ*) or "His soul has withdrawn from his body" (*ne 'kra afi ne ho*). These two sentences, one with *honhom* as subject and the other with *ɔkra*, do, in fact, say the same thing; they express the same thought, the death-of-the-person. The departure of the soul from the body means the death of the person, and so does the cessation of breath. Yet this does not mean that the *honhom* (breath) is identical with the *ɔkra* (soul). It is the *ɔkra* that "causes" the breathing. Thus, the *honhom* is the tangible manifestation or evidence of the presence of the *ɔkra*. [In some dialects of the Akan language, however, *honhom* has come to be used interchangeably with *sunsum* ("spirit"), so that the phrase *honhom bɔne* has come to mean the same thing as *sunsum bɔne*, that is, evil spirit. The identification of the *honhom* with the *sunsum* seems to me to be a recent idea, and may have resulted from the translation of the Bible into the various Akan dialects; *honhom* must have been used to translate the Greek *pneuma* (breath, spirit).] The clarification of the concepts of *ɔkra*, *honhom*, *sunsum* and others bearing on the Akan conception of the nature of a person is the concern of this chapter.

2. *SUNSUM* (SPIRIT)

Sunsum is another of the constituent elements of the person. It has usually been rendered in English as "spirit." It has already been observed that *sunsum* is used both generically to refer to all unperceivable, mystical beings and forces in Akan ontology, and specifically to refer to the activating principle in the person. It appears from the anthropological accounts that even when it is used specifically, "spirit" (*sunsum*) is not identical with soul (*ɔkra*), as they do not refer to the same thing. However, the anthropological accounts of the *sunsum* involve some conceptual blunders, as I shall show. As for the mind— when it is not identified with the soul—it may be rendered also by *sunsum*, judging from the functions that are attributed by the Akan thinkers to the latter.

On the surface it might appear that "spirit" is not an appropriate rendition for *sunsum*, but after clearing away misconceptions engendered by some anthropological writings, I shall show that it is appropriate but that it requires clarification. Anthropologists and sociologists have held (1) that the *sunsum* derives from the father,[9] (2) that it is not divine,[10] and (3) that it perishes with the disintegration of the *honam*,[11] that is, the material component of a person. It seems to me, however, that all these characterizations of the *sunsum* are incorrect.[12]

Let us first take up the third characterization, namely, as something that perishes with the body. Now, if the *sunsum* perishes along with the body, a physical object, then it follows that the *sunsum* also is something physical or material. Danquah's philosophical analysis concludes that "*sunsum* is, in fact, the matter or the physical basis of the ultimate ideal of which *ɔkra* (soul) is the form and the spiritual or mental basis."[13] Elsewhere he speaks of an "interaction of the material mechanism (*sunsum*) with the soul," and assimilates the *sunsum* to the "sensible form" of Aristotle's metaphysics of substance and the *ɔkra* to the "intelligible form."[14] One might conclude from these statements that Danquah also conceived the *sunsum* as material, although some of his other statements would seem to contradict this conclusion. The relation between the *honam* (body) and the *sunsum* (supposedly bodily), however, is left unexplained. Thus, philosophical, sociological, and anthropological accounts of the nature of the person give the impression of a tripartite conception of a human being in Akan philosophy:

ɔkra (soul)	}	immaterial
Sunsum ("spirit")	}	material (?)
Honam (body)	}	material

As we shall see, however, this account or analysis of a person, particularly the characterization of the *sunsum* ("spirit") as something material, is not satisfactory. I must admit, however, that the real nature of the *sunsum* presents perhaps the greatest difficulty in the Akan metaphysics of a person and has been a source of confusion for many. The difficulty, however, is not insoluble.

The functions or activities attributed to the *sunsum* indicate that it is neither material nor mortal nor derived from the father. Busia says that the *sunsum* "is what moulds the child's personality and disposition. It is that which determines his character and individuality."[15] Danquah says: "But we now know the notion which corresponds to the Akan '*sunsum*' namely, not 'spirit' as such, but personality which covers the relation of the 'body' to the 'soul' (*ɔkra*)."[16] That the *sunsum* constitutes or rather determines the personality and character of a person is stated by Danquah several times.[17] Rattray observed that the *sunsum* is the basis of character and personality.[18] Eva Meyerowitz also considered the *sunsum* as personality.[19] My own researches indicate that the views of Busia and Danquah regarding the connection between *sunsum* and personality are correct, but that they failed to see the logical implications of their views. There are indeed sentences in the Akan language in which *sunsum* refers to a person's personality and traits. Thus, for "He has a strong personality" the Akans would say, "His

sunsum is 'heavy' or 'weighty'" (*ne sunsum yɛ duru*). When a man is
generous they would say that he has a good *sunsum* (*ɔwɔ sunsum pa*).
When a man has an impressive or imposing personality they would say
that he has an overshadowing *sunsum* (*ne sunsum hyɛ me so*). In fact
sometimes in describing a dignified person they would simply say, "He
has *spirit*" (*ɔwɔ sunsum*), that is, he has a commanding presence. And
a man may be said to have a "gentle" *sunsum*, a "forceful" *sunsum*, a
"submissive" or "weak" *sunsum*. Thus, the concept of the *sunsum*
corresponds in many ways to what is meant by personality, as was
observed by earlier investigators.

It is now clear that in Akan conceptions the *sunsum* ("spirit") is the
basis of a man's personality, and, in the words of Busia, "his ego."[20]
Personality, of course, is a word that has been variously defined by
psychologists. But I believe that whatever else that concept may mean,
it certainly involves the idea of a set of characteristics as evidenced in
a person's behavior—thoughts, feelings, actions, etc. (The sentences
given above demonstrate that it refers to more than a person's physical
appearance.) Thus, if the *sunsum* is that which constitutes the basis of
an individual's personality, it cannot be a physical thing, for qualities
like courage, jealousy, gentleness, forcefulness, and dignity are
psychological, not sensible or physical. The conception of personality
as the function of the *sunsum* makes a material conception of the latter
logically impossible. (Some Western philosophers and theologians in
fact identify personality with the soul.[21]) On the basis of the
characteristics of *sunsum*, Parrinder describes it as the
"personality—soul," perhaps using the term for the first time.[22]

As noted, certain statements of Danquah suggest a physicalistic
interpretation of the *sunsum*. On the other hand, he also maintains that
"it is the *sunsum* that 'experiences,'"[23] and that it is through the *sunsum*
that "the *ɔkra* or soul manifests itself in the world of experience."[24]
Elsewhere he says of the *sunsum*: "It is the bearer of conscious
experience, the unconscious or subliminal self remaining over as the
ɔkra or soul."[25] It is not clear what Danquah means by the "bearer" of
experience. Perhaps what he means is that the *sunsum* is the subject of
experience—that which experiences. Experience is the awareness of
something. Since a purely material thing, such as wood or a dead body,
cannot experience anything, it follows that the *sunsum*, *qua* subject of
experience, cannot be material. If, as Danquah thought,[26] it is the
sunsum that makes it possible for the destiny (*nkrabea*) of the soul to

be "realized" or "carried out" on earth, then, like the ɔkra (soul), an aspect of whose functions it performs, the *sunsum* also must be spiritual and immaterial. Danquah's position on the concept of the *sunsum*, then, is ambivalent, as is Busia's. Busia says that one part of a person is "the personality that comes indirectly from the Supreme Being."[27] By "personality" Busia must, on his own showing,[28] be referring to the *sunsum*, which must, according to my analysis, derive directly from the Supreme Being, and not from the father. (What derives from the father is the *ntoro*, to be explained directly.) It must, therefore, be divine and immortal, contrary to what he and others thought. That *sunsum* cannot derive from the child's father is proved also by the fact that trees, plants, and other natural objects also contain *sunsum*.

The explanation given by most Akans of the phenomenon of dreaming also indicates, it seems to me, that *sunsum* must be immaterial. In Akan thought, as in Freud's, dreams are not somatic but psychical phenomena. It is held that in a dream it is the person's *sunsum* that is the "actor." As an informant told Rattray decades ago, "When you sleep your '*Kra* (soul) does not leave you, as your *sunsum* may."[29] In sleep the *sunsum* is said to be released from the fetters of the body. As it were, it fashions for itself a new world of forms with the materials of its waking experience. Thus, although one is deeply asleep, yet one may "see" oneself standing atop a mountain or driving a car or fighting with someone or pursuing a desire like sexual intercourse; also, during sleep (that is, in dreams) a person's *sunsum* may talk with other *sunsum*. The actor in any of these "actions" is thought to be the *sunsum*, which thus can leave the body and return to it. The idea of the psychical part of a person leaving the body in sleep appears to be widespread in Africa. The Azande, for instance, maintain "that in sleep the soul is released from the body and can roam about at will and meet other spirits and have other adventures, though they admit something mysterious about its experiences... During sleep a man's soul wanders everywhere."[30]

The idea that some part of the soul leaves the body in sleep is not completely absent from the history of Western thought, even though, as Parrinder says, "the notion of a wandering soul is [are] foreign to the modern European mind."[31] The idea occurs, for instance, in Plato. In the *Republic* Plato refers to "the wild beast in us" that in pursuit of desires and pleasures bestirs itself "in *dreams* when the *gentler part of the soul* slumbers and the control of reason is withdrawn; then the wild beast in us, full-fed with meat and drink, becomes rampant and shakes off sleep to go in quest of what will gratify its own instincts."[32] The context is a discussion of tyranny. But Plato prefaces his discussion with remarks on the *psychological* foundation of the tyrannical man, and says that desire (Greek: *epithumia*) is the basis of his behavior.

It is not surprising that both scholars of Plato and modern psychologists have noted the relevance of the above passage to the analysis of the nature of the human psyche. On this passage the classical scholar James Adam wrote: "The theory is that in dreams the part of the soul concerned is not asleep, but awake and goes out to seek the object of its desire."[33] The classicist Paul Shorey observed that "The Freudians have at least discovered Plato's anticipation of their main thesis."[34] The relevance of the Platonic passage to Freud has been noted also by other scholars of Plato such as Renford Bambrough[35] and Thomas Gould,[36] and by psychologists. Valentine, a psychologist, observed: "The germ of several aspects of the Freudian view of dreams, including the characteristic doctrine of the censor, was to be found in Plato."[37]

It is clear that the passage in Plato indicates a link between dreams and (the gratification of) desires.[38] In Akan psychology the *sunsum* appears not only as unconscious but also as that which pursues and experiences desires. (In Akan dreams are also considered predictive.) But the really interesting part of Plato's thesis for our purposes relates to *the idea of some part of the human soul leaving the body in dreams.* "The wild beast in us" in Plato's passage is not necessarily equivalent to the Akan *sunsum*, but one may say that just as Plato's "wild beast" (which, like the *sunsum*, experiences dreams) is a *part* of the soul and thus not a physical object, so is *sunsum.*

It might be supposed that if the *sunsum* can engage in activity, such as traveling through space or occupying a physical location—like standing on the top of a mountain—then it can hardly be said not to be a physical object. The problem here is obviously complex. Let us assume, for the moment, that the *sunsum* is a physical object. One question that would immediately arise is: How can a purely physical object leave the person when he or she is asleep? Dreaming is of course different from imagining or thinking. The latter occurs during waking life, whereas the former occurs only during sleep: *wɔnda a wɔnso dae,* that is, "Unless you are asleep you do not dream" is a well-known Akan saying. The fact that dreaming occurs only in sleep makes it a unique sort of mental activity and its subject, namely *sunsum*, a different sort of subject. A purely physical object cannot be in two places at the same time: A body lying in bed cannot at the same time be on the top of a mountain. Whatever is on the top of the mountain, then, must be something nonphysical, nonbodily, and yet somehow connected to a physical thing—in this case, the body. This argument constitutes a *reductio ad absurdum* of the view that *sunsum* can be a physical object.

But, then, how can the *sunsum*, qua nonphysical, extrasensory object, travel in physical space and have a physical location? This question must be answered within the broad context of the African belief in the activities of the supernatural (spiritual) beings in the physical world. The spiritual beings are said to be insensible and intangible, but they are also said to make themselves felt in the physical world. They can thus interact with the physical world. But from this it cannot be inferred that they are physical or quasiphysical or have permanent physical properties. It means that a spiritual being can, when it so desires, take on physical properties. That is, even though a spiritual being is nonspatial in essence, it can, by the sheer operation of its power, assume spatial properties. Debrunner speaks of "temporary 'materializations,' i.e., as spirits having taken on the body of a person which afterwards suddenly vanish."[39] Mbiti observed that "Spirits are invisible, but may make themselves visible to human beings".[40] We should view the "physical" activities of the *sunsum* in dreaming from the standpoint of the activities of the spiritual beings in the physical world. As a microcosm of the world spirit, the *sunsum* can also interact with the external world. So much then for the defense of the psychical, nonphysical nature of *sunsum*, the subject of experiences in dreaming.

As the basis of personality, as the coperformer of some of the functions of the *ɔkra* (soul)—undoubtedly held as a spiritual entity—and as the subject of the psychical activity of dreaming the *sunsum* must be something spiritual (immaterial). This is the reason for my earlier assertion that "spirit" might not be an inappropriate translation for *sunsum*. On my analysis, then, we have the following picture:

   ɔkra (soul)   }   immaterial (spiritual)
   Sunsum ("spirit") }   immaterial (spiritual)
   Honam (body) }   material (physical)

In their conception of the nature of the person the Akans distinguish the *ntoro* and the *mogya* (blood). In contrast to the *sunsum* and *ɔkra*, which definitely are of divine origin, the *ntoro* and the *mogya* are endowed by human beings. The *ntoro* is held as coming from the father of the child. It has been confused with *sunsum*. Thus, Busia says that the two terms are synonymous, and hence renders *ntoro* as "spirit." He writes: "*Ntoro* is the generic term of which *sunsum* is a specific instance."[41] Rattray also translated *ntoro* by "spirit," though he thought it corresponded with the semen.[42] He said elsewhere that the *ntoro* is "passed into the woman by a male during the act of coition."[43] One of my discussants stated that *ntoro* is derived from the father's semen, but the *sunsum*, he said, comes from the Supreme Being.[44] The *ntoro* appears to be the basis of inherited characteristics and may therefore be simply translated as "sperm-transmitted characteristic," even though spiritual as well as physiological qualities are attributed to it. Both *ntoro* and *mogya* (blood, which is believed to be transmitted by the mother) are genetic factors responsible for inherited characteristics, on the basis of which the Akan thinkers have created proverbs such as:

> The crab does not give birth to a bird.
> The offspring of an antelope cannot possibly resemble a deer's offspring.
> The antelope does not leap for its offspring to crawl.[45]

The introduction of inherited characteristics into the constitution of a person introduces an element of complexity into the Akan concept of the person.

NOTES

1. I say "a conception" because I believe there are other conceptions of the person held or discernible in that philosophy (see above, 47, 55).
2. Kwasi Wiredu, "The Akan Concept of Mind," *Ibadan Journal of Humanistic Studies*, in press, 9. The page references are to the typescript.
3. *ibid.*, 10; my italics.
4. Wiredu, "The Akan Concept of Mind," 9.
5. *ibid.*
6. *ibid.*, 19.
7. Bernard Williams, *Descartes: The Project of Pure Enquiry* (Pelican Books London, 1978), 78; also, *Descartes, Philosophical Writings*, trans. and ed. Elizabeth Anscombe and Peter T. Geach (Edinburgh University Press, Edinburgh, 1954), xxxvii, n. 2, and xvii.
8. Wiredu, "The Akan Concept of Mind," 19.
9. K. A. Busia, "The Ashanti of the Gold Coast," in Daryll Forde (ed.), *African Worlds*, 197; M. Fortes, *Kinship and the Social Order* (University of Chicago Press, Chicago, 1969), 199, n. 14; Robert A. Lystad, *The Ashanti, A Proud People* (Rutgers University Press, New Brunswick, N.J., 1958), 155; Peter K. Sarpong, *Ghana in Retrospect: Some Aspects of the Ghanaian Culture* (Ghana Publishing Corp., Accra, 1974), 37.
10. Busia, 197; Lystad, 155; E. L. R. Meyerowitz, *The Sacred State of the Akan* (Faber and Faber, London, 1951), 86; and "Concepts of the Soul among the Akan," *Africa*, 26.
11. Busia, 197; Lystad, 155; P. A. Twumasi, *Medical Systems in Ghana* (Ghana Publishing Corp., Accra, 1975), 22.
12. Here the views of W. E. Abraham are excepted, for he maintains, like I do, that the *sunsum* is not "inheritable" and that it "appears to have been a spiritual substance." W. E. Abraham, *The Mind of Africa* (University of Chicago Press, Chicago, 1962), 60.
13. J. B. Danquah, *The Akan Doctrine of God* (Lutterworth Press, London, 1944), 115.
14. *ibid.*, 116.
15. Busia, 197; also 200.
16. Danquah, 66.
17. *ibid.*, e.g., 67, 75, 83, 205.
18. R. S. Rattray, *Ashanti*, 46.
19. E. L. R. Meyerowitz, *The Akan of Ghana, Their Ancient Beliefs* (Faber and Faber, London, 1958), 98, 150, and 146; also her *Sacred State*, 86.
20. Busia, 197.
21. Corliss Lamont, *The Philosophy of Humanism* (Ungar, New York, 1974), 81-95. Malcolm J. McVeigh, *God in Africa* (Calude Stark, Cape Cod, Massachusetts, 1974), 26, 37.

22. E. G. Parrinder, *West African Psychology*, 32, 46, 70.
23. Danquah, 67.
24. *ibid.*
25. *ibid.*, 112.
26. *ibid.*, 66-7, 115.
27. Busia, 200.
28. *ibid.*, 197.
29. R. S. Rattray, *Religion and Art in Ashanti*, 154.
30. E. E. Evans-Pritchard, *Witchcraft, Oracles and Magic among the Azande*, 136; also E. G. Parrinder, *West African Religion*, 197.
31. Parrinder, *West African Religion*, 197.
32. Plato, *The Republic*, 571, beginning of Book IX.
33. James Adam (ed.), *The Republic of Plato*, 2d ed. (Cambridge University Press, Cambridge, 1975), Vol. 2, 320.
34. Plato, *The Republic*, ed. and trans. by Paul Shorey (Loeb Classical Library, Harvard University Press, Cambridge, Mass., 1935), 335.
35. Plato, *The Republic*, trans. by A.D. Lindsay (J. M. Dent, London, 1976), 346.
36. Thomas Gould, *Platonic Love* (Routledge and Kegan Paul, London, 1963), 108ff and 174ff.
37. Charles W. Valentine, *Dreams and the Unconscious* (Methuen, London, 1921), 93; also his *The New Psychology of the Unconscious* (Macmillan, New York, 1929), 95.
38. Wilfred Trotter, *Instincts of the Herd in Peace and War* (T. F. Unwin, London, 1916), 74.
39. H. Debrunner, *Witchcraft in Ghana* (Waterville Publishing House, Accra, 1959), 17.
40. Mbiti, *African Religions and Philosophy*, 102.
41. Busia, 197; also K. A. Busia, *The Position of the Chief in the Modern Politial System of Ashanti*, 1.
42. Rattray, *Ashanti*, 1, 45, 46, 48.
43. Rattray, *Religion and Art*, 319.
44. Interview with Opanin Twum Barimah, Kibi, 17 August 1974.
45. All three proverbs refer to the idea of giving birth (*awo*) and the belief that offsprings take on the characteristics of their parents. All the three seek to assert resemblance between parents and offsprings in respect of their characteristics. The first proverb means that the characteristics of the offspring of the crab will (have to) be those of the crab and not those of the bird, and the proverb is uttered when someone is utterly convinced of the character resemblances between a child and its parent(s). The other two proverbs must be understood in the same way. All such character resemblances are, according to Akan thinkers, attributable to the *ntoro*. The postulation of *ntoro* therefore is intended

to answer questions about resemblances—particularly character resemblances (not so much physical resemblances)—between children and their parents.

Questions for Chapter 9
The Concept of a Person

1. TRUE or FALSE?

   a. On Gyekye's account, Akans believe that a person is made up of three different elements.
   b. On Gyekye's account, the Akan conception of a person is Cartesian.
   c. Gyekye agrees with Wiredu that the Akans believe that a person has material component.
   d. Gyekye claims that a belief in life after death is necessary for a belief in dualism.

2. On Gyekye's account, the Akans believe that the *sunsum* is not responsible for:

   (A) personality.
   (B) inherited characteristics.
   (C) dreaming.
   (D) thinking.

3. On Gyekye's account the *ɔkra* may not be translated as:

   (A) consciousness.
   (B) soul.
   (C) mind.
   (D) the spirit.

4. Compare and evaluate Oguah, Wiredu and Gyekye's arguments as well as accounts of the Akan conception of a person.

Chapter 10

Philosophy, Logic and the Akan Language

Kwame Gyekye

Ɔnantefo sen ɔse as ɛm. —The traveller is more knowledgeable than his or her father. (Akan proverb)

PROLOGUE

Here, Kwame Gyekye argues, as Wiredu does, that some but not all philosophical problems are language-dependent; since philosophical problems about, say, the ontological argument and about the distinction between subjects and predicates on the basis of the completeness or incompleteness of the expression do not arise in the Akan language, though they do in English. (Gyekye's biographical sketch appears in Chapter 9.)

Here is part of his argument:

"In the ontological argument for the existence of God the claim is made that existence is an attribute (that is, predicate)...The Akan verb for "to exist" is *wɔ hɔ.* Thus, *Onyame wɔ hɔ* translates the English "God exists" or "There is God." There is, however, no direct equivalent of the noun "existence" in Akan; it would be rendered by "that something is there (exists)" (*se biribi wɔ hɔ*). Thus, the question whether existence is an attribute becomes in Akan something like: "Is that something is there an attribute?" The bizarre nature of this question in Akan makes implausible the thesis about the reality of God that derives from the concept of existence. The ontological argument, then, loses its plausibility when considered within the context of the Akan language. Because of the qualities of the language, it is more than likely that a thinker using Akan would never have raised the ontological argument...The logical distinction based on the concepts of "completeness" and "incompleteness," respectively, is invalid not only in respect of Akan grammar but Chinese grammar as well, according to Tsu-Lin Mei...The discussion on existence, predication, and identity point up the fact that some logical or philosophical puzzles and confusion generated in ancient philosophy by the Greek verb "to be" (*einai*) evaporate when such matters are examined in, say, the Akan language. The Akan language is well equipped to handle logical matters relating to existence, predication, and identity. The implication here is that some philosophical or logical problems are relative to language. I use the word "some" here advisedly, for I do not believe that all philosophical problems relating to fatalism, bases (sources) of morality, civil disobedience, human rights, the existence of God, political legitimacy, moral obligation, among others, are relative to some natural language or other. Such philosophical problems, in my view, do in fact arise from common human experiences. This is why it is possible for thinkers from different cultural backgrounds and using different languages to arrive at similar conclusions."

Philosophy, Logic and the Akan Language

Kwame Gyekye

1. EXISTENCE, PREDICATION, AND IDENTITY

Philosophers acquainted with ancient Greek philosophy are of course aware of the logical puzzles or confusions generated by the ambiguity inherent in the Greek verb *einai*, "to be." Often it is not clear whether the word was used to indicate existence, copulation (predication), identity, or some other relation. For instance, the opening sentence of Protagoras' (481-411 B.C.) work *On Truth* reads as follows: "Man is the measure of all things, of what is (*esti*), that it is (*esti*), of what is not, that it is not (*ouk esti*)." (*Esti* is the present tense third-person singular of *einai*.) It is possible to interpret the verb *einai* here as existential; it is equally possible, particularly since the subject is truth, to interpret the verb as "to be so," "to be the case," or "to be true," which is another meaning of *einai*.[1] In fact Kahn claims that this latter meaning is philosophically "the most fundamental value of *einai* when used alone (without predicates)."[2] Thus, the minds of scholars of Plato are much exercised about whether Plato in the *Sophist* intends *einai* existentially or predicatively. Owen, a foremost scholar of Aristotle, points out that Aristotle nowhere distinguishes the predicative and existential uses of *einai*.[3] Graham observes: "It is well known that Greek philosophy hardly ever distinguishes between the existential and copulative functions of *einai*, 'to be.'"[4]

In English and most other Indo-European languages the problem relating to existence and predication is not as acute as it is in Greek. In English, for instance, in addition to the word "exist," the expression "there is" also indicates simple existence. German "*es gibt*" and French "*il y a*" are equivalents of the English "there is" in terms of their functions. Although "exist" in

1. Lions exist

is a grammatical predicate, it is generally held not to be a logical predicate,[5] so that (1) is strictly not a predicate statement. It is an existential statement, asserting the existence of something—in this case, lions. Similarly,

2. There are lions

is also an existential statement.

In English, however, the same verb, "to be," is used to express existence, predication, and identity, as in

3. There are lions (existence)
4. Lions are fierce animals (predication: class membership)
5. Lions are the kings of the forest (identity).

Let us now turn to see how the Akan language handles existence, predication, and identity. Akan is more than adequate in meeting the logical difficulties inherent in the Greek *einai*. It may also have some advantages over English for these questions, for it has three separate verbs for expressing existential, predicative, and identity statements.

2. EXISTENCE

In Akan existence is expressed by the word *wɔ*: "to be somewhere," "to be or exist in a place,"[6] to which the deictic word *hɔ* ("there") is added. The complete existential expression is thus *wɔ hɔ*, "there is," "exists." [This is what is represented in modern logic by the formula $(\exists x) Fx$.] Thus,

God exists: Nyame *wɔ hɔ*.

The *hɔ* part of this existential expression is, in my view, not "semantically empty," as Boadi thought.[7] In Akan the existential verb involves location—and this is not peculiar to Akan[8]—and it is the *hɔ* that, it seems to me, contains the locative implication of the existential expression *wɔ hɔ*. Therefore, the *hɔ* cannot be semantically empty. And although *wɔ* and *hɔ* do not appear as a unitary lexical item—neither do "be" and "there" in English—nevertheless, insofar as it is the two together that adequately express the notion of existence, that is, existential locative, it would be a mistake to deny the *hɔ* a semantic function. In fact the two words constitute a semantic unit.

3. PREDICATION

The predicative "be" in Akan is *yɛ*, which is used to indicate both class membership and class inclusion. As examples:

1. *anoma no yɛ patu.*
   (The bird *is* an owl.)
2. *bepow no yɛ tenten.*
   (The mountain *is* tall.)
3. *nnipa nyinaa yɛ Onyame mma.*
   (All men *are* children of God.)

Statements (1) and (2) indicate class membership, whereas (3) indicates class inclusion.

4. IDENTITY

Identity statements in Akan are expressed by *ne*, "to be (identical with)."

1. *Onyame ne panyin.*
   (God *is* the elder.)
2. *Owusu ne sukuu no hwɛfo.*
   (Owusu *is the* principal of the school.)
3. *sukuuhwɛfo no ne Owusu.*
   (The principal of the school *is* (the same as) Owusu.)

Thus, *ne* necessarily involves and makes use of the concepts of definite description and proper name. The thought expressed in (1) and (2) would change if we substituted *yɛ* (the predicative "is") for *ne*. Thus,

Onyame yɛ panyin
(God *is* an elder.)

would not be an identity, but a predicative statement indicating class membership.

There is yet another word in the Akan language that expresses identity, but only in a limited or special sense. The verb *de* ("to be") is used in statements such as:

1. *ne din de Owusu*
   (His name *is* Owusu.)
2. *nsuo no din de Volta*
   (The river's name *is* Volta.)

In such cases the grammatical subject is generally the word "name" and the grammatical predicate must be a proper name. However, a proper name can be used as the grammatical subject, as in

Owusu ne ne[9] din
(Owusu *is* his name.)

In the latter case *de* becomes *ne*. (Christaller may be correct in saying that *de* is an old form of *ne*.[10]) Sometimes *ne* is used in place of *de* for emphasis, as in:

ne din ne Owusu
(His name certainly *is* Owusu.)

It is thus clear that the Akan language sharply separates the existential and copulative functions of the verb "to be" and that it has different words to express existence, predication, and identity. Consequently puzzles, confusions, or mistakes arising out of the use of such an ambiguous verb as the Greek *einai* cannot arise within Akan. So, if ancient philosophers such as Protagoras, Parmenides, Plato, and Aristotle had written in Akan, they would have been able to avoid the ambiguities of *einai*.

5. THE ONTOLOGICAL ARGUMENT

In the ontological argument for the existence of God the claim is made that existence is an attribute (that is, predicate). This implies that the attribution of existence to an object adds something to its characterization: It provides new information apart from asserting the existence of the object.

Now let us consider this claim within the context of Akan. The Akan verb for "to exist" is *wɔ hɔ*. Thus, Onyame *wɔ hɔ* translates the English "God exists" or "There is God." There is, however, no direct equivalent of the noun "existence" in Akan; it would be rendered by "that something is there (exists)" (*sɛ biribi wɔ hɔ*). Thus, the question whether existence is an attribute becomes in Akan something like: "*Is that something is there* an attribute?" The bizarre nature of this question in Akan makes implausible the thesis about the reality of God that derives from the concept of existence. The ontological argument, then, loses its plausibility when considered within the context of the Akan language. Because of the qualities of the language, it is more than likely that a thinker using Akan would never have raised the ontological argument.

6. SUBJECT AND PREDICATE

Here I wish to discuss, within the context of the Akan language, the logical criterion that P. F. Strawson, the distinguished Oxford philosopher, advances as a basis for a distinction between the subject and predicate of a sentence. The traditional view is that a predicate is an expression that provides an assertion about something, this something being referred to as the subject. Thus, in the sentence

Owusu walks

the predicate "walks" asserts something about Owusu, with Owusu, being that about which something is asserted, as the subject. Strawson rejects this characterization on the grounds that in the above sentence one might be talking about walking, and not necessarily about Owusu.[11] I think Strawson is right here. The traditional definition of the predicate as that which makes an assertion about something is not satisfactory.

In his arguments for the logical criterion for distinguishing between subject and predicate, Strawson uses the terms "complete" and "incomplete" to characterize the subject and predicate, respectively, terms which had been used by the German mathematician-philosopher Gottlob Frege (1848-1925) for practically the same purpose. Strawson's intention is to defend the Fregean characterizations of the subject and predicate. Subject expressions, he says, are complete, or better, are nearer completion, whereas predicate expressions are incomplete because they hardly ever occur alone. According to Strawson, the main difference between what are called subject expressions like "Socrates," "John," and "Owusu," and predicate expressions like "is wise," "smokes," and "walks," is that a subject expression "might be completed into any kind of remark (or clause), not necessarily a proposition, or it might stand by itself as designating an item in a list; but the expression 'is wise' demands a certain kind of completion, namely, completion into a proposition or propositional clause."[12] Thus, he explains that subject expressions "introduce their terms in a grammatical style (the substantival) which would be appropriate to *any kind of remark* (command, exhortation, undertaking, assertion) or to none,"[13] whereas predicate expressions "introduce their terms in a very distinctive grammatical style, viz., the assertive or propositional style."[14] The minimal claim Strawson makes is that "is wise" and "smokes" occur only in propositions; thus, they introduce their terms in the propositional style. A predicate expression, therefore, is an expression that can be completed *only* into a proposition or propositional clause, whereas a subject expression is an expression that can be completed into any kind of remark, not necessarily a proposition or propositional clause.

Strawson's thesis is based on the characteristics of English grammar, for in English the verb introducing the predicate expression is inflected to agree with the subject expression in number and in person. Verbs in Akan, however, are not inflected for person or for number. Strawson's theory may therefore produce problems when considered within the context of Akan. Let us consider the following sentence:

> *Owusu* nante
> (Owusu *walks.*)

In Strawson's theory the predicate expression, *nante*, is completable only into a proposition. But in Akan *nante* (unlike its equivalent "walks" in the above sentence) does not demand to be completed only into a proposition or propositional clause. It can be completed into other kinds of remark (or clause) that are not propositions. As examples:

> 1. *nante* can be used as a (grammatical) *subject*, as in:
>   nante *yɛ yaw*
>   (walking or to walk is painful) or
>   nante *yɛ ma honam*
>   (walking is good for the body).
> 2. *nante* can be used as imperative:
>   nante! (walk!)
> 3. *nante* can be used in asking a *question*:
>   nante? (walk?)

Thus, the predicate expression *nante* in Akan performs functions that "walks" cannot perform in English. Strawson's criterion collapses.

The picture, however, appears slightly different when the predicate expression is introduced by the verb "to be." Consider the Akan sentence

> *barima no yɛ kɛse*
> (the man *is big*)

Although the predicate expression *yɛ kɛse* cannot perform all the functions performed by nante, nevertheless it is not completable only into a proposition or propositional clause, for *yɛ kɛse* can be used in a command, as in

yɛ kɛse!
(Be big!)

Of course in English "is big" cannot be used for a command, but in Akan *yɛ kɛse* can. In Akan the copulative (predicative) *yɛ* can be translated as "am," "are," "be," depending on the type of sentence. Thus,

Be big!: *yɛ kɛse*
He *is* big: *ɔyɛ kɛse*
I *am* big: *me yɛ kɛse*
They *are* big: *wɔ yɛ kɛse,* etc.

The English sentence "Socrates is wise" can be rendered into Akan in three ways:

1. Socrates yɛ *onyansafo*
(Socrates *is* a wise man)
2. Socrates wɔ *nyansa*
(Socrates *possesses* wisdom)
3. Socrates nim *nyansa*
(Socrates *perceives* wisdom; *nim* literally means "to know").

Expression (1) indicates a case where a part of the predicate expression, namely, *onyansafo* (wise man), itself designates a complete symbol, for *onyansafo* can be, and is, used as a subject expression, as in the well-known Akan proverb *onyansafo wobu no bɛ na wɔnka no asɛm* ("The wise man is spoken to in proverbs, not in speeches or words").

Similarly, in (2) and (3) a part of the predicate expression, namely *nyansa* (wisdom), can be used as a subject, as in

nyansa *yɛ ade papa*
[*Wisdom* is a good thing (a virtue).]

It is obvious that Strawson's observation that the expression "is wise" or "smokes" ("walks" in my example) demands a certain kind of completion, namely, completion into a proposition or propositional clause, exploits some facts about English grammar: (a) the fact that the verb is inflected, as a result of which the expression "smokes," for instance, cannot perform any other function than being coupled with a subject expression like "Raleigh" to form a proposition;[15] (b) the fact that the verb must agree with the subject in person and number, as a result of which the expression "smokes," for instance, can be coupled only with a third-person singular subject expression. (As we have seen, neither of these applies to Akan.) Thus, it is clear that Strawson's observations were influenced by the characteristics of English. But Strawson seems to deny this: "It should be noticed that, in drawing this distinction between A-expressions [that is, subject expressions] and B-expressions [that is, predicate expressions], I am not merely exploiting the fact that English is a comparatively uninflected language, especially as regards its noun-forms..."[16] (but the English verb is inflected in the present tense.) The denial seems to imply that Strawson sees his criterion as applicable regardless of language. The facts he exploits, however, are not congruent with Akan grammar, for instance.

The idea behind the description of the subject expression as complete is that such an expression can occur alone and can be used in itself as salutation, command, and exclamation ("Owusu!"). Questions ("Owusu?") and assertions ("Owusu.") may also consist only of the proper name "Owusu." Predicate expressions behave differently in English; they can hardly occur alone—hence their incompleteness. In asking a question and in issuing a command in English, one says "walk" instead of "walks." But in Akan the case is different in respect of predicate expressions. The predicate expression *nante* (walk), like the subject expression, can occur alone and can be used in itself, as already noted, as command ("*nante!*"), as question ("*nante?*"), and as assertion ("*nante*"). If the predicate is "incomplete" because it cannot occur alone and also because it is completable only into a proposition, then it is difficult to see why predicate expressions in Akan should be depicted as "incomplete," for, after all, they can perform the functions that subject expressions are supposed to perform. Strawson's theory regarding the character and behavior of the predicate is therefore invalid with respect to the grammar of the Akan language.[17]

7. CONCLUSIONS

First, we may conclude that it is neither safe nor proper for philosophers or logicians to generalize for other natural languages a particular philosophical thesis or logical theory or principle that has been influenced or determined by the features of some particular language (or family of languages). Thus, the logical distinction based on the concepts of "completeness" and "incompleteness," respectively, is invalid not only in respect of Akan grammar but Chinese grammar as well, according to Tsu-Lin Mei.[18] Mbiti's analysis of the so-called African concept of time, which was based on a couple of East African languages, is incorrectly attributed to other African languages. Generalizations on such matters that are based on the characteristics of one or two natural languages ought to be made with circumspection. Thus Lemmon, after referring to the logical connectives, incautiously wrote: "This book is written in English, and so mentions *English* sentences and words; but the above account could be applied, by appropriate translation, to all languages I know of. *There is nothing parochial about logic,* despite this appearance to the contrary."[19] It is not clear how many and what kind of languages Lemmon knows. If one examines sentences and words in a number of languages, one would reject Lemmon's view that "there is nothing parochial about logic," at least as regards the aspects that are demonstrably language-oriented.

This is not to say, however, that the whole system of logic necessarily derives from the grammatical rules of language. I believe that there are logical rules or principles that can be said to be language-neutral and may operate in all natural languages. Such rules or principles that transcend the limits of languages, it seems to me, really belong to the realm of thought; that is, they can be known to be true by reflection. I suppose that the hypothetical syllogism $[(p \rightarrow q) \wedge (q \rightarrow r)] \rightarrow (p \rightarrow r)$ and the disjunctive syllogism $[(p \vee q) \wedge \sim p] \rightarrow q$ are among such logical principles whose validity can be ascertained by thought, and so can be said to be true in all languages.

Second, it is clear from our examination of the type of arguments used by Western dualist philosophers on the mind-body problem and from our remarks on the ontological argument that some philosophical theses formulated on the basis of one language lose their validity or plausibility or importance when translated into another language. Thus, despite the materialism apparent in the Akan language, the Akan philosophy of mind and body is nevertheless *not* materialistic, but thoroughly and undoubtedly dualistic.

Third, the discussions on existence, predication, and identity point up the fact that some logical or philosophical puzzles and confusions generated in ancient philosophy by the Greek verb "to be" (*einai*) evaporate when such matters are examined in, say, the Akan language. The Akan language is well equipped to handle logical matters relating to existence, predication, and identity. The implication here is that some philosophical or logical problems are relative to language. I use the word "some" here advisedly, for I do not believe that all philosophical problems relating to fatalism, bases (sources) of morality, civil disobedience, human rights, the existence of God, political legitimacy, moral obligation, among others, are relative to some natural language or other. Such philosophical problems, in my view, do in fact arise from common human experiences. This is why it is possible for thinkers from different cultural backgrounds and using different languages to arrive at similar conclusions.

Finally, because languages have different and peculiar structures, a philosophical or logical thesis that is *clearly* based on the characteristics of one language should not necessarily or precipitately be generalized to other languages, unless the evidence is extremely persuasive. Where such evidence is lacking, one should make circumspect statements and speak in terms of probabilities rather than certainties.

Notes

1. Aristotle, *Metaphysics*, 1017a33-5.
2. Charles H. Kahn, "The Greek Verb 'To Be' and the Concept of Being," *Foundations of Language*, Vol. II, 1966, 250.
3. G. E. L. Owen, "Aristotle on the Snares of Ontology," in R. Bambrough (ed.), *New Essays on Plato and Aristotle* (Routledge and Kegan Paul, London, 1965), 84ff.
4. A. C. Graham, "'Being' in Linguistics and Philosophy," *Foundations of Language*, Vol. 1, 1965, 224.
5. Of course, there is a dispute of long standing in Western philosophy as to whether existence is a logical predicate. The general view is that it is not. But see Kwame Gyekye, "A Note on Existence as a Predicate," *Second Order*, Vol. III, No. 2, July 1974, 97-101.
6. J.G. Christaller, *Dictionary*, 560.
7. L. A. Boadi, "Existential Sentences in Akan," *Foundations of Language*, Vol. 7, 1971, 19.
8. Thus, Charles H. Kahn, "The Greek Verb 'To be'", 258, said that there is a "close connection between the ideas of existence and location in Greek philosophical thought." John Lyons also wrote: "In fact, the existential 'be' copula does not normally occur in English without a locative or temporal complement; and it might appear reasonable to say that *all existential sentences are at least implicitly locative...*" John Lyons, "A Note on Possessive, Existential and Locative Sentences," *Foundations of Language*, Vol. III, 1967, 390; my italics.
9. The second *ne* in "Owusu ne *ne* din" is genitive.
10. Christaller, *Grammar*, 110.
11. P. F. Strawson, "Proper Names," *Proceedings of the Aristotelian Society*, Suppl. Vol. XXXI, 1957, 193. The same doctrine appears in his *Individuals, An Essay in Descriptive Metaphysics* (Doubleday, New York, 1963), 143-6.
12. *ibid.*, "Proper Names," 196; *Individuals*, 153.
13. *ibid.*, "Proper Names," 193-4; my italics.
14. *ibid.*, 194.
15. It is strange indeed why Strawson fastens on the third person singular "walks." If he had chosen the first or second person (singular and plural), he might have arrived at different conclusions, for we can say "walk!" (imperative) or "walk?" (interrogative).
16. Strawson, "Proper Names," 195, n. 3.
17. This section on the subject and predicate was inspired by the two papers of Tsu-Lin Mei, "Subject and Predicate, A Grammatical Preliminary," *Philosophical Review*, Vol. LXX, April 1961, 153-75, and "Chinese Grammar and the Linguistic Movement," *Review of*

Metaphysics, Vol. XIV, No. 3, March 1961, 487-92. In both papers, Tsu-Lin Mei rejects Strawson's conclusions as invalid in respect of Chinese grammar.

18. Tsu-Lin Mei's arguments are in the two papers of his referred to at the preceding note.

19. E. J. Lemmon, *Beginning Logic* (Nelson, London, 1971), 6; my italics, except for the word "English."

Questions for Chapter 10
Philosophy, Logic and the Akan Language

1. TRUE or FALSE?

    a. According to Gyekye, there is nothing parochial about Logic.
    b. According to Gyekye, all the rules of Logic are rules of language.
    c. According to Gyekye, all problems about the existence of God are relative to language.
    d. On Gyekyes account, 'existence' in Akan involves location.

2. Gyekye claims that the following philosophical problems are relative to language:

    (A) Logical distinctions based on completeness and incompleteness of concepts.
    (B) Problems about human rights.
    (C) The sources of morality.
    (D) All logical matters relating to existence, predication, and identity.

3. State and evaluate Gyekye's arguments for the claim that:

    (a)   some philosophical problems are relative to language.
    (b)   some philosophical problems are not relative to language.

Chapter 11

Truth and the Akan Language

Kwasi Wiredu

Atokoro sæ nokwapem. —**One lie destroys a thousand truths.**
(**Akan proverb**)

PROLOGUE

In exploring issues about logic and truth in the Akan language, Kwasi Wiredu (whose biographical sketch appears in Chapter 8) notes, as Gyekye does, that not all logical or philosophical problems and theories are universal. For example, he argues, that even though the concepts of *Truth* in the cognitive (non-moral) sense and *Equivalence* in terms of 'if and only if' are expressible in the Akan language as *nea ete saa* and *ne nyinaa kosi faako*, they are not literally and directly translatable. Hence some of the important Western philosophical problems about, say, how facts are related to true propositions, or how 'if and only if' is related to equivalence, or whether the correspondence theory is acceptable do not arise in Akan language and culture.

Wiredu argues, partly, as follows:
"...let us concentrate on '*Ete saa*' which is certainly the most unproblematic rendition of the cognitive concept of truth in Akan. The interesting point now is that in this language the concept of fact will also be rendered in terms of the notion of '*ete saa*' i.e. of what is so. A fact is simply '*nea ete saa*,' what is so. Consider now how the correspondence theory would sound in this language. Suppose we formulate it as 'A statement is true means that it corresponds with facts.' This would become something like '*Asem no te saa kyerese ene*

nea ete saa di nsianim' which translates into English literally as 'The statement is so means that it coincides, corresponds with what is so.' This has the beauty of a tautology, but it teaches little wisdom. It seems to me unlikely that thinking in this language, one could be easily tempted into correspondence formulations of this sort."

J. T. Bedu-Addo, whom Wiredu refers to in the Notes (particularly the third note following Wiredu's article), was educated at the University of the Gold Coast (now University of Ghana) and Queen Mary College where he earned his bachelor's and doctorate degrees respectively. He is, currently, living in Nigeria and working at the Obafemi Awolowo University as a Reader in Philosophy.

Bedu-Addo disagrees with Wiredu's conception of truth in Akan. He argues that the Akan word for truth in both the moral and cognitive senses is '*nokware*' or, more precisely, *nokwaredi* and not *nea ete saa* as Wiredu will have us believe. According to Bedu-Addo, truth is ultimately an epistemological concept rather than a moral one. Hence the Akan word for moral truth is the same as that for cognitive truth. Further, *nokware* provides a better translation of English sentences involving 'truth' and 'facts' than other Akan words. Additionally, the Akan phrase *nea ete saa* also applies to things, such as chairs, and not just statements; and it suggests a certain relationship between statements and facts and, hence, problems about how true statements are related to facts.

"If you ask an Akan the meaning of the phrase *nea ete saa (ma otse dem)*," Bedu-Addo writes in "On the Concept of Truth in Akan" (in *Philosophy in Africa: Trends and Perspectives.* Ile-Ife, Nigeria: University of Ife Press, 1985.), "the idea of propositions and statements is not likely to occur to him at all; for the phrase literally means 'that which is like that'" (70). He proceeds: "...Now, since it is the same concept of truth that operates in the sphere of morality where intention to be honest or deceitful is involved, it is not at all an easy matter to justify the claim that the main preoccupation with truth in traditional Akan society was moral..." (74).

Truth and the Akan Language

Kwasi Wiredu

1. THE PROBLEM OF DEFINING TRUTH

...But what exactly is that problem? I do not think that the problem can be said to be one of giving the meaning of the phrase 'is true.' I find no problem with the ordinary lexical definition of truth as agreement with reality. What presents a problem is to clarify what it is that is said to agree with reality and also to explain what we mean by reality in this context. Again, we might alternatively but equivalently note another ordinary discourse definition of truth. To say that something is true is to say that it is so. The problem is: What is it that may be said to be so or not so? And what are we saying of that thing, whatever it is, when we say it is so? I believe that it is a special merit of Tarski's equivalence that it presents a potentially ideal context for raising one of these questions, namely: What is the ontological status of the second component of the original equivalence? The classical theories of truth of Western philosophy give various answers to this question, though it is not always clear that the theorists are aware that this is the question being tackled in the appropriate parts of their theories. The Correspondence theory, in effect, construes that component as fact in some non-linguistic sense. The Pragmatic theory, in its Deweyan form at least, in effect, construes it as representing a warranted conclusion; while the coherence theory, in effect, construes it as an element well integrated into a received system. Much confusion, would, I think, have been avoided had it been clearly realized that this was the issue at stake.

Truth, then, is correspondence with reality. But it is not the correspondence of a statement or belief with reality. It is the correspondence of the ideational content of a statement or belief with reality; and reality is not a fact but the referent of the ideational import of a fact. Common (English) idiom sometimes metaphorically objectifies fact, but philosophy can do better than be misled by idiom A fact is always a fact *that* P, and as argued, the P, which represents a judgment consists of an ideational content and a claim of reference, instantiation

Excerpted from "Truth: The Correspondence Theory of Judgment," *African Philosophical Inquiry*, Vol. 1, No. 1, 1987 (28-30), by permission of Ibadan University Press.

or correspondence. Reality is what the ideational content refers to, not the claim that there is such a reference. Correspondence, then, is the essence of truth, but it is also a constitutive intension of judgment. To reach a correspondence theory of judgment is to see through the correspondence theory of truth.

2. THE CONCEPT OF TRUTH AND THE AKAN LANGUAGE

I would like to conclude with a brief remark on how this problem of truth stands in the context of my own vernacular, Akan, a subject which I have previously discussed at some length in 'The Concept of Truth in the Akan Language.'[1] In this language, the most usual word for truth is *Nokware*. But in fact, this word primarily means truthfulness. In some contexts it expresses the cognitive concept of truth which is more unambiguously expressed in Akan by the phrase *ete saa*, and slightly less unambiguously by *eye ampa* and *ewom*. Now *Ete saa* translates literally into English as 'it is so.' The literal meanings of the other two phrases are respectively 'It is a good statement or piece of discourse' and 'It is in it.' It will distract us unnecessarily to embark on the etymological analysis of these phrases. So let us concentrate on '*Ete saa*' which is certainly the most unproblematic rendition of the cognitive concept of truth in Akan. The interesting point now is that in this language the concept of fact will also be rendered in terms of the notion of '*ete saa*' i.e. of what is so. A fact is simply '*nea ete saa*,' what is so. (Indeed in one of our best known dictionaries, '*Nokware*' is given as one of the meanings of 'fact.')[2] Consider now how a correspondence theory would sound in this language. Suppose we formulate it as 'A statement is true means that it corresponds with fact.' This would become something like '*Asem no te saa kyerese ene nea ete saa di nsianim*' which translates into English literally as 'The statement is so means that it coincides, corresponds with what is so.' This has the beauty of a tautology, but it teaches little wisdom.[3] It seems to me unlikely that thinking in this language, one could be easily tempted into correspondence formulations of this sort. Indeed, in this language, it is pretty clear that the problem of truth must be the problem of clarifying the idea of something being so. My answer is that to say that something is so means that an ideational content applies or corresponds to an object or situation. I hope that this answer, even in its present unelaborated form,[4] goes some way towards demystifying the problem of truth. The elaboration must await another occasion.

NOTES

1. Presented at a conference at the University of Ibadan in 1981 and included in the proceedings of the conference edited by Prof. P. O. Bodunrin under the title *Philosophy in Africa: Contemporary Perspectives* (Ile-Ife, Nigeria: University of Ife Press, 1985).

2. See Rev. J. G. Christaller, Rev. Ch. W. Locher, Rev. J. Zimmermann, *A Dictionary, English, Tshi (Asante), Akra*, Basel: 1874.

3. In an elaborate and elegant critique of my views on the concept of truth in the Akan language and on truth generally, Prof. Bedu-Addo disputes my Akan trivialization of the correspondence theory of truth. (His paper entitled 'Wiredu on Truth as Opinion and the Akan Language,' which was presented at a later conference, is also included in the proceedings of the conference mentioned in footnote 1 above). In particular, he denies that *nokware* primarily means truthfulness on the ground that the word is ambiguous, meaning now truthfulness, now truth in the cognitive sense, depending on context. This of course, is a *non sequitur*, for one of the senses of an ambiguous word may predominate over the others as the primary. Indeed, frequently when we speak of the meaning of a word we mean its primary meaning. We need not however, pursue this issue since in any case, he allows that *ete saa* expresses the cognitive sense of *nokware* when this word is cognitively used. The cognitive sense of *nokware* is, of course, expressed in English by such a phrase as 'it is true,' and Bedu-Addo says, "Now the phrases *ete saa* and *ente saa* mean 'it is like that' and 'it is not like that' respectively, and as such they are quite regularly used in Akan to express 'it is true' and 'it is not true.'" Moreover, he himself asserts that "the correct Akan rendition of a sentence like 'It is a fact that it is raining' is *'Eye nokware se nsu reto,'*" a rendition in which *nokware* translates 'fact.' And here, of course, what is operative is the cognitive use of the word *nokware*. Thus, on his own showing, *ete saa* expresses the cognitive sense of the word *nokware* which in English is expressed by 'it is true,' and the same Akan word *nokware* in its cognitive usage also expresses what is expressed by the English word 'fact.' But if this is so, then it supports my claim that the thesis that truth is correspondence with fact reduces to a tautology in Akan! Bedu-Addo's critique deserves a point-by-point rejoinder, but this is not the place for it; it should already, however, be clear that it avails naught to rescue the correspondence thesis in its Akan rendition from total trivialization.

Bedu-Addo maintains also that there is no way in Akan in which a sentence like 'It is a fact that it is raining' can be translated into English in terms of the notion of *ete saa* or *nea ete saa*. This surprising opinion is clearly due to his mechanical attachment to these two phrases in the rendition of the *notion* expressed by them. In fact, however the phrase *Nea ete ne se* is an idiomatic variant of *nea ete saa* which is very commonly used to render just such a thought as is expressed by 'It is a fact that...'.   The whole English sentence becomes *Nea ete ne se nsu reto*. Note, in any case, that if he is being consistent then his contention can only have a syntactical rather than a semantical significance for his position as seen in the previous paragraph, is that *ete saa* and *nokware* express the same concept when the latter is used cognitively, and *nokware* in that sense translates 'fact.'

4. There is the need to indicate, for example how the proposed truth-defining analysis of judgement can be extended to truth-predications concerning statements like '2+2=4.'

Questions for Chapter 11
Truth and the Akan Language

1. TRUE or FALSE?

   a. According to Wiredu, there is no difference in Akan language and thought between the moral and cognitive concepts of truth.
   b. According to Wiredu, a theory of truth is not of any real significance.
   c. Wiredu claims that the correspondence theory is tautological in English.
   d. According to Wiredu, some philosophical problems are not really philosophical problems.

2. Wiredu denies that:

   (A) truth is corresponce with reality.
   (B) the corresponce theory is translatable into Akan.
   (C) the problem of truth is the problem of giving the meaning of "It is true."
   (D) there is an Akan concept of truth.

3. Give a critique of both Wiredu and Gyekye's theses on the relationship between language and philosophy. Are there any differences between the two?

4. What are the implications of Gyekye's and Wiredu's theses for Appiah's conception of philosophy as well as other conceptions of philosophy?

Chapter 12

Society and Ideology, and Consciencism

Kwame Nkrumah

Woyε me-noko-medi a, wunya asaman nhui. —**If you are selfish you inherit the land of ghosts.** (Akan proverb)

PROLOGUE

Kwame Nkrumah was born on 18th September 1909 in the village of Nkroful in the western part of the land of the Akans called Nzima. He was a graduate of Achimota College in Ghana, Lincoln University in Pennsylvania and, thereafter, the University of Pennsylvania. Subsequently, he pursued a doctorate in philosophy at the University College of London; but in 1947 he abandoned that for politics in Ghana. He was the first Prime Minister and also first president of modern or post-colonial Ghana until he was overthrown in a coup d'etat on 24th February 1966. After his overthrow, he lived in Guinea as the guest of President Sekou Toure until he died of cancer in a Romanian hospital in Bucharest on 27th April 1972.

In his book *Consciencism*, Kwame Nkrumah argues for practising scientific socialism in post-colonial Africa as a way of recapturing, in a modern society, the egalitarianism of traditional African society. Here are portions of his argument:

"The traditional face of Africa includes an attitude towards man which can only be described, in its social manifestation, as being socialist. This arises from the fact that man is regarded in Africa as primarily a spiritual being, a being endowed originally with a certain inward dignity, integrity and value. This idea of the original value of man imposes duties of a socialist kind upon us.   Herein lies the theoretical basis of African communalism...In the traditional African society, no sectional interest could be regarded as supreme; nor did legislative and executive power aid the interests of any particular group. The welfare of the people was supreme...With true independence regained, however, a new harmony needs to be forged, a harmony that will allow the combined presence of traditional Africa, Islamic Africa and Euro-Christian Africa, so that this presence is in tune with original humanist principles underlying African society...In socialism, the principles underlying communalism are given expression in modern circumstances...Socialism, therefore can be and is the defence of the principles of communalism in modern setting...The evil of capitalism consists in its alienation of the fruit of labour from those who with the toil of their body and the sweat of their brow produce this fruit. This aspect of capitalism makes it irreconcilable with those basic principles which animate the traditional African society. Capitalism is unjust; in our newly independent countries it is not only too complicated to be workable, it is also alien...In sum, the restitution of Africa's humanist and egalitarian principles of society requires socialism. It is materialism that ensures the only effective transformation of nature, and socialism that derives the highest development from this transformation."

Society and Ideology, and Consciencism

Kwame Nkrumah

'Coercion' could unfortunately be rather painful, but it is signally effective in ensuring that individual behaviour does not become dangerously irresponsible. The individual is not an anarchic unit. He lives in orderly surroundings, and the achieving of these orderly surroundings calls for methods both explicit and subtle.

One of these subtle methods is to be found in the account of history. The history of Africa, as presented by European scholars, has been encumbered with malicious myths. It was even denied that we were a historical people. It was said that whereas other continents had shaped history, and determined its course, Africa had stood still, held down by inertia; that Africa was only propelled into history by the European contact. African history was therefore presented as an extension of European history. Hegel's authority was lent to this a-historical hypothesis concerning Africa, which he himself unhappily helped to promote. And apologists of colonialism lost little time in seizing upon it and writing wildly thereon. In presenting the history of Africa as the history of the collapse of our traditional societies in the presence of the European advent, colonialism and imperialism employed their account of African history and anthropology as an instrument of their oppressive ideology.

Earlier on, such disparaging accounts had been given of African society and culture as to appear to justify slavery, and slavery, posed against these accounts, seemed a positive deliverance of our ancestors. When the slave trade and slavery became illegal, the experts on Africa yielded to the new wind of change, and now began to present African culture and society as being so rudimentary and primitive that colonialism was a duty of Christianity and civilization. Even if we were no longer, on the evidence of the shape of our skulls, regarded as the missing link, unblessed with the arts of good government, material and spiritual progress, we were still regarded as representing the infancy

From *Consciencism: Philosophy and Ideology for Decolonization* by Kwame Nkrumah, New York, Monthly Review Press. (62-63 & 68-77). Copyright © 1970 by Monthly Review Press. Reprinted by permission of Monthly Review Foundation.

of mankind. Our highly sophisticated culture was said to be simple and paralysed by inertia, and we had to be encumbered with tutelage. And this tutelage it was thought, could only be implemented if we were first subjugated politically.

The history of a nation is, unfortunately, too easily written as the history of its dominant class. But if the history of a nation, or a people, cannot be found in the history of a class, how much less can the history of a continent be found in what is not even a part of it— Europe. Africa cannot be validly treated merely as the space in which Europe swelled up. If African history is interpreted in terms of the interests of European merchandise and capital, missionaries and administrators, it is no wonder that African nationalism is in the forms it takes regarded as a perversion and neocolonialism as a virtue.

In the new African renaissance, we place great emphasis on the presentation of history. Our history needs to be written as the history of our society, not as the story of European adventures. African society must be treated as enjoying its own integrity; its history must be a mirror of that society, and the European contact must find its place in this history only as an African experience, even if as a crucial one. That is to say, the European contact needs to be assessed and judged from the point of view of the principles animating African society, and from the point of view of the harmony and progress of this society.

When history is presented in this way, it can become a map of the growing tragedy and the final triumph of our society. In this way, African history can come to guide and direct African action. African history can thus become a pointer at the ideology which should guide and direct African reconstruction...

The need for subtle means of social cohesion lies in the fact that there is a large portion of life which is outside direct central intervention. In order that this portion of life should be filled with order, non-statutory methods are required. These non-statutory methods, by and large, are the subtle means of social cohesion. But different societies lay different emphases on these subtle means even if the range of conformity which they seek is the same. The emphasis which a particular society lays on a given means depends on the experience, social-economic circumstances and the philosophical foundation of that society.

In Africa, this kind of emphasis must take objective account of our present situation at the return of political independence. From this point of view, there are three broad features to be distinguished here. African society has one segment which comprises our traditional way of life; it has a second segment which is filled by the presence of the Islamic tradition in Africa; it has a final segment which represents the infiltration of the Christian tradition and culture of Western Europe into Africa, using colonialism and neocolonialism as its primary vehicles. These different segments are animated by competing ideologies. But since society implies a certain dynamic unity, there needs to emerge an ideology which, genuinely catering for the needs of all, will take the place of the competing ideologies, and so reflect the dynamic unity of society, and be the guide to society's continual progress.

The traditional face of Africa includes an attitude towards man which can only be described, in its social manifestation, as being socialist. This arises from the fact that man is regarded in Africa as primarily a spiritual being, a being endowed originally with a certain inward dignity, integrity and value. It stands refreshingly opposed to the Christian idea of the original sin and degradation of man.

This idea of the original value of man imposes duties of a socialist kind upon us. Herein lies the theoretical basis of African communalism. This theoretical basis expressed itself on the social level in terms of institutions such as the clan, underlining the initial equality of all and the responsibility of many for one. In this social situation, it was impossible for classes of a Marxian kind to arise. By a Marxian kind of class, I mean one which has a place in a horizontal social stratification. Here classes are related in such a way that there is a disproportion of economic and political power between them. In such a society there exist classes which are crushed, lacerated and ground down by the encumbrance of exploitation. One class sits upon the neck of another.

In the traditional African society, no sectional interest could be regarded as supreme; nor did legislative and executive power aid the interests of any particular group. The welfare of the people was supreme.

But colonialism came and changed all this. First, there were the necessities of the colonial administration. For its success, the colonial administration needed a cadre of Africans, who, by being introduced to a certain minimum of European education, became infected with European ideals, which they tacitly accepted as being valid for African societies. Because these African instruments of the colonial administration were seen by all to be closely associated with the new sources of power, they acquired a certain prestige and rank to which they were not entitled by the demands of the harmonious development of their own society.

In addition to them, groups of merchants and traders, lawyers, doctors, politicians and trade unionists emerged, who, armed with skills and levels of affluence which were gratifying to the colonial administration, initiated something parallel to the European middle class. There were also certain feudal-minded elements who became imbued with European ideals either through direct European education or through hobnobbing with the local colonial administration. They gave the impression that they could be relied upon implicitly as repositories of all those staid and conservative virtues indispensable to any exploiter administration.   They, as it were, paid the registration fee for membership of a class which was now associated with social power and authority.

Such education as we were all given put before us right from our infancy ideals of the metropolitan countries, ideals which could seldom be seen as representing the scheme, the harmony and progress of African society. The scale and type of economic activity, the idea of the accountability of the individual conscience introduced by the Christian religion, countless other silent influences, these have all made an indelible impression Upon African society.

But neither economic nor political subjugation could be considered as being in tune with the traditional African egalitarian view of man and society. Colonialism had in any case to be done away with. The African Hercules has his club poised ready to smite any new head which the colonialist hydra may care to put out.

With true independence regained, however, a new harmony needs to be forged, a harmony that will allow the combined presence of traditional Africa, Islamic Africa and Euro-Christian Africa, so that this presence is in tune with the original humanist principles underlying African society. Our society is not the old society, but a new society enlarged by Islamic and Euro-Christian influences. A new emergent ideology is therefore required, an ideology which can solidify in a philosophical statement, but at the same time an ideology which will not abandon the original humanist principles of Africa.

Such a philosophical statement will be born out of the crisis of the African conscience confronted with the three strands of present African society.   Such a philosophical statement I propose to name *philosophical consciencism*, for it will give the theoretical basis for an ideology whose aim shall be to contain the African experience of

Islamic and Euro-Christian presence as well as the experience of the traditional African society, and, by gestation, employ them for the harmonious growth and development of that society.

Every society is placed in nature. And it seeks to influence nature, to impose such transformations upon nature, as will develop the environment of the society for its better fulfillment. The changed environment, in bringing about a better fulfillment of the society, thereby alters the society. Society placed in nature is therefore caught in the correlation of transformation with development. This correlation represents the toil of man both as a social being and as an individual. This kind of correlation has achieved expression in various social-political theories. For a social-political theory has a section which determines the way in which social forces are to be deployed in order to increase the transformation of society.

Slavery and feudalism represent social-political theories in which the deployment of forces is not a problematic question. In both slavery and feudalism, workers, the people whose toil transforms nature for the development of society, are dissociated from any say in rule. By a vicious division of labour, one class of citizen toils and another reaps what it has not sown. In the slave society, as in the feudal society, that part of society whose labours transform nature is not the same as the part which is better fulfilled as a result of this transformation. If by their fruits we shall know them, they must first grow the fruits. In slave and feudal society, the fruit-eaters are not the fruit-growers. This is the cardinal factor in exploitation, that the section of a society whose labours transform nature is not the same as the section which is better fulfilled as a result of this transformation.

In every non-socialist society, there can be found two strata which correspond to that of the oppressor and the oppressed, the exploiter and the exploited. In all such societies, the essential relation between the two strata is the same as that between masters and slaves, lords and serfs. In capitalism, which is only a social-political theory in which the important aspects of slavery and feudalism are refined, a stratified society is required for its proper functioning, a society is required in which the working class is oppressed by the ruling class; for, under capitalism, that portion of society whose labours transform nature and produce goods is not the portion of society which enjoys the fruits of this transformation and productivity. Nor is it the whole of society which is so enhanced.

This might indeed be termed a contradiction. It is a social

contradiction in so far as it is contrary to genuine principles of social equity and social justice. It is also an economic contradiction in so far as it is contrary to a harmonious and unlimited economic development.

Capitalism is a development by refinement from feudalism, just as feudalism is a development by refinement from slavery. The essence of reform is to combine a continuity of fundamental principle, with a tactical change in the manner of expression of the fundamental principle. Reform is not a change in the thought, but one in its manner of expression, not a change in what is said but one in idiom. In capitalism, feudalism suffers, or rather enjoys reform, and the fundamental principle of feudalism merely strikes new levels of subtlety. In slavery, it is thought that exploitation, the alienation of the fruits of the labour of others, requires a certain degree of political and forcible subjection. In feudalism, it is thought that a lesser degree of the same kind of subjection is adequate to the same purpose. In capitalism, it is thought that a still lesser degree is adequate. In this way, psychological irritants to revolution are appeased, and exploitation finds a new lease of life, until the people should discover the *opposition* between reform and revolution.

In this way, capitalism continues with its characteristic pompous plans for niggardly reforms, while it coerces one section of a society somehow into making itself available to another section, which battens on it. That development which capitalism marks over slavery and feudalism consists as much in the methods by means of which labour is coerced as in the mode of production. Capitalism is but the gentleman's method of slavery.

Indeed, a standard ruse of capitalism today is to imitate some of the proposals of socialism, and turn this imitation to its own use. Running with the hare and hunting with the hounds is much more than a pastime to capitalism; it is the hub of a complete strategy. In socialism, we seek an increase in levels of production in order solely that the people, by whose exertions production is possible, shall raise their standard of living and attain a new consciousness and level of life. Capitalism does this too, but not for the same purpose. Increased productivity under capitalism does indeed lead to a rise in the standard of living; but when the proportion of distribution of value between exploited and exploiter is kept constant, then any increase in levels of production must mean a greater *quantity*, but not *proportion*, of value accruing to the exploited. Capitalism thus discovers a new way of seeming to implement reform, while really genuinely avoiding it. It creates the welfare state.

Whereas capitalism is a development by refinement from slavery and feudalism, socialism does not contain the fundamental ingredient of capitalism, the principle of exploitation. Socialism stands for the negation of that very principle wherein capitalism has its being, lives, and thrives, that principle which links capitalism with slavery and feudalism.

If one seeks the social-political ancestor of socialism, one must go to communalism. Socialism has characteristics in common with communalism, just as capitalism is linked with feudalism and slavery. In socialism, the principles underlying communalism are given expression in modern circumstances. Thus, whereas communalism in an untechnical society can be *laissez faire*, in a technical society where sophisticated means of production are at hand, if the underlying principles of communalism are not given centralised and correlated expression, class cleavages arise, which are the result of economic disparities, and accompanying political inequalities. Socialism, therefore, can be and is the defence of the principles of communalism in a modern setting. Socialism is a form of social organisation which, guided by the principles underlying communism, adopts procedures and measures made necessary by demographic and technological developments.

These considerations throw great light on the bearing of revolution and reform on socialism. The passage from the ancestral line of slavery via feudalism and capitalism to socialism can only lie through revolution: it cannot lie through reform. For in reform, fundamental principles are held constant and the details of their expression modified. In the words of Marx, it leaves the pillars of the building intact. Indeed, sometimes, reform itself may be initiated by the necessities of preserving identical fundamental principles. Reform is a tactic of self-preservation.

Revolution is thus an indispensable avenue to socialism, where the antecedent social-political structure is animated by principles which are a negation of those of socialism, as in a capitalist structure (and therefore also in a colonialist structure, for a colonialist structure is essentially ancillary to capitalism). Indeed, I distinguish between two colonialisms, between a domestic one, and an external one. Capitalism at home is domestic colonialism.

But because the spirit of communalism still exists to some extent in societies with a communalist past, socialism and communism are not in the strict sense of the word 'revolutionary' creeds. They may be described as restatements in contemporary idiom of the principles underlying communalism. On the other hand, in societies with no history of communalism, the creeds of socialism and communism are fully revolutionary, and the passage to socialism must be guided by the principles of scientific socialism.

The nature and cause of the conflict between the ruling class and the exploited class is influenced by the development of productive forces, that is, changes in technology; the economic relations which these forces condition; and the ideologies that reflect the properties and psychology of the people living in that society. The basis of a socialist revolution is created when the class struggle within a given society has resulted in mass consent and mass desire for positive action to change or transform that society. It is then that the foundation is laid for the highest form of political action — when a revolution attains its excellence, and workers and peasants succeed in overthrowing all other classes.

I have explained how society's desire to transform nature reflects itself in different social-political theories. I wish now to suggest how the same desire reflects itself in philosophy. Just as social-political theories, to the extent that they deploy forces for the harnessing and development of nature, fall into two lots, so do philosophies. From this standpoint, the two real social-political alternatives facing society are either that one section should produce, and another section batten thereon, or that all sections should produce and all sections should be fulfilled by the value created by labour.

In the same way, there are two real philosophical alternatives. These alternatives coincide with idealism and materialism. I explained how idealism was connected with a tiered society, how through its mode of explaining nature and social phenomena by reference to spirit, idealism favoured a class structure of a horizontal sort, in which one class sat upon the neck of another.

I also explained how materialism, on the other hand, was connected with a humanist organization, how through its being monistic, and its referring all natural processes to matter and its laws, it inspired an egalitarian organization of society. The unity and fundamental identity of nature suggests the unity and fundamental identity of man in society. Idealism favours an oligarchy, materialism favours an egalitarianism.

Individuals have both idealist and materialist tendencies in them. So have societies both idealist and materialist streaks. But these streaks do not exist in equipoise. They are connected by a conflict in which now one streak predominates, now the other.

By reason of the connection of idealism with an oligarchy and of materialism with an egalitarianism, the opposition of idealism and materialism in the same society is paralleled by the opposition of conservative and progressive forces on the social level. When in the dialectical opposition of capitalism to socialism, the former for a time becomes triumphant, social progress is not thereby altogether arrested, though it is seriously attenuated. But since it is not arrested, it is hardly cause for wonder that the workers of today in many respects enjoy better circumstances of life than even a good many feudal lords of the past. To confess to this degree of progress is not to say, however, that capitalism has been without its shanty towns and slums, its captive workers languishing and finally dying in public squares, victims of hunger, cold and disease.

The question is not whether there has been discernible progress under capitalism, but rather whether what progress is admitted can be said to be adequate. Here we discern one of capitalism's deadly sins. Under this social-political system, man's materialist approach to nature loses its bearings. It sheds its humanist stimulus under the impulse of the profit motive. If happiness is defined in the context of society, then happiness becomes that feeling which an individual derives, from a given economic, political and cultural context, that he is in a position to make good his aspirations. Since capitalist development is unfortunately a process in which a rapacious oligarchy is pitted against an exploited mass, happiness, according to this definition, is denied to many. The achievements of the capitalist oligarchy define new limits of what is attainable by the individual, and thereby push outward the frontiers of legitimate aspirations. But capitalism is a system in which these limiting aspirations are by definition denied to the people, and only reserved for a few.

The evil of capitalism consists in its alienation of the fruit of labour from those who with the toil of their body and the sweat of their brow produce this fruit. This aspect of capitalism makes it irreconcilable with those basic principles which animate the traditional African society. Capitalism is unjust; in our newly independent countries it is not only too complicated to be workable, it is also alien.

Under socialism, however, the study and mastery of nature has a humanist impulse, and is directed not towards a profiteering accomplishment, but the affording of ever-increasing satisfaction for the material and spiritual needs of the greatest number. Ideas of transformation and development, in so far as they relate to the purposes of society as a whole and not to an oligarch purpose, are properly speaking appropriate to socialism.

On the philosophical level, too, it is materialism, not idealism, that in one form or another will give the firmest conceptual basis to the restitution of Africa's egalitarian and humanist principles. Idealism breeds an oligarchy, and its social implication is obnoxious to African society. It is materialism, with its monistic and naturalistic account of nature, which will balk arbitrariness, inequality and injustice. Materialism suggests a socialist philosophy.

In sum, the restitution of Africa's humanist and egalitarian principles of society requires socialism. It is materialism that ensures the only effective transformation of nature, and socialism that derives the highest development from this transformation.

Questions for Chapter 12
Society and Ideology

1. TRUE or FALSE?

   a. According to Nkrumah, philosophy implies an ideology.
   b. According to Nkrumah, every society has an ideology.
   c. According to Nkrumah, traditional African societies were class-less societies.
   d. According to Nkrumah, the African conception of a person is Christian.

2. According to Nkrumah, the social-political ancestor of socialism is:

   (A) capitalism.
   (B) communalism.
   (C) communism.
   (D) none of the above.

3. What is the difference, if any, between Marxism and consciencism?

4. State and evaluate Nkrumah's argument(s) for socialism in Africa.

5. State and evaluate Nkrumah's argument(s) against capitalism in Africa.

Chapter 13

The Political Heritage Of Africa In Search Of Democracy

Kofi Abrefa Busia

Onipa bɔne biako te man mu a, ne nkoa ne nnipa nyinaa. —**If there is one bad person living in a State, he or she alone is everyone in the State. (Akan Proverb)**

PROLOGUE

Kofi Abrefa Busia was a native of Wenchi in the Brong Ahafo region of the Akan society. He was born on 11th July 1913 and educated at Achimota college in Ghana and Oxford University where he later taught and died. His involvement in politics as a member of the opposition party in Ghana under Kwame Nkrumah's one-party socialist government, sent him into self-exile in 1959 as a Professor of Sociology in Holland and England. After the overthrow of Nkrumah's government, he returned to head the government of Ghana as Prime Minister of the Second Republic from 1969 until his overthrow in a coup d'etat in 1972. He died in exile in Oxford, England, on 28th August 1978 as a result of heart failure.

Kofi Busia agrees with Kwame Nkrumah that the traditional African society was egalitarian. He disagrees, however, about using socialism to recapture the traditional egalitarianism. One of his reasons is that both the authoritarianism and one-party system associated with socialism are inconsistent with traditional African democratic values and institutions.

In the excerpts from his *Africa in Search of Democracy* reprinted below, he tries to show how liberal the traditional Akan political system of the Ashantis is. He also tries to show that a liberal multi-party democracy rather than a one party system can better capture traditional cohesion and democracy in post-colonial multi-ethnic African societies. One-party States and governments, he argues, are not uniquely African: "Arguments to justify the one-party State or authoritatianisms cannot be based on the grounds of tradition. There were tribes which had hardly any institutional checks on their rulers, or where these were so ineffective as to make the system autocratic; but it is stretching the point too far to argue from this that one-party rule is a uniquely African innovation, uniformly in accord with her tradition.   One-party governments can, in this twentieth century, be found in all continents, and cannot be appropriated by Africa as her own unique attribute. In the political system of the Ashanti, one might note three features which differ from those observed in one-party governments...The first feature to note about the Ashanti system is that it was based on decentralization which gave a large measure of local autonomy to the smaller units...So strong was the value of solidarity that the chief aim of the councillors was to reach unanimity, and they talked till this was achieved. Some have singled out this feature of talking till unanimity was reached as the cardinal principle of African democracy...The traditions of free speech and interchange of views do not support any claim that the denial of free speech or the suppression of opposition is rooted in traditional African political systems...A third noteworthy feature was that there were traditional political systems which, like those of the Ashanti, allowed the people to choose their own rules, and, as we have seen, there were alternatives to choose from...The social reality is, however, more complex than that. The new African States are composed of many different tribes...The social situation which is the background to the nation-building and the political experiments going on in Africa is very different from that in which the traditional political systems developed; there is a difference in scale, the areas being larger, and the populations bigger and more heterogeneous; in technology, the means of transport and communications, and the mechanisms of control are vastly more efficient; the tasks of government are more numerous. The impact of Europe has impelled social changes within which old institutions no longer function..."

The Political Heritage

Kofi Abrefa Busia

There are protagonists who have attempted to justify contemporary authoritarianism in some of the new African States by contending that it is in accord with the spirit and practice of traditional political systems; others, on the contrary, have maintained that traditional political institutions were democratic, and that it was the European Colonial Powers who destroyed democracy in Africa. This controversy calls for an examination of the traditional systems...

It would be more concrete to illustrate some principles of political structure by taking a particular instance; and for this purpose we may choose the Ashanti of Ghana. Their system falls into the first of the two categories stated above; it is this category which is the more apposite to the problem of democratic government with which we are concerned.

The Ashanti system is matrilineal, and a lineage, which is the basic political unit, consists of members who trace their descent from a common ancestress. The community, large or small, consists of lineages that share the common territory. Where every member of the community belongs to a lineage, all can be represented through the lineage system. This is what happens in the traditional political organization: Each lineage is a political unit, and the head, chosen by the members of the lineage represents it on what becomes the governing council. It is a council of lineage heads who look after the affairs of the community as a whole.

The political organization is thus based on small social groups joining with other social groups to form a larger unit. It is based on the recognition of the sectional interests of the component groups; but it is also realized that these have to be harmonized with the wider interests of the larger unit. This principle should be noted as it has relevance to the contemporary problem of welding different tribes into a nation. The problem of building a larger political unit out of smaller units is not a new one.

A political unit has a chief, recognized as the head of the political

Reprinted by permission of Routledge, Chapman & Hall Ltd., London, from *Africa in Search of Democracy* by K. A. Busia, (17, 22-34) New York: Frederick A. Praeger Inc., © 1967 by K. A. Busia.

communities. Among the Ashanti, in every political community there is a 'royal' lineage, sometimes there are several, from which the chief is chosen. Usually there are several eligible candidates who belong to the lineages from which a chief is chosen. No one becomes a chief automatically. Kin-right, that is, eligibility because one belongs to a particular lineage, must be reinforced by election by those to whom custom assigns that right. The principle is one which ensures that kin-right is combined with popular choice.

When a chief was selected and initiated into his office, he became at once a judge, a commander-in-chief, a legislator, and the executive and administrative head of his community. It was not many offices, but a single composite office to which various duties and activities, rights and obligations were attached.

An office which combined so many duties needed to be watched, lest the holder became a tyrant. The political system of the Ashanti provided for this contingency. It had checks and balances. The chief's manifold duties, and the rights and responsibilities he exercised, and his high prestige, gave him much power; but he was given a Council to hold him in check. The chief was bound by custom to act only with the concurrence and on the advice of his Council. If he acted arbitrarily, and without consultation and approval by his Council, he could be deposed. That was one way in which the chief's powers were curbed. This feature should also be noted. Those who elected the chief, also had the power to depose him if he did not perform the duties of his office satisfactorily.

There was another way in which the chief's authority was limited, particularly in the chiefdoms spread over a large territory. Some chiefdoms in Ashanti were very large; and, as is well known, Ashanti became a large and powerful confederation of chiefdoms with a king at the head.

Without roads, and with the lack of means of transport and communication, the problems of administration of a large chiefdom were difficult. Apart from technical difficulties, the Ashanti were careful to prevent their chief from becoming tyrannical, and they developed a delicate balance between central authority and regional autonomy. This was an important aspect of their political structure. In matters of administration, each lineage or village managed its own affairs with a minimum of interference from the chief. That is to say, each chiefdom was run on a policy of decentralization, and there was a careful balance between the central authority of the chief on the one hand and the local autonomy of the component units of the chiefdom on the other. If the chief abused his power, his subordinate chiefs, the members of his Council, could destool him. On the other hand, if a subordinate chief or councillor tried to become too powerful, the chief could destool him. In each case, there were constitutional procedures to protect the individuals concerned, and to check arbitrariness or vindictiveness.

The best kind of democracy is the one which enables as many people as possible to share in the making of decisions, and in the actual functions of government. In the Ashanti system, the fact that each lineage, village, or part of a chiefdom managed as much of its own affairs as was consistent with the unity of the whole chiefdom enabled many to share in decision-making in local affairs; for the head of each unit was, like the chief at the centre, obliged to act only on the concurrence and with the advice of his own local council.

However autocratic a chief was permitted to appear, he really ruled by the consent of the people. There was a balance between authority on the one side, and obligation on the other. A chief or king had the power to raise taxes, or exact tribute, or ask his people to work on his farm, or even call them to take up arms to defend the chiefdom. But he had the corresponding obligation to dispense justice, or to protect the interests of his people, or ensure their welfare by certain ritual acts and observances. The ruler's subjects knew what duties they owed him; they also knew what duties he owed them, and they could exert pressure to make him discharge those duties.

There can be no true democracy where there is no free expression of opinion in public affairs or criticism of the ruling body. Any member of the community could take part in the public discussions of community affairs, or in the public hearings and "anyone—even the most ordinary youth—will offer his opinion, or make a suggestion with an equal chance of its being heard as if it proceeded from the most experienced sage."[5]

The members of a chief's council were, in one aspect, representatives of the people; in another sense, they and the chief constituted the government. As representatives of a section of the chiefdom, they were to protect the sectional interests of those whom they represented, and to see to it that the chief did not abuse his power; but as members of the council which had responsibility for the affairs of the whole community, they were to help to ensure the welfare of all, and to see that the people obeyed and supported the constituted authority. They shared responsibility with the chief. It is never easy to reconcile the two functions.

Somebody has to keep the government or the constituted authority to the mark. None can do this better than those over whom the government rules. The Ashanti system provided opportunities for the 'commoners,' those who were ruled, to express criticism, either through their lineage heads, or through a chosen leader recognized as spokesman for the commoners; through him the body of free citizens could criticize the government and express their wishes when they thought that undesirable measures were being contemplated or enforced; in the last resort, they could depose their rulers. Democracy cannot survive, unless people are able to make the government express their will; unless they have the power to choose their rulers and to change them. These principles are discernible in the indigenous political system of the Ashanti.

Though the system was designed to check any tendency towards absolute despotism, it could not prevent a ruler from failing to observe the accepted practices, and becoming a tyrant; but it could be maintained that the despotism was a violation of the system.

The pervasive influence of religion spread into the political system of the Ashanti. The most important aspect of Ashanti chieftaincy was undoubtedly the religious one. An Ashanti chief filled a sacral role. His stool, the symbol of his office, was a sacred emblem. It represented the community, their solidarity, their permanence, their continuity. The chief was the link between the living and the dead, and his highest role was when he officiated in the public religious rites which gave expression to the community values. He then acted as the representative of the community whose members are believed to include those who are alive, and those who are either dead, or are still unborn. This sacral aspect of the chief's role was a powerful sanction of his authority.

This is but a brief sketch of the political system of one of the many tribes of Africa. It cannot stand for the whole. But there are features and principles which are applicable to others. For example, there is remarkable identity with what the Kenya Government has written about the traditional system in that part of the continent:

Political democracy in the African traditional sense provided a genuine hedge against the exercise of disproportionate political power by economic power groups. In African society a man was born politically free and equal and his voice and counsel were heard and respected regardless of the economic wealth he possessed. Even where traditional leaders appeared to have greater wealth and hold disproportionate political influence over their tribal or clan community, there were traditional checks and balances including sanctions against any possible abuse of power. In fact, traditional leaders were regarded as trustees whose influence was circumscribed both in customary law and religion. In the traditional African society, an individual needed only to be a mature member of it to participate fully and equally in political affairs.[6]

Neither authoritarianism nor the one-party State can be traced to traditional political systems like these. Arguments to justify the one-party State or authoritarianism cannot be based on the grounds of tradition. There were tribes which had hardly any institutional checks on their rulers, or where these were so ineffective as to make the system autocratic; but it is stretching the point too far to argue from this that one-party rule is a uniquely African innovation, uniformly in accord with her tradition. One-party governments can, in this twentieth century, be found in all continents, and cannot be appropriated by Africa as her own unique attribute.

In the political system of the Ashanti, one might note three features which differ from those observed in one-party governments. As has been pointed out, the Ashanti political organization was one in which smaller political units based on the lineage amalgamated to form larger units. This posed the familiar problem of how to safeguard the sectional interests of the smaller units, and at the same time promote the common interests shared by all in the larger unit. There was always the danger that one would override the other. There was frequent temptation for those at the head of the larger unit to move towards the centralization of authority. The first feature to note about the Ashanti system is that it was based on decentralization which gave a large measure of local autonomy to the smaller units. The tendency towards centralization characteristic of one-party governments runs counter to this traditional feature.

When a council, each member of which was the representative of a lineage, met to discuss matters affecting the whole community, it had always to grapple with the problem of reconciling sectional and common interests. In order to do this, the members had to talk things over: they had to listen to all the different points of view. So strong was the value of solidarity that the chief aim of the councillors was to reach unanimity, and they talked till this was achieved. Some have singled out this feature of talking till unanimity was reached as the cardinal principle of African democracy. They have even gone farther to maintain that it is the essential mark of a democratic form of government, and that any government which has this is therefore democratic. This is going too far, for there are other important elements of a democracy. The principle is, however, noteworthy. The members of a traditional council allowed discussion, and a free and frank expression of opinions, and if there was disagreement, they spent hours, even days if necessary, to argue and exchange ideas till they reached unanimity. Those who disagreed were not denied a hearing, or locked up in prison, or branded as enemies of the community.

The councils could afford to spend hours or days of talk till they reached unanimity. They could do this because the volume of business was small, compared with what modern governments have to get through. In the new situation, local councils and legislative assemblies have wide and complex problems on which to make decisions, and there is no time to talk till unanimity is reached on every issue. So they now resort to voting, and accept and act on what the majority agree upon. But the traditional practice indicates that the minority must be heard, and with respect and not hostility. The traditions of free speech and interchange of views do not support any claim that the denial of free speech or the suppression of opposition is rooted in traditional African political systems.

The traditional systems were not perfect; imperfection is written upon all human institutions. There have been bad chiefs and councillors; there have been instances of corruption and exploitation and abuse of power; but the machinery was devised, and when it functioned well could check those in power and protect those who were ruled, and regulate behaviour for the peace and well-being of the community.

A third noteworthy feature was that there were traditional political systems which, like those of the Ashanti, allowed the people to choose their own rulers, and, as we have seen, there were alternatives to choose from. Within each kinship group there were several from whom the electors could choose. Moreover, the electors retained the right to change those whom they had chosen. This right to change their office-holders was exercised whenever the rulers failed to discharge their responsibilities and obligations in accordance with the established norms.

The hereditary element imposed a limitation on the choice of office-holders and rulers. The electors could change the office-holders, but they could replace them only by other members of the same lineage. The change of government did not call for institutions through which a minority could convert itself into a majority so as to take over the reins of power. The alternation of rulers and officeholders could only take place within the framework of the lineage system.

In the traditional political systems of Africa, the primary loyalties were centred on lineage and tribe. This was universal throughout the continent, and examples could be found from every part, north, south, central, east, or west. We may mention a few more examples. Among the Bantu, the political system was based on the kinship structures of the tribes. The chief was the head of a community held together by bonds of kinship. His office combined executive, judicial and ritual functions performed on behalf of the tribe. Among the Ngwato of Bechuanaland, the in habitants of a village or ward generally belonged to the same tribal community and came under the leadership of a hereditary headman. Within each ward, each family, a patrilineal group, managed its own affairs under its elder. Among the Bemba, the matrilineal lineage was the basis of the political organization. Descent was traced through the mother, and membership of the lineage determined succession to different offices in the community. African political systems were tribal structures.

There were many reasons why the tribes held together. A tribe inhabited a common territory; its members shared a tradition, real or fictitious, of common descent; and they were held together by a common language and a common culture. The environment, and the state of technology compelled co-operation in the activities on which their survival depended, whether it was food-growing, or herding cattle, or hunting, or building a home; and the most natural unit of organization, both for production and distribution was the kinship group. The same kinship structure was the basis of group religious ceremonies, especially when these were directed towards ancestors. The tribe's common language was a bond of unity, as also of differentiation from other tribes. From cradle to grave, every activity motivated the individual to maintain his membership of his lineage and tribe.

The tribal solidarity of the past invades the present. It sets problems of political organization for the new States of Africa. It has been a source of tensions and instability. It has led to civil war in the Congo. Nigeria tried to contain its tribal tensions in a federation, in an effort to achieve and maintain democratic government. Others are attempting to contain the tensions through the establishment of one-party regimes, employing varying degrees of coercion and persuasion. In so far as traditional political structures have any relevance to the contemporary situation, the legacy of tribalism is the most general problem it has set.

It is remarkable that this should be so, despite the fact that the kinship system has been assailed on all sides by economic, political, social as well as religious changes. There are now many different ways of earning a living; people move to towns, harbours, mining and industrial areas in search of employment; cash economies, specialization, urbanization, and social differentiation have all upset the balance of dependence and the reciprocities of the family and lineage; the authority of tribal chiefs was undermined under colonial rule; and new religious doctrines and formal education threaten the beliefs which sustained the tribe. Yet in spite of these disruptive forces, the solidarity of the lineage and loyalty to the tribe continue to pose dilemmas for the creation of the modern State and its collective organs.

Some approach this problem by assuming that tribal loyalty represents a narrow loyalty which is inimical to the State. They start from the assumption that loyalty to the State is 'modern' and loyalty to the tribe is anachronistic. They seem to assume that one cannot be loyal to one's lineage or tribe, and to a larger unit at the same time. A very experienced President of an African State, one who has weathered many political storms, said calmly when asked about this: "No President or Prime Minister in Africa today can keep his place for long without the backing of large tribes." There are more than a hundred tribes in his State. The fact is that the tribe is not only a territorial unit but is also a unit bound together by some of the most enduring of human ties and values: shared memories and traditions, language, affectionate relationships, and a sense of security and belonging.

Some have argued that the process of nation-building requires that tribal groups should be smashed, by coercive measures, if necessary. Even in large cities of Africa, organizations based on tribal affiliations flourish and gain enthusiastic and loyal support, affording evidence that tribal cohesion is a cherished social value. It has a long tradition.

The value placed on social cohesion is an argument in favour of the establishment of the one-party State. Everyone would belong to the one party, and thus the tradition of solidarity would be carried on through the party organization. The State replaces the tribe.

The social reality is, however, more complex than that. The new African States are composed of many different tribes. A state can claim to be a common territory for all the tribes within it, but common descent, real or fictitious, cannot be maintained among tribes, some of which have a history of different origins and migrations, such as the Buale, Senufo, Guro of the Ivory Coast; the Yoruba, Hausa, Ibo of Nigeria; Ewe, Fanti, Dagomba of Ghana, to mention only a few examples from West Africa. Instead of the bond of a common culture and language, there are language and cultural differences which tend to divide rather than unite.

The social situation which is the background to the nation-building and the political experiments going on in Africa is very different from that in which the traditional political systems developed; there is a difference in scale, the areas being larger, and the populations bigger and more heterogeneous; in technology, the means of transport and communications, and the mechanisms of control are vastly more efficient; the tasks of government are more numerous. The impact of Europe has impelled social changes within which old institutions no longer function.

The most persistent legacy of traditional political systems is the value of tribal cohesion which was given expression in lineage and tribal organization. It is still a highly desired social value which the various forms of the one-party organization and other political experiments seek to preserve and express within the larger unit of the State.

References

1. H. S. Maine, *Lectures on the Early History of Institutions* (New York, 1888), 72-4.
2. Republic of Kenya: Sessional Paper No. 10 of 1963/5, para. II.
3. *African Political Systems*, M. Fortes and E. E. Evans-Pritchard (eds.) (O. U. P., 1940).
4. *African Political Systems*, 5.
5. Brodie Cruickshank, *Eighteen Years on the Gold Coast of Africa* (London, 1854).
6. Republic of Kenya: Sessional Paper No. 10 of 1963/5, para 9.

Questions for Chapter 13
The Political Heritage

1. TRUE or FALSE?

   a. According to Busia, the Ashanti (Akan) system did not permit rulers to be tyrants.

   b. According to Busia, an Ashanti (Akan) chief played a political but not a religious role.

   c. According to Busia, in all respects, the Ashanti (Akan) political system is representative of African political systems.

   d. According to Busia, arguments for justifying one-party states can be based on African traditions.

2. According to Busia, the solidarity of ethnic or tribal African societies of the past:

   (A) hinder political organization in the new African States.

   (B) helps to ensure social cohesion in the new African States.

   (C) provides a good argument in favor of one-party states in Africa.

   (D) ensured that European colonialism could not adversely affect the traditional African institutions.

3. In what way(s) were traditional African societies democratic? Define democracy and compare the arguments of Busia and Nkrumah on this issue.

4. State and evaluate Busia's arguments for (the practice of) liberal democracy in Africa.

5. State and evaluate Busia's arguments against (the practice of) democratic centralism in Africa.

Chapter 14

Business Ethics And Capitalism In A Poor Country

Safro Kwame

Sikanibere na εde bɔne nyinna ba. —**The love of money generates every kind of evil. (Akan proverb)**

PROLOGUE

In the article reprinted below, Safro Kwame (whose biographical sketch appears in Chapter 2) uses the ethics of the business practices in the Akan and Ga societies of Ghana—which are currently not very different from what they were at the time he wrote this article—to argue against both popular capitalistic and popular socialistic practices in parts of Africa. Part of his argument is as follows: Given the economic conditions in poor countries such as are to be found in Africa and other parts of the so-called Third World, certain capitalistic practices such as using the free market to determine prices of basic goods are disastrous. Similarly certain socialistic practices such as central planning that is tainted with corruption are disastrous; and so is the use of guns by military governments to control prices. Part of the reason for this is that people tend to invent rather than discover what is right or wrong from prevailing conditions; and those conditions need to change to match the values being imposed by the capitalist, socialist or military government in order to avoid disaster or serious problems.

Here is a selection from the article:

"The economic practice of profiteering, often preceded by hoarding, the creation of artificial shortage and overpricing, is better known in the West African country of Ghana as *kalabule*...If murder and the unnecessary infliction of pain are bad, so is *kalabule* done with a clear view of the consequences. To put basic goods out of the economic reach of persons when it is obvious that the lack of such basics leads to starvation and death, is tantamount to murder...That Akans who are Christians could subscribe to *kalabule* which conflicts with Christian and Akan ethics, indicates (though it does not prove) that ethics is human-made or invented from the prevailing conditions rather than God-given or society-given to be discovered whatever the conditions are. If we wish to make or invent Akan-like or Christian-like ethics, we would have to create the conditions conducive to the making of it. I have suggested that the adoption of wholesale capitalism in conditions of acute shortage of basic goods is unconducive to the invention or practice of or belief in Akan and Christian ethics. In consequence, I have recommended central planning only with respect to the necessities of life when supply is greatly inadequate. I do not for a moment think that central planning (in whatever form) is sufficient for ensuring progress, development or that moral standards are high. I merely note its importance for poor countries. Hence, the attack by the Friedmans, if intended to show that central planning does not ensure development, is at best uninteresting...The problem of *kalabule* and the solution to it are economic. Hence, the prevailing African attempt to solve such problems by means of coup d'états and the consequent almost exclusive appeal to force, side-track the issue."

Business Ethics and Capitalism in a Poor Country

Safro Kwame

In Africa and other parts of the Third World, it is not uncommon for persons to sell goods far above approved (government controlled) prices,[1] reaping windfall profits in the process. The economic practice of profiteering, often preceded by hoarding, the creation of artificial shortage and overpricing, is better known in the West African country of Ghana as *kalabule*.[2] Here in Ghana much of business is taken up by the distribution of goods and services which is largely, though not exclusively, in the hands of women. Business ethics, for Ghanaian businessmen and women, is largely dictated by the maximization of profit. In oversimplified terms, business ethics for *kalabule* businessmen and women states that it is not wrong to maximize profits.

In Ghana, as in other African countries, it is usual for women to queue continually for basic commodities such as soap, sugar, flour and milk while the men are off to work, and resell them to the men and other workers when they (the men) return from work. It is common for *kalabule* businesswomen to buy a cake of soap and a tin of evaporated milk for approximately ¢2[3] each, in those days, yet resell them at ¢10 and ¢12 respectively, even though most Ghanaians—in those days—earn only slightly above the ¢12 minimum wage.

In sub-Saharan Africa, it is easy to sell basic goods such as soap and sugar at the highest price possible, because most African countries, like their counterparts elsewhere in the Third World, can neither produce nor buy enough of anything to meet national demand. Agricultural production constitutes the main activity of over seventy percent of the 300 million people of Sub-Saharan Africa. Sub-Saharan Africa is the region most dependent on agriculture. Yet agricultural production, according to the 1980 World Development Report, continues to be almost uniformly sluggish with food output per person declining in 25 countries (World Bank 1980, 86). Being mainly an agricultural production region, the Sub-Saharan depends on the outside world, especially Europe and North America, for both luxuries and basics.

Reprinted by permission of Kluwer Academic Publishers from "Doin' Business in an African Country," by Safro Kwame in *Journal of Business Ethics* 2, 1983 (263-268) © 1983 by D. Reidel Publishing Company.

Ghana's import program for 1979 was estimated in 1978 to be ¢2,432.6 million with a total of ¢475.00 million being provided for the importation of basic consumer goods. Imports included imputs for textiles, beer, tobacco, soap, milk, beverage, matches and toilet rolls and finished products such as sugar, meat, canned fish and baby food (G.C.B., 1978, 1 and 2).

Unfortunately, export earnings, which determine the capacity to import, grow (if at all) unsatisfactorily in developing countries due to falling demand and falling prices (World Economic Survey, 1978, 32). While Ghana's exports, for example, grew slowly, the Quarterly Economic Review of the Ghana Commercial Bank indicates that demand for imports grew at a high rate (*op. cit.*, 1). Local food production, the Review adds, could not meet growing demand (*ibid.*, 1). In the Quaterly Economic Review of July–December 1980, the Research Department of the Ghana Commercial Bank writes:

> While the economy was faced with increasingly high cost of crude oil, the price of cocoa, the country's major export, declined about 14 per cent during the year. This seriously curtailed further funds that could have been spent on essential goods and services. The supply of goods and services was, therefore, further worsened despite attempts by the government to improve the flow of goods and check prices... During the period, therefore, the government sought for a loan of ¢34.9 million to import 73,500 tonnes of cereals to supplement local production (G.C.B., 1981, 1).

Paradoxically, imports into Africa include food. It is noteworthy that Africa imports much of its food requirement. Grain imputs into Sub-Saharan Africa between 1965 and 1975 rose from 1.6 to 2.6 million tonnes, and it is expected to rise to 4.5 million tonnes by 1985 (World Bank, 1980, 85). According to the Food and Agriculture Organization of the United Nations Organization, "the level of food imports is rising and many developing countries could face grave difficulties in meeting their food deficits over the next decade. (F.A.O., 1979, p. 77). In Africa, the balance of trade has continued to decrease from 1.9 billion dollars in 1974 to 14.7 billion dollars in 1978. In these conditions, it is obvious that most African countries cannot meet even the demand for food and other basic goods. Hence, the business practice of *kalabule* is bound to lead to starvation for most Africans and even death for some.

No wonder half of the population of Sub-Saharan Africa is absolutely poor (World Bank, 1980, 86). An absolutely poor person, according to the World Development Report, is one who lives in conditions that fall short of the requirements of any reasonable definition of human decency (*ibid.*, 32). Typically, a poor person in Sub-Saharan Africa spends almost his whole income on food which consists of a monotonous diet of gari, yam or cassava. Many of such persons are so malnourished that they are unable to work hard. The physical and mental development of their children is impaired; such children also have low resistance to infection. While most poor persons are sick with malaria, measles or diarrhea, their children are likely to suffer from food-deficiency diseases such as kwashiorkor and marasmus if they are "lucky enough to survive the first year of life."

Any system of distribution or marketing that permits businessmen and women to maximize their profits in the sale or distribution of basic goods that are in short supply, is bound to aggravate the situation for an already starving people. I hesitate to describe such a system of distribution which ensures suffering and death for the majority of people in a society as moral. If murder and the unnecessary infliction of pain are bad, so is *kalabule* done with a clear view of the consequences. Murder is the deliberate killing of a human being. To put basic goods out of the economic reach of persons when it is obvious that the lack of such basics leads to starvation and death, is tantamount to murder. So long as rationing could ensure that most persons have these basic goods at (cheaper) government-controlled prices, the practice of *kalabule* could be said to inflict unnecessary suffering on the impoverished peoples of Africa.

It is surprising that many of Ghana's *kalabule* businessmen and women are Christians or adherents to Akan ethics (or both), since neither Christian nor Akan ethics permits disrespect and unconcern for human beings and their lives. An Akan proverb states that it is the human being, not money or clothing, that matters:

Mefre sika a, sika nnyeso; mefre natama a, ntama nnye so: Onipa ne asem.

Saint Luke reports Jesus as saying that "it is easier for a camel to go through the eyes of a needle than for a rich man to enter the Kingdom of God" which Christians seek (Luke, 18:25). For it is difficult for rich persons, such as *Kalabule* businesswomen who overprice goods and profiteer in order to maximize profits, to follow Jesus' instruction to give up treasure on earth in favour of treasure in heaven by distributing their wealth to the poor (Luke, 18: 22).[4]

It certainly would not surprise Mackie that *kalabule* could be a nation-wide practice in a society such as Ghana in which the major ethnic group is Akan, and Christians form a national majority. Perhaps, Mackie wrote, the truest teachers of moral philosophy are the outlaws and thieves for whom rules of justice and good behaviour are rules of convenience with no pretence of receiving them as innate laws of nature (Mackie, 1977, 10-11). Values, for Mackie, are not part of the fabric of the world to be discovered (*ibid.*, 15); they have to be made, tailored to suit our goals and desires:

> The objective values which I am denying would be action-directing absolutely, not contingently upon the agent's desires and inclinations (Mackie, 1977, 29).

Hence, if this view is accepted in so far as *kalabule* ethics conflicts with Christian and Akan ethics, we have to make a choice depending on our desires concerning the type of society we wish to build—one that is concerned about the plight of its members or one that is indifferent to the suffering of the majority.

If ethics is discovered rather than invented, we would have to decide, without recourse to our desires, preferences and inclinations, whether it is the Akan-Christian ethics (which might not be entirely compatible with each other) or rather the ethics associated with *kalabule* that is real. I do not see how this can be done so successfully as to eliminate moral scepticism, in the light of diversity and variability in moral values as well as of our conflicting claims to moral knowledge. Certainly if we share with Singer the assumption that suffering and death from lack of food, shelter or medical care are bad (Singer, 1972, 231), we ought to abandon *kalabule* ethics in favour of ethics of the Akan-Christian type. But for those who disagree (supposing that some do) and rather believe for example that it is good to die or suffer for lack of food, shelter or medical care through no fault of the victim, it is, as far as I can see, difficult to argue them out of disagreement. I see, however, that the above-given considerations on murder and the unnecessary infliction of pain may go some way in making such disagreers less certain; and, in any case, there are very few, if any, practitioners of *kalabule* who so disagree.

Experience has shown that mass suffering and starvation associated with *kalabule* are precisely what the practice of capitalism, also called free private enterprise, does to people who can neither produce nor buy their needs in sufficient quantities. Samuelson tells us that "the price mechanism, working through supply and demand in competitive markets, operates to answer the three fundamental problems or economic organization in our [American] mixed private enterprise system" (Samuelson, 1976, 55). The three problems concern WHAT commodities shall be produced and in what quantities, HOW they shall be produced and FOR WHOM (The rich or the poor, the rich man's dog or the poor man's daughter?). "In a system of free private enterprise," Samuelson remarks, "no individual or organization is consciously concerned with the triad of economic problems. WHAT, HOW, and FOR WHOM." (*ibid.*, 41). "This fact," he adds, "is really remarkable" (*ibid.*, 41).

It surely is remarkable that the profit motive of suppliers (sellers) and the basic and nonbasic needs of demanders (buyers) operating in a market should determine the What, How and For Whom rather than any conscious planning on the part of individuals and organizations. In a rich society of abundance, such as the United States of America, one can afford not to be "consciously concerned;" in poor countries such as those of sub-Saharan Africa, it may be immoral (or cruel) to do so in the face of the mass suffering and starvation we have noted. Galbraith realizes this:

> The poor country has no such easy-going options. It must use its resources for the right things; if it fails to do so—if funds go into fancy housing, a glittering airport or official Cadillacs—the cries of outrage and horror will come first of all from the most rugged American free-enterprisers (Galbraith, 1971, 180).

This, in Galbraith's opinion, indicates that free enterprise—which he takes to be the practice of letting the market decide—is a product of well-being (*ibid.*, 180).

Planning, Galbraith continues, is dictated by poverty (*ibid.*, 180). Yet, paradoxically, an unplanned economy is easier and cheaper to run because the distribution and production of even necessities of life are the result of what Samuelson terms "the unconscious automatic price mechanism" (*op. cit.*, 43) which lacks central direction and master planning. In other words, an unplanned economy is easier or cheaper to run because, in a sense, it is neither planned nor run. Often it is neither run nor planned because (in a rich society of abundance) there is no need to do so. In the face of acute scarcity, mass suffering and starvation, however, there is a need to do so—as every war-torn capitalist country would confirm. The problem with most of the poor countries of the South is that they are almost permanently in war-torn conditions.

The price mechanism is a product of the market economy and the problem with it (the price mechanism), as almost every economist would tell you, is that it operates beautifully and with entirely good consequences only in the unearthly perfect market. In the real-life imperfect market filled with psychological egoists, the profit motive of sellers and the inelastic demand of buyers of necessities are, as indicated by the African situation, incapable of preventing *kalabule*. With private ownership of the means of production, the price mechanism is incapable of ensuring that what is produced and how it is produced is for those who are badly in need or even those with the greatest contribution. Capitalism, Cairncross points out, embraces both the price mechanism and a particular set of institutions governing the ownership and control of property just referred to above (Cairncross, 1973, 181). Both operate on individual profit. An official endorsement of capitalism, thus, stands in danger of raising psychological egoism to the level of ethical egoism. Such endorsement could be taken as saying that people seek their selfish interests in a market economy and they ought to (be permitted to) do so.

The principle of capitalism rests on the profit motive. The mainspring of the capitalist system, Macpherson wrote, "is that men do act as their calculation of net gain dictates" (Macpherson, 1973, 181). "As long as prices still move in response to these calculated decisions, and as long as prices still elicit the production of goods and determine their allocation," Macpherson continued, "we may say that the essential nature of the system has not changed" (*ibid.*, 181-82). The basic principle of 'kalabuleism', we noted, is the maximization of profit. It seems to me that in the Christian countries of the North, such as the United Kingdom and the United States of America, the reason for relative absence of most of the adverse or 'unethical' effects of *kalabule* is that the Northern countries are countries of relative abundance (not scarcity).

If the practice of capitalism in conditions of scarcity is likely to lead to the 'evil' practices of *kalabule* (assuming that we accept them as evil), it is immoral to recommend capitalism to poor countries such as are found in Africa and other parts of the South. Yet the Friedmans recommend capitalism to poor countries on the grounds that "it is moral and progressive." "Free trade at home and abroad," according to Milton and Rose Friedman, "is the best way that a poor country can promote the well being of its citizens" (Friedman, 1980, 31). The Friedmans cite correlations between capitalism and development, against central planning and the authoritarian allocation of goods and services:

> Intellectuals everywhere take for granted that free enterprise capitalism and a free market are devices for exploiting the masses, while central economic planning is the wave of the future that will set their countries on the road to rapid economic progress....The facts themselves are different. Wherever we find any large element of individual freedom, some measure of progress in the material comforts at the disposal of ordinary citizens, and widespread hope of further progress in the future, there we also find that economic activity is organized mainly through the free market. Wherever the state undertakes to control in detail the economic activities of its citizens, wherever, that is, detailed central economic planning reigns, there ordinary citizens are in political fetters, have a low standard of living and have little power to control their own destiny (Friedman, 1980, 46).

To substantiate their argument, Milton and Rose Friedman refer to the contrast that existed between East and West Germany (*ibid.*, 47). They ask:

> Which [East or West Germany] has prospered? Which had to erect a wall to pen in its citizens? Which must man it today with armed guards, assisted by fierce dogs, minefields, and similar devices of devilish ingenuity in order to frustrate brave and desperate citizens who are willing to risk their lives to leave their communist paradise for the capitalist hell on the other side of the wall? (Friedman, 1980, 47.)

Malaya, Singapore, Korea, Taiwan and Japan—all relying extensively on private markets, the Friedmans wrote, are thriving (*ibid.*, 48). Their peoples, they continued, are full of hope (*ibid.*, 48). By contrast, they added, India, Indonesia and Communist China—all relying on central planning—have experienced economic stagnation and political repression (*ibid.*, 49).

What the Friedmans forget is that correlation is not causation, and to identify the one with the other is to expose oneself to the fallacy of false cause. Nothing that the Friedmans have 'said' indicates that capitalism is the cause of economic progress and the humane treatment of persons. In fact we have cited the Ghanaian experience as a counterexample, since *kalabule* was at its height immediately before and after the 112-day 'moral revolution' which sought to do away with *kalabule* in Ghana. In Ghana, the price-control system of the pre-'moral revolution' administration of ex-General Kutu Acheampong did give way to the laissez-faire economic activity of market women, when *kalabule* was at its height. After the uprising of 4th June 1979, a 'moral revolution' which sought to use executions to abolish *kalabule* ethics was launched. But the *kalabule* ethics, guided by the maximization of profits operating in a free market system, re-emerged in the 1979-81 Limann administration that was capitalist in all but theory. Hence, the launching of the 'holy war' against 'kalabuleism' in the wake of the forcible overthrow of the Limann administration on 31st December 1981.

In my opinion, the attempt to fight the business ethics of *kalabule* by way of indiscriminate violence and terrorism through the use of machine guns, in the name of a moral revolution or a holy war, is misplaced. If suffering and death resulting from business practices that seek to maximize profits are intuitively immoral, so are suffering and death resulting from terrorizing the society by machine guns. Experience has shown that in such conditions of 'machine-gun ethics,' the supply of even locally produced basics such as food disappear from the markets creating starvation and suffering. The subsequent attempt to use guns to get goods back on the market at controlled prices results in further killing or harming of poor non-*kalabule* persons (among others). Such 'moral revolutionaries' and 'holy warriors' seem not to appreciate that sanctions are external to morality and that ethics are made or invented not discovered. To invent ethics, we noted, the conditions must be conducive to the creation of the kind of values we are interested in. In a society of scarcity and capitalists, we are unlikely to have the resources with which to invent anything but *kalabule* ethics. If the prevailing conditions are not conducive to making non-*kalabule* ethics, it is futile to force people to embrace any other ethics. The mark of ethical conduct in a society of adult human beings, is that the members of the society can discriminate between good and evil and conduct themselves well by the use of reason, unlike children and subhumans. If ethics is to be discovered, then we need not force people to give up one system of ethics for the other, because there is no evidence that at any point in time all or several societies have discovered exactly the same ethical system. Further, if people ought to be forced in order that they do what they do, what guarantee is there that they do what they do because it is good and not because of fear?

In conclusion, I wish to note the following. That Akans who are Christians could subscribe to *kalabule* which conflicts with Christian and Akan ethics, indicates (though it does not prove) that ethics is human-made or invented from the prevailing conditions rather than God-given or society-given to be discovered whatever the conditions are. If we wish to make or invent Akan-like or Christian-like ethics, we would have to create the conditions conducive to the making of it. I have suggested that the adoption of wholesale capitalism in conditions of acute shortage of basic goods is unconducive to the invention or practice of or belief in Akan and Christian ethics. In consequence, I have recommended central planning only with respect to the necessities of life when supply is greatly inadequate.

I do not for a moment think that central planning (in whatever form) is sufficient for ensuring progress, development or that moral standards are high. I merely note its importance for poor countries. Hence the attack by the Friedmans, if intended to show that central planning does not ensure development, is at best uninteresting. Central planning—in the recommended form of rationing—which is tainted with corruption, would be tantamount to the practice of capitalism. In fact corrupt rationing would lead to 'kalabuleism;' since it would replace the equitable system of rationing with inequities in supply to individuals which would permit those with more than what the rationing system would have permitted them to have to sell at whatever price to those who received less than their ration. The problem of *kalabule* and the solution to it are economic. Hence the prevailing African attempt to solve such problems by means of coup d'états and the consequent almost exclusive appeal to force, side-track the issue. To the extent that 'moral revolutions' and 'holy wars' rely on armed force rather than the reason (logic) of economic considerations associated with ideologies, to that extent would they be counterproductive in the attempt to revolutionalize business ethics; especially if the 'moral revolutionaries' and 'holy warriors' are motivated by the belief that revolutionary ethics are discoverable on earth or in heaven, in our past or future.

Notes

1. Also called 'reasonable prices' in some parts of Africa.
2. Pronounced as 'kaela-'buli' as in 'Carla-bully'.
3. Read as 'Two Cedis' (Ghanaian currency).
4. Most *kalabule* businesswomen I have spoken to accept this Akan proverb and seek entry into the 'kingdom of God'.

References

Caincross, A. *Introduction to Economics*, 5th ed. (Butterworth & Co. Ltd., 1973).

Economic Survey 1978: Current Trends in the World Economy (UN, New York: UN, 1980).

F.A.O., *Fighting World Hunger* (L 8403/E/79 Rome).

Friedman, Milton and Rose Friedman. *Free to Choose* (New York: Avon Books, 1980).

Galbraith, J. K. *Economics, Peace and Laughter* (Harmondsworth: Penguin Books Ltd., 1971).

GCB 1978. *Quarterly Economic Review* (Econ. Research Department of Ghana Commercial Bank).

GCB 1981. *Quarterly Economic Review* (Research Department of Ghana Commercial Bank).

Luke, The Gosple according to *The Holy Bible*, Revised Standard Version.

Mackie, J. L. *Ethics: Inventing Right and Wrong* (Harmondsworth: Penguin Books, 1977).

Macpherson, C. B. *Democratic Theory* (Oxford Univ. Press, 1973).

Samuelson, Paul. *Economics* (New York: McGraw-Hill Inc., 1976).

Singer, Peter. 'Morality, Famine and Affluence', in *Philosophy and Public Affairs* (1973).

World Bank. *World Development Report* (Washington D.C.:IBRD, 1980).

World Economic Survey 1978: Current Trends in the World Economy. (New York: UN, 1980).

Questions for Chapter 14
Business Ethics and Capitalism

1. TRUE or FALSE?

   a. Safro Kwame claims that African countries should practice socialism.
   b. Safro Kwame claims that Christian and Akan ethics are similar in certain respects.
   c. Safro Kwame suggests that African countries should use soldiers to enforce price control.
   d. According to Safro Kwame, it is immoral to advocate capitalism.

2. *Kalabule* is (as described in the text) not a form of:

   (A) government.
   (B) capitalism.
   (C) business practice.
   (D) business ethic.

3. Safro Kwame suggests that our moral rules and values are

   (A) invented by human beings.
   (B) determined by God.
   (C) given by nature.
   (D) none of the above.

4. Compare Safro Kwame's conclusion and arguments with Busia's as well a Nkrumah's.

5. What form of government or ideology would you recommend for African countries and why?

6. 'Any system of distribution or marketing that permits business persons to maximize profits in the sale or distribution of basic goods is immoral.' Discuss.

7. Do you agree that military governments are, from moral, economic, and political points of view, dangerous in Africa and other parts of the so-called Third World?

Chapter 15

Polygamy And The Emancipation Of Women: An African Perspective

Florence Abena Dolphyne

Ayere dodow ye ohia na ɛnyɛ hwee. —**There is nothing but poverty in polygamy.** (Akan proverb)

PROLOGUE

Florence Abena Dolphyne was educated at the University of Ghana at Legon and at the University of London where she obtained a Ph.D in Linguistics. She is currently, Dean of the Faculty of Arts at the University of Ghana, Legon. She has chaired the University of Ghana's Linguistics Department and taught at the University of Ibadon, Michigan State University, Fourah Bay College, and the University of California at Los Angeles.

Here, she tries to explain (1) the distinction between the women's movement in the Western world and its counterpart in Africa, and (2) what women's emancipation means to African women. Her account is drawn from her experiences as the (former) chairperson of the National Council on Women and Development in Ghana as well as her experiences and those of other women in other parts of sub-Saharan Africa.

According to Dolphyne, there are so many differences in priorities and conceptions among Western and African women that, in spite of her working for the total emancipation of women, she does not consider herself a feminist. Those differences relate to polygamy, the bride-wealth or bride-price, female circumcision, prostitution, and lesbianism.

For example, while lesbianism and prostitution are major issues of concern to many African women and their advocates, polygamy, extra-martial relations, and the division of domestic labor are not. Further, in her view, some of the arguments of Western feminists such as those against high fertility and bride-wealth do not take African culture into consideration and are un-African.

Here is a sample of Dolphyne's arguments:
"At the End-of-Decade Conference held in Nairobi, Kenya, in 1985, the rather hostile reception given the lesbian women's group attending the Forum again highlighted the fact that there are certain women's rights that are non-issues to African women. For most African women living in rural areas with no good drinking water, with no hospital or clinic within easy reach, no motorable roads to centres where certain essential services can be obtained, living in a drought-stricken area where there is a constant threat of famine and so on, the issue of women's rights is inextricably linked with that of survival. Their concerns relate to the provision of the basic necessities of life that will relieve them from the anxieties inherent in their existence, so that they can direct their energies towards making a worthwhile contribution to the achievement of a sustainable improvement in the conditions in which they live, and to the development of their society...For most African women, there-fore, the emancipation of women and the status of women in society are closely linked with national development, and during the Decade most of the activities initiated for women in Africa were women in development programmes...In traditional African societies, men have usually married more than one woman in order to have more hands to help them work on their farms...More wives meant more children, and the larger a man's farm, the more wives and children he had. Thus, over the years, the number of wives a man had was seen as a reflection of his affluence...In modern times...the usefulness of wives as free labour has been considerably reduced, but the practice of polygamy still persists... One of the main reasons for this state of affairs is that all African societies believe that a woman must be married, and marriage confers on a woman a high degree of respectability in her community...The freedom of movement that a polygamous marriage makes possible for women can also be seen in the activities of market women...Some women who support polygamy have even argued that it is justified on account of the ratio of women to men in their countries, although one is yet to find an African country whose census figures show that women are around 65 per cent of the population,

which will be a basis for at least some of the men being entitled to no more than two women each ...For the present, most African women, especially the rural majority, believe that polygamy as practised in African societies, is to be preferred to the situation one finds in Western societies where, in the strict monogamous system, a man may be married to one woman but keeps one or more mistresses...It is quite clear that African societies are, in general, not yet ready to consider polygamy, or monogamy with extra-marital relations, as a major issue."

Polygamy And The Emancipation Of Women: An African Perspective

Florence Abena Dolphyne

1. PREFACE

Ever since International Women's Year in 1975 highlighted the issue of the equality of men and women, women's issues, which previously were the concerns of voluntary women's societies, have attained national and international significance. During that year and throughout the ten years of the United Nations Decade for Women that followed, there were numerous research studies into the condition of women in different societies. There also were many conferences and seminars held at regional and international levels all over the world which afforded women the opportunity to identify, discuss and find ways of removing the obstacles that had been, and still were impeding womens emancipation and their full integration into the economic, social and political life of their various countries. From these research studies and discussions one thing became clear, that in spite of the differences in culture, in levels of education and in economic and industrial development of their countries, women the world over suffered similar types of injustice and discrimination within the family structure, in employment, in education and in access to professional training and so on. The difference between countries was one of degree, and as the evidence of discrimination built up, it became more and more obvious that, in order to achieve the objectives of the Decade, namely, Equality, Development and Peace, women, from developing as well as the industrialized countries, have to work together to fight the injustices that society has subjected them to for centuries.

It was in the spirit of women's solidarity therefore that many of the discussions of women's issues were conducted. The objective was to help women articulate their problems in clear terms and to work together in finding solutions to these problems.

It was disturbing for me, therefore, that at the Forum sessions (the

Reprinted by permission of the author and publisher, from *The Emancipation of Women: An African Perspective* by Florence Abena Dolphyne, Accra, Ghana: Ghana Universities Press, © 1991 by Florence Abena Dolphyne.

meetings organized for representatives of Non-Governmental Organizations) of the Mid-Decade Conference held in Copenhagen, Denmark, in 1980, there was a clear polarization of positions held by women from the Western world in particular and women from Africa on certain burning issues about which both groups were obviously concerned, and for which both groups were equally anxious to find solutions. These issues related to certain traditional practices in African societies such as polygamy, bride-wealth (or bride price as it has been referred to by some anthropologists) and female circumcision. Both groups were equally of the opinion that these practices were an obstacle to the emancipation of women on the African continent. What they were not agreed on were the measures to be taken to eradicate them and the timing of such measures. The majority of the women from Western countries were for immediate legislation banning such practices. To them this was an obviously logical proposition: if all of us agree that these traditional practices are inimical to the welfare and total emancipation of women, then let the governments in those countries where these traditions persist legislate to make them illegal, and thereby set in motion the process that would put an end to them. This point of view was particularly strong at the sessions where female circumcision was discussed. At some of these sessions, gruesome details were given about the operation itself and the risks to the woman's health in later life, if she does not die from tetanus or some other form of infection after the circumcision.

The African women were put on the defensive. They tried to explain that these practices are deeply rooted in the traditions of the societies that practice them, and have religious and cultural significance in such societies. They pointed out that as educated African women, they realize that the principles underlying these practices are no longer tenable and they fully appreciate the need to work towards the total eradication of such practices. They have themselves been pressing for such eradication. However, what was needed most at this time, when most of the affected societies have a very high proportion of non-literate population living in rural areas, was education to make them aware of the health-hazards of female circumcision, for example, and improvement in their living conditions which will lower infant mortality —one major reason for frequent child-bearing in African women. Education and professional or vocational training were also needed to make young women economically independent and therefore make it unnecessary for a girl to be married off by her parents to a wealthy old man, who already has four wives, in order to ensure that she is well taken care of. They pointed out that many educated African women living in urban centres no longer practice these traditions, and it is clear that only sustained systematic education will achieve the results that everybody at the Conference was hoping for.

The educational programmes and the overall improvement in the living conditions of rural African societies that the African women participants at these discussions were asking for were too long-term for the Western women. They wanted to see immediate results, and the more radical among them felt the African women had let the side down, they had betrayed the women's cause.

While African women attending the Forum discussions were being accused of not being radical enough, their colleagues at the main Conference for government delegations were being accused of being too radical. They were not concentrating on what many of their Western counterparts considered to be "women's issues"—appropriate technology for women, organizing women's trade groups into viable co-operatives, and so on. Instead, they were dabbling in international political issues like racism in South Africa and the conflict in the Middle East, which, according to them, should be properly discussed at the United Nations General Assembly. Presumably, these are issues that should be properly discussed by men, since the delegations that go to the General Assembly are dominated by men.

The African women argued that all issues are women's issues; that in any situation of deprivation, as was found in South Africa, or of war, as in the Middle East, or of poverty and hunger, as can be seen in a number of African countries, it is women and children who are the most vulnerable. For example, there is the Palestinian woman who has to bring up her children in the violent environment of a refugee camp, not knowing from one day to the next whether or not the camp would be raided, but fully conscious that she is raising her sons to be used as pawns in a conflict that seems to go on for ever. Then there is the South African woman who has to cope with bringing up her children single-handed in a squatter camp or in a remote settlement for blacks, miles away from her husband who works in a mine and who can only see his family for a short period once a year. There is also the woman in an African village who watches helplessly while her child dies of malnutrition and preventable diseases. For all these women, the issue of women's emancipation cannot be separated from the politics that brought about their particular situation. For all of them, the major problem is one of survival, and a necessary prerequisite for an improvement in their condition is that for the Palestinian woman, a satisfactory solution to the politics that created the war situation in the Middle East must be found. For the South African woman, the structures that suppress people on account of the colour of their skin in racist South Africa just have to be dismantled; and, for the woman in the developing African country, the inequities inherent in the present trade relations between industrialized countries and raw-material-producing Third World countries must be dealt with. In other words, the situation in which the former determine not only the price at which they sell their manufactured goods to developing countries, but also the price at which they buy raw materials from the developing countries, just has to change, because that is the main reason why African governments are unable to earn enough from their exports to provide basic education and adequate health facilities for all their citizens. By all means let us devise new appropriate   technology to lighten the work-load of rural women, let there be programmes to educate women on primary health care, sanitation and such important matters; women should study the laws of their countries and agitate for the deletion or amendment of those laws that are discriminatory against women; and so the list of "women's concerns" continues. But it is also necessary for women to discuss, and to try to find solutions to international political issues that have far-reaching effects on the lives of women and their children in many countries.

Since that Conference, I have become more and more conscious of the difference in approach to women's issues between Western women, especially 'feminists,' and African women who are actively working for women's emancipation. I myself, as Vice-Chairman and later as Chairman of the National Council on Women and Development, the national machinery set up by the Ghana Government to ensure that the objectives of International Women's Year and the subsequent United Nations Decade for Women are achieved in Ghana, always knew that I was working for the total emancipation of women in Ghana. However, I never considered and still do not consider myself a 'feminist,' for the term evokes for me the image of an aggressive woman who, in the same breath, speaks of a woman's right to education and professional training, her right to equal pay for work of equal value, her right to vote and to be voted for in elections at all levels, etc. as well as a woman's right to practice prostitution and lesbianism. It is this image of the feminist which made African men, some in highly-placed positions in government, and some women as well, rather uncomfortable about the idea of an international year for women. During 1975, it was usual for people to say that the whole idea of the equality of the sexes was foreign to Africa. Indeed, it was not until after the United Nations General Assembly had endorsed the Mexico International Women's Year Conference recommendation that 1976-1985 be declared the United Nations Decade for Women, that many countries in Africa began setting up offices like the Ghana National Council on Women and Development for ensuring that the objectives of the Decade were achieved in those countries. This is because it became clear from the details contained in the Mexico Programme of Action adopted at the 1975 International Women's Year Conference, that there was more at stake than the question of who cooked the dinner or changed the baby.

At the End-of-Decade Conference held in Nairobi, Kenya, in 1985, the rather hostile reception given the lesbian women's group attending the Forum again highlighted the fact that there are certain women's rights that are non-issues to African women. For most African women living in rural areas with no good drinking water, with no hospital or clinic within easy reach, no motorable roads to centres where certain essential services can be obtained, living in a drought-stricken area where there is a constant threat of famine and so on, the issue of women's rights is inextricably linked with that of survival. Their concerns relate to the provision of the basic necessities of life that will relieve them from the anxieties inherent in their existence, so that they can direct their energies towards making a worthwhile contribution to the achievement of a sustainable improvement in the conditions in which they live, and to the development of their society.

For most African women, therefore, the emancipation of women and the status of women in society are closely linked with national development, and during the Decade most of the activities initiated for women in Africa were women in development programmes...

2. POLYGAMY

An Asante (Ghana) folktale that provides a rationale for polygamy goes like this: A man who had been married for about two years decided to take on a second wife. His wife thought there was no need for that since she felt they were getting on perfectly happily. She already had one child, and was likely to have more. The man argued that she alone could not provide for him all the things he needed at the times he needed them, but the woman insisted he had no basis for that claim. To prove his point, the man one day said he wanted to eat Asante kenkey, a preparation from corn-dough, and the woman had that day to prepare it for him. The woman accepted the challenge and started by beating the maize in a very deep mortar to remove the skin from the maize, for the kenkey is made from polished maize. After removing the skin, she pounded the maize in another mortar to break it up. She then ground it on a big grinding stone to get a smooth paste, for this was the age when there were no cornmills. By this time she was not only physically exhausted, but both palms were in blisters, and she had difficulty mixing the corn-dough to the right consistency for making the kenkey. She eventually gave up, went to the elders of her family and asked them to go and apologize to the man on her behalf for being so stubborn, and to tell him that she was perfectly agreeable to his marrying a second wife. And that, according to the story, is how men started marrying more than one wife.

This story illustrates how society conditions its members into accepting the norms of the society. A young girl in a village would hear this story told over and over again, and by the time she is of age she would know that it is not possible for one woman to satisfy the needs of her husband, and therefore she should be prepared to share her husband with co-wives. It is for this reason that while the more radical feminists would want to see legislation banning the traditional practices that are seen to be demeaning to a woman's status in society, it is clear to most African women fighting for women's emancipation that such legislation will at best affect only a fraction of the educated women living in urban communities. The rest of the population will continue to practice them until the inimical effects of the particular traditional practice have been demonstrated to them in no uncertain terms, or until, as suggested above in the case of child-marriage, something new and seen to be beneficial, such as formal education, has been put in its place.

In traditional African societies, men have usually married more than one woman in order to have more hands to help them work on their farms. More wives meant more children, and the larger a man's farm, the more wives and children he had. Thus, over the years, the number of wives a man had was seen as a reflection of his affluence. In recent years, formal education has meant a reduction in the labour provided by children, and hired labour has also meant a reduction in the value of the labour provided by wives, although they became useful supervisors of the hired labour. In modern times, therefore, the usefulness of wives as free labour has been considerably reduced, but the practice of polygamy still persists.

One of the main reasons for this state of affairs is that all African societies believe that a woman must be married, and marriage confers on a woman a high degree of respectability in her community. And so whatever her level of education, professional status or economic independence, an African woman would not normally choose to remain single, although it is also true to say that higher education and professional status do confer a very high degree of respectability on a woman, irrespective of her marital status. One must add that marriage also confers respectability on a man. An unmarried man is normally regarded as irresponsible: he cannot even assume responsibility for a wife and children. A woman is also expected to have children to prove her womanhood, and it is true to say that the respect and status that motherhood confers on a woman is greater than that conferred by marriage per se. A young woman who has children outside marriage is generally regarded as a disgrace to herself and to her family, and so to have children, a woman must be married, and it does not matter how many wives the man already has. For these reasons, one finds that some of the strongest opponents to any legislation banning polygamy are women, even highly educated women.

There are other reasons why many women find polygamy a convenient arrangement. There are women who have been able to continue their education and have professional training after marriage and the birth of one or two children because as the third or fourth wife, they found willing and competent mothers for their children in the senior co-wives. Understandably, this can only happen if the junior wife gives them due respect, and there is harmony in the home.

The freedom of movement that a polygamous marriage makes possible for women can also be seen in the activities of market women. In, especially, the non-Moslem parts of West Africa, retail trade in agricultural produce and in manufactured goods is dominated by women. They have full control over the money they earn, and many of them have, without the help of husbands, brothers or other male relation, been able to give their children education and professional training. Many of these women are married in a polygamous system, and they find it a very convenient arrangement, for a woman can travel for days buying goods from one part of the country and transporting them to the market centres without having to worry about a husband whose meals have to be ready at specific times. There will be another wife to take care of that while she is away. Of course, it also can happen that if the man is not too well organized, and has not made proper arrangements, he may go hungry because each wife expects one or the other co-wife to be cooking for him. This situation is summed up in an Asante (Ghana) proverb which translates as "It is hunger that killed the man with many wives," a statement which implies that although traditional society approves of polygamy, it also feels that a man can have a wife too many.

Some educated women, especially those of the Moslem faith, whose religion does not give any protection against polygamy because it allows a man up to four wives, will tell you that they would not mind being the second, third or fourth wife. Their reason is that they will have time to concentrate on their profession when it is not their turn to keep house for the husband. The cynics among them will add that while monogamy does not guarantee a husband's fidelity, in a polygamous marriage, a woman at least has some idea of where her husband is likely to be when he is not with her.

Some women who support polygamy have even argued that it is justified on account of the ratio of women to men in their countries, although one is yet to find an African country whose census figures show that women are around 65 per cent of the population, which will be a basis for at least some of the men being entitled to no more than two women each. The fact is that since most women do not have any formal education, and since they do not need to undergo any formal vocational training, having learnt whatever trade their mothers are engaged in from observation and participation, there are, at any given time, more girls who are ready for marriage than there are marriageable men. The young men of their age or a little older will still be in school or will be struggling to acquire some property, such as their own farm, which will enable them to pay for the bride-wealth required, and also make them capable of maintaining a wife and children. Girls, therefore, marry men who are often many years older than they are, and it is not unusual to find a woman in traditional society addressing her husband as 'Master' or by some other title that duly reflects his superior position. She never calls him by his name.

For the present, most African women, especially the rural majority, believe that polygamy as practised in African societies, is to be preferred to the situation one finds in Western societies where, in the strict monogamous system, a man may be married to one woman but keeps one or more mistresses. This is what is happening in many 'monogamous' marriages among educated Africans. There is also the modern trend of successive polygamy where a man in his life-time may be married to several women, only he divorces one before he marries the next—a system that creates problems for children born in each succeeding marriage. The polygamous system in traditional African societies at least gives equal status to co-wives, although usually the most senior commands respect and the newest wife is the favoured one.

One should not, however, underrate the emotional strain that individual women go through in polygamous marriages, especially in modern times. In the past, a woman married for economic security, and she would put up with infidelity and with other forms of cruelty on the part of her husband as long as he provided for her and her children. Now that women are becoming economically independent, they have other expectations in marriage, the major ones being affection and companionship. This is particularly true of educated women. When these expectations are not fulfilled because a husband is seriously involved in extramarital relations, some women decide to break off the marriage, especially if they can, on their own, take full responsibility for the upbringing of their children. This has led to the creation of the impression that education, especially higher education, for women is responsible for the increase in divorce rate. Men and women of the older generation, in particular, cannot appreciate the feeling of betrayal that a woman, who has had a happy marriage with her husband and shared confidences with him for many years, has when her husband decides to take on another wife, or when he starts having children outside his officially monogamous marriage. A woman who decides to divorce her husband because he has a serious relationship with another woman is, therefore, considered to be over-reacting, and she cannot normally expect much sympathy from either friends or relations, especially if there are children in the marriage. She will be told that divorce is bad for the children. Older women in her family will tell her about several instances in which a woman had patiently tolerated her husband's infidelity, and then several years later he had come back to her, having realized the uselessness of those other relationships. In other words, if the woman waits long enough, she will have her husband back, and the marriage will be as good as new. Of course, they never tell of those cases where the women have stayed on and suffered in silence, ending up growing old prematurely, losing their interest in life and, sometimes, even losing their minds. They do not also tell of the rivalries that can and do develop between brothers and sisters from different mothers, not to mention the rivalries between co-wives and the effect they have on their children.

It is quite clear that African societies are, in general, not yet ready to consider polygamy, or monogamy with extramarital relations, as a major issue. This is why educated African women working for women's emancipation do not treat it as a priority, for they feel the time is not yet right for serious discussion on the issue. Moreover, the effect, on women, of polygamy and extra-marital relations on the part of husbands is still a very private issue, and when one considers the obvious and demonstrable inimical effects that practices like child-marriage, bride-wealth and circumcision have on women, it is difficult to accord polygamy the same priority status among pressing issues that affect women in Africa.

In recent years, many men, especially those in the urban centres, have become keenly conscious of the need to educate and provide a fairly high standard of living for their children. This, coupled with the economic hardships that almost all African countries are experiencing, have made many men come to the realization that it is difficult enough for them to cope with a small family, and they would not even contemplate acquiring a second wife who will insist on having her quota of children, at least three or four, much less a third and a fourth.

It would appear, therefore, that the desire for a better standard of living for one's family, and the economic constraints of modern life are the two major factors that will eventually make men see the undesirability of marrying more than one woman at a time. It may be mentioned here that the Christian religion, with its insistence on monogamy, has helped to reduce the incidence of polygamy to some extent. Moreover, some men, who grew up in polygamous homes and suffered from the rivalries that existed between co-wives and between their children, no longer consider marriage to more than one woman a worthwhile venture.

One practical way of reducing the incidence of polygamy is to encourage professional and vocational training for girls, so that they marry at a later age when it is possible for them to find husbands among their own age group. Such professional training will also mean that a woman will be reasonably economically independent, so that it would not be necessary for her to become a second or a third wife to a man simply because he is well-to-do and therefore able to provide for her. In other words, the need for economic security will no longer be a motive for a girl to get into marriage, whether polygamous or not.

3. WIDOWHOOD

...One may mention the practice in many African societies where the successor to the dead man may inherit his widow(s) as well. In some of these societies, the widow has the right to choose a husband from among the dead husband's brothers. The widow may also refuse to re-marry into her husband's family, although in such a situation, her family, in most cases, will have to return the bride-wealth that was given at her marriage. Returning the bride-wealth indicates that the marriage between her family and her dead husband's is broken, and that she is free to re-marry.

A typical feminist reaction to a widow being married by the dead husband's relation is that it makes a woman part of a man's estate that may be disposed of or inherited at his death. However, given the fact that the women in many of these societies have no independent source of livelihood, such re-marriage into the husband's family guarantees that she and her children will be taken care of. The only way to put an end to such a practice is, as suggested under polygamy, to give women skills that will make them economically independent, so that marriage will not be the only avenue open to them in their search for economic security.

Questions for Chapter 15
Polygamy and the Emancipation of Women

1. TRUE or FALSE?

   a. According to Dolphyne, all African societies believe that a woman must be married.
   b. According to Dolphyne, some of the strongest opponents to legislation against polygamy are women.
   c. Dolphyne's reaction to a widow being married by the dead husband's relatives is that it makes a woman part of the man's estate.
   d. According to Dolphyne, African societies consider monogamy with extra-marital relations as a major issue, but do not consider polygamy as a major issue.

2. According to Dolphyne, which of these is a non-issue for African women?

   (A) Women's rights.
   (B) The emancipation of women.
   (C) National development.
   (D) The provision of basic necessities.
   (E) All of the above.
   (F) None of the above.

3. State and evaluate all the arguments against feminism presented in Dolphyne's account.

4. Is polygamy defensible?

Chapter 16

Feminism and African Philosophy

Safro Kwame

Mmea nyinaa yɛ baako. —All women are the same. (Akan proverb)

PROLOGUE

Safro Kwame (whose biographical sketch appears in Chapter 2) expresses his concern about how the larger questions about the existence of African philosophy have drowned out more important philosophical questions such as equality and justice for Africans living in African societies and elsewhere. Concerning women, he believes that there are at least two senses in which, from an African perspective on human equality, women may be said to be significantly alike. In the negative or first sense suggested by the traditional African philosophy of the Akans of Ghana, women all over the world may be said to be equally selfish, evil or in some way inferior to men. This, he argues, calls into question the suggestion by some African and non-African women that traditional Akan and African societies provide a refutation of the belief that all women are oppressed. The second, more positive sense acknowledges that in a general sense almost all women everywhere are oppressed and we need to do something about that. In that sense Kwame, more so than Dolphyne, believes that (1) feminism, properly interpreted, has a major role to play in Africa and (2) unless feminism—like philosophy—is appropriated by one race or group, African feminism—unlike African philosophy—is not needed.

In part, his argument is as follows:

"One approach to African philosophy consists in extracting it from the proverbs, beliefs and practices of African societies. Without going into the metaphilosophical debate between the so-called ethnophilosophers who favor this approach and the so-called professional philosophers who oppose it, I would simply like to note that the following is an account of a conception of women on one view of African philosophy. A brief examination of the proverbs of the Akan society, for example, will give us insight into the Akan conception of women. Not surprisingly, it is a conception that is opposed to that of Omolade, Callaway, Smock and others. Here are some of the relevant Akan proverbs that were and still are popular in Akan society:

Ɔbaa twa bomma a, etweri barima dan mu. (Even if a women creates a taking drum, she stores it in a man's house.)

Ɔbea ho yɛfɛ a, efi ne kunu. (If a woman is beautiful, it is because of her husband.)

These are representative of the bulk of the proverbs on women compiled by Akrofi as reflecting Akan beliefs and ideas. "Twi proverbs," he notes, "are a reflection of the philosophy of the Akan."...There is some independent confirmation of this invidiously sexist conception of women in most contemporary African societies...Writing from her own experience as an Akan woman living in a modern African society, Ama Ata Aidoo, for example, notes that "the position of a woman in Ghana is no less ridiculous than anywhere else."...For example, she recalls "as a child living among adult females that everything which had to do exclusively with being a woman was regarded as dirty." If bell hooks is right about 'talking back' being a sign of equality and vice versa, it should be obvious to those who are familiar with both the traditional and contemporary African society that African women are seldom considered as the equals of men... My suggestion is that, even though African philosophy or at least one version of it indicates that there is sexism of an invidious kind in African societies, there is very little evidence that African philosophers have significantly fought or even addressed it. To do that, I believe we do not need a special kind of feminism; for feminist philosophy, whether liberal, radical, socialist or post-modern is—as Alison Jaggar points out—inspired by a determination that women's concerns, interests, capacities, and achievements should receive full and fair appreciation and evaluation. At least, it ought to be so inspired, if it already is not."

Feminism And African Philosophy[1]

Safro Kwame

1. INTRODUCTION

There is, in both feminist and non-feminist circles, a myth about the Akan society that needs to be broken. The myth is that the existence of African societies, particularly matrilineal ones such as that of the traditional Akan, falsifies the thesis of the universal oppression of women. Barbara Omolade, for example, insists that "even the most cursory examination of cultures and history of black women, for example, would force feminists to raise questions about the universal oppression of women under patriarchy."[2]

Using the Akans of Ghana as her example, Barbara Callaway writes:

> The concepts of modernization and development, as defined in much of the accepted literature, assume the 'emancipation of women' as part of these processes, but the Ghanaian case indicates the fallacy of this view.[3]

In reviewing the literature on Akan and other matrilineal societies Dorothy Vellenga remarks that "in fact, the study of matrilineal societies gives rise to real questions about the universal subordination of women."[4] In noting that only 4 to 6 percent of members of national and local councils and boards in Ghana in the 1970's were women, Christine Oppong and Katharine Abu made the following remark: "This is certainly in contrast to the parallel and complementary roles of females and males in traditional political and military spheres." [5]

My two-fold objective, here, is as follows. First, I wish to undermine this view of both the Akan society and African women, and the attendant view of the thesis of universal oppression of women. Secondly, I wish to propose an Akan conception of women and an African philosophy of women. Let me start with a critique of the arguments of the afore-mentioned authors, before turning to the Akan or African conception of women.

2. THE TRADITIONAL AFRICAN SOCIETY

Omolade's account presents the life-styles of token women in West Africa in an attempt to overgeneralize and glorify the past. She writes that "African women in traditional culture were human, were citizens, and were valuable members of society,"[6] as if recognition of this could not co-exist (albeit, inconsistently) with sexist and racist practices. Being a human being, a citizen, and a valuable member of society are not sufficient to eliminate the irrational belief in a person's inferiority or to ensure that one is not a victim of any kind of invidious discrimination. Indeed, part of the critique of sexism as well as racism and slavery is that it is inconsistent with the recognition that women and, in case of slavery and racism, blacks are valuable human citizens. In other words it can exist in spite of the (logical) inconsistency.

In the first place, Omolade admits that "men and women had clearly designated roles and tasks."[7] She adds: "But this did not undermine the rights of women to participate in the tribal decision-making process, i.e., tribal and family councils; to have redress against mistreatment even by their husbands; and to have the right to own property and accumulate personal wealth and goods from their labor."[8] Here again it needs to be noted that if participation in decision-making processes and having legal right to redress and property ownership were sufficient for ensuring equality of the sexes, then the United States of America, for example, could be said to have achieved equality of the sexes in the 1960's. But it cannot, in spite of the right of women to vote, own property, and seek redress for spouse abuse. Further it ought to be pointed out that not all or even a majority of African women are able to acquire substantial wealth, power, or property. Omolade seems to forget that the history of these traditional African societies even as narrated by traditional Africans and written by modern Africans themselves is dominated by male chiefs, kings and important male figures. The important women— the Cleopatras, the Queens of Sheeba and Yaa Asantewas (the Akan counterparts of Joan of Arc)—were marginal as both Dolphyne and Appiah seem to recognize.[9]

Secondly, Omolade argues that "African women were valued as childbearers, a sign to many feminists of oppression and restriction." "But," she continues, "Africans viewed motherhood as an honor necessary for the tribe's continuance.[10] It needs to be recalled that sexist and racist societies saw women and blacks as providing sexual and manual services that were necessary to the society's continuance and, yet, discriminated against women and blacks. Valuing a woman as a childbearer need not involve perceiving women as more than human-making factories. We need to remember that in most of the traditional African societies women worked equal hours with the men on the farms in the morning but did the housework alone while the men drank palm wine under shady trees. Men were, generally, given preference in education and in dining, and women were, often, the recipients of the residues of food and other necessities. Population and development in West Africa shows that there are and have been, for a long time in West Africa, female farmers without adequate access to land and services.[11]

Thirdly, Omolade argues that the African economic system in Africa was not, in itself, sexist:

> There was no economic system in Africa where women were either appendages, household ornaments, or worthless dradges. African women were workers encouraged to work and participate in the survival of the tribe and clan. Wealthy men were proud of their wives for working and managing market stalls which traded goods and crafts. Their activities enhanced the family's status and wealth. Thus African women captured as slaves were brutally wrested from a society where they participated as human beings with firmly entrenched rights and status. It is not surprising, therefore, that from the beginning African women as well as men independently and collectively resisted enslavement. They did not want to leave Africa and clearly understood that their human rights were left on its shore.[12]

Even if it is true that the traditional economic system in Africa was not designed to oppress or degrade women, it does not mean that it cannot and has not been used to do that. Further it cannot be denied that some women have been so victimized. I am acquainted with both relatives and non-relatives in Ghana, Nigeria, and Togo who were treated like household ornaments and appendages of their husbands, economically, socially, and politically. It may be equally true that differences in sex and race were not 'designed' to oppress or degrade human beings even though it has, historically, been used for that purpose. The unwillingness of Africans to accept enslavement in the Americas is no more surprising than the unwillingness of twentieth-century African-American women to accept residency in apartheid South Africa. But to say that African-American women are unwilling to accept citizenship in apartheid South Africa is not to say that they are not victims of sexism or racism in twentieth-century America. No one that I know of is willing to trade visceral or insidious sexism or racism for outright enslavement, whether or not they are currently experiencing sexism or racism. The reason, I presume, has to do with 'human nature' however one chooses to characterize the details. Hence, the

unwillingness of African women to submit to slavery in the Americas
does not prove that the traditional African society was non-sexist.

Using the words of politicians like President Leopold Senghor, the
matrilineality of Akan society, and the power of a few Akan women as
her evidence, Callaway, like Omolade, comes to blame the white
colonialists for sexism in present-day Africa.[13] Concerning the
traditional Akan society she writes:

> Women are seldom accorded actual sovereignty in these states, but there
> were women who participated in the exercise of power and who occupied
> positions either on a par with or complementary to that of the king, or
> 'Ohene.' In Ashanti, 'Ohemaa' or queen mother, was the chiefs'
> counterpart. She was the senior female of the royal lineage and was
> usually either the mother or the sister of the 'Ohene.' As the
> representative of the women, she was a major power in the community.
> As joint ruler, she had prerogatives far greater than those held by any
> man other than the 'Asantehene' (King of the Ashanti) himself. She had
> a separate palace and her own court, and numerous functionaries
> performed under her direction. She supervised all "feminine matters such
> as marriages, birth, children's education, and dealt with questions relating
> to adultery, divorce, and female initiation ceremonies.[14]

Note that she admits that the king is more powerful than the queen-
mother and she was seldom accorded sovereignty. Also it is noteworthy
that the State allows for only one queen-mother. Her privileges do not
translate into privileges for the other women. In any case, her role was
sex-specific not androgynous. She supervised all "feminine matters."
Callaway also notes that "a matrilineal society is not matriarchal,
although in Akan culture there were important political roles for
women."[15] She quotes an Akan proverb "the rain beats the leopards skin
but it does not wash out the spots," (*Osu hwe sebo a, ne ho na ɛfɔw; na
ne nworannworan de, ɛmpopa*), in support of blaming colonialism for
the prevailing system of sexism. She fails to note that the same proverb
generates a contrary conclusion namely colonialism cannot wash out the
egalitarianism of the traditional society. In this respect, Callaway is
guilty of not just gross generalization but also special pleading.

Like Callaway, Audrey Smock uses the matrilineality of the Akan
society and token Akan women to make a case for sexual equality in
the traditional society.[16] She writes that despite male political
predominance, women held significant social and political roles and
came close to achieving equality in many respects."[17] "Although the

chief outranked the queen-mother," she continues, "a capable woman filling that office could command considerable authority in her own right."[18] She adds that "On occasion, Akan women even served as chiefs. Yaa Asantewa, for example, an Ashanti woman, led the Ashanti warriors in the final Anglo-Ashanti war of 1900-1901."[19] She acknowledges the practice of polygamy but remarks that "it would be erroneous to assume, however, that the existence of plural marriages necessarily lowered women's status."[20] She adds, "Polygamy first and foremost represented the manner in which men could display wealth. Having more than one wife also increased the number of children available to work with the father and therefore enhanced his economic prospects."[21]

By Smock's own admission, the Akan society is one which allowed polygamy but not polyandry and in which men were dominant and women were occasionally chiefs and warriors but mostly a form of wealth for men. It would be a 'non-sequitur' to argue analogously that Great Britain in the 1990's or even 1980's was a non-sexist society merely because the Queen, Prime Minister and several wealthy people were women or because women in general were content with their lot. One should not be deluded by the lack of significant disparities among members of simple, 'under-developed,' communitarian societies into thinking that they are egalitarian societies. In my opinion, the real test of egalitarianism comes with development, technology, and capitalism which generate opportunities, wealth, goods and services to be distributed either equally or unequally.

Remember that these allegedly non-sexist traditional societies are the same societies that believe God is male and in their folktales blame women for God's distancing himself from humanity as a result of the noisy fufu-pounding activities of women. This is more or less a traditional African version of the Biblical story of Adam and Eve in which a woman is seen as the cause of the break in close personal relations between two males viz man and God. Kwasi Wiredu appropriately warns us against the patriotic but uncritical attempt by Africans to glorify our past as if our traditional societies were perfect societies.[22]

Certainly the ideal feminist society is not a polygynous one in which women are occasionally chiefs and warriors, but mostly queen-mothers, cooks, baby-sitters, hewers of wood and drawers of water with statuses that are usually subordinate to men and roles that are mostly sexually determined. If it were, I doubt that all women—African and non-

African—would want to realize that ideal. I do not deny that some Western anthropologists have viewed traditional African societies in terms of Western societies and concluded on the basis of such ethnocentricity that African societies are, in all respects, as sexist as Western ones. Neither do I deny that colonialism and development have augmented the sexual differences in African societies. I merely deny that the traditional African society captures the feminist ideal of a non-dualistic and unoppressive society.

3. THE CONTEMPORARY AFRICAN SOCIETY

In the light of the above-noted remarks, it should not surprise Oppong and Abu to note that, in practice, women are underrepresented in high and decision-making levels at the workplace and that women are unequal to men even though legally they are supposed to be equal.[23] This, they claim, is in contrast to the traditional society as depicted by people like Kwame Arhin.[24] What they fail to note is that the logic of Arhin's account is such that it does not support the thesis that traditional African societies had equal as well as complementary roles for men and women that were changed by the European colonial powers. In the Akan society that Arhin discusses, political power translates into military command.[25] Thus, if there were many supreme female political authorities in Akan history, then there would have been many female supreme commanders in the history of Akan society.[26] But there is no evidence to suggest that there was more than a few of such female commanders.[27] Arhin writes:

> With the exception of Yaa Asantewa, however, the Akan know of no parallels to the British Boadicea; there are only examples of those who urged on their male counterparts to fight to the death in order to retrieve the national honour...The main female military role, albeit played far behind the battlelines, was to engage in what was known as *mmomomme twe*, perform pantomime dances and sing dirges in support of the men at war.[28]

Arhin notes that while the Akan vested the right of succession in the royal matrilineage, they left the question of the successor among the eligible males open.[29] He admits that it is extremely unlikely that the colonial authorities would have recognized a woman as an occupant of a major male stool, given "the British bias towards patriliny and male chauvinism.[30] He concludes that "the Akan saw the woman in general as an educator, a moral guardian and a conciliator in the political process and adds that male and female essentially complemented each other."[31] But to conclude from all this that the Akan or African woman had parallel and equal roles to the man is to jump to a conclusion. It is as if one concluded, from the claim that the slave and the master had complementary roles, that slaves and masters were equal. Simply stated the Akan woman appears in Arhin's account as an "overburdened creature"—as Arhin characterized the Akan woman[32]—whose political head, the queen-mother or 'ohemma,' appeared powerful merely because, prior to modernization and specialization, she played the triple role of queen, medical doctor, and director of social services.[33] Felix Akuffo notes that the increasing inequality of women vis-a-vis men in Akan society is partly due to "the traditional view that a girl's place is in the kitchen and that, whatever the level of her education, she will one day be married and cared for by a man."[34] This view and interpretation of traditional Akan philosophy of women is consistent with the standard interpretation of the Akan proverbs to be discussed in the next section.

Dorothy Vellenga's view that the study of matrilineal societies in Africa has raised serious questions about the universal subordination of women, is based on the suggestion of these studies that African matrilineages enable women to be independent of their husbands and, in cases, make men dependent on women.[35] However in studying the matrilineal African societies of the Akans and other ethnic groups in Africa, she comes, in effect, to deny this. She notes that in the matrilineal areas more women—47 percent—work for their husbands as against 26 percent in patrilineal areas.[36] Additionally, polygyny is more widespread in matrilineal areas.[37] Vellenga concludes her study by noting that within the emerging class system in the southern half of Ghana which is predominantely Akan, women, because of their gender, clearly face different and more severe disabilities than men.[38] The process of Ghana's incorporation into the world capitalist economy, she adds, has possibly escalated male-female tensions while rural women bear the main brunt of the adverse effects of developments.[39] "In Ghana," she writes, "these tensions have surfaced in attacks on independent women entrepreneurs, mostly petty traders, whom the government has blamed for Ghana's economic problems."[40]

Claire Robertson sees the late 1970's and early 1980's destruction of the popular women-dominated 'Mokola'-type markets in the Akan and Ga areas of Ghana as containing "a specifically misogynist element, giving it the earmarks of a classic witch-hunt."[41] Her reason is that it is

apparent that the policies of the male-dominated Ghanaian governments
of the 1960's and 1970's were to blame for Ghana's economic
problems.[42] She writes:

> In fact, the attack on Mokola can be seen as an effort by the men to
> destroy one of the last realms of influence left to women. Certainly "fear
> woman" has played a role in the persecution; the men do not want to be
> dependent on the women in any area.[43]

While I do not wish to absolve these so-called businesswomen of the
disastrous impact of their selfish and greedy capitalistic practices known
as *Kalabule,*[44] I agree with Robertson that the men who run the system
and country were ultimately to blame for Ghana's economic disaster.
As my economics teacher used to say to me in those days, "those semi-
literate market women outwitted the college-trained economists."[45] They
seem to have a practical knowledge of the country's economy that the
government economists lacked. In any case, my point is that this
African conception of women that exhorts men to beware of women is
not new. It is buried in the traditional African philosophy of women that
the male-dominated African philosophers have left largely untouched.

4. AN AFRICAN CONCEPTION OF WOMEN

One approach to African philosophy consists in extracting it from the
proverbs, beliefs and practices of African societies. Without going into
the mataphilosophical debate between the so-called ethnophilosophers
who favor this approach and the so-called professional philosophers who
oppose it, I would simply like to note that the following is an account
of a conception of women on one view of African philosophy. A brief
examination of the proverbs of the Akan society, for example, will give
us insight into the Akan conception of women. Not surprisingly, it is a
conception that is opposed to that of Omolade, Callaway, Smock and
the others discussed above. Here are some of the relevant Akan
proverbs that were and still are popular in Akan society:

1. *'Obaa twa bomma a, etweri barima dan mu'* (Even if a woman creates
   a talking drum, she stores it in a man's house).
2. *'Mmea nyinaa ye baako'* (All women are the same).
3. *'Obea ho yɛfɛ a, efi ne kunu'* (If a woman is beautiful, it is because of
   her husband).
4. *'Mmea pɛ nea sika wɔ'* (Women are in love with money).
5. *'Mmea se, "Wo ho yɛ fɛH a ɛne ka'* (If women say "You are handsome,"

it means you are in financial trouble).

The Akan scholar, C.A. Akrofi, in his collection of Akan proverbs entitled *Twi Mmebusem* (Twi Proverbs) interprets the first proverb as "however great a woman, she is dependent on a man" and the second as "all women are alike."[46] Literally, the second proverb claims that all women are one and may be interpreted as 'women are similar,' 'all women are alike,' 'every women is the same' or 'there is only one kind of woman.' But, however it is interpreted, it usually has a negative connotation in Akan society and it is often taken to mean that all women are equally unfaithful, bad, evil, or even worthless.

These are representative of the bulk of the proverbs on women compiled by Akrofi as reflecting Akan beliefs and ideas. "Twi proverbs," he notes, "are a reflection of the philosophy of the Akan."[47] "Through the proverbs," he adds, "we also see mirrored Akan customs concerning men, women, and children."[48] These proverbs are derogatory of women and invidiously sexist in overtone. The Akan conception of women or rather part of that conception suggested by these proverbs is a conception of greedy, worthless, and evil parasites or something close to that conception—if you think my characterization is too negative. This, at best, is an unfortunate case of gross generalization which is inconsistent with most Akans' conception of their mothers who are obviously women. Certainly it is inconsistent with my conception of most of the African women I have encountered in my life; and these include my mother.

Nevertheless there is some independent confirmation of this invidiously sexist conception of women in most contemporary African societies as reflected in the lyrics of the popular Nigerian musician and social commentator Fela Anikulapo Kuti. In his song 'Lady' which is popular in Black communities in Africa as well as America and has recently been re-released by South African trumpeter Hugh Masekela, the traditional African woman is contrasted with her Westernized counterpart.[49] The real and traditional African woman, according to the lyrics of 'Lady' acknowledges that the man is her master and she is willing to do anything he says, cook for him, and serve him. The 'Lady,' by contrast, is regrettably domineering and different.

Writing from her own experience as an Akan woman living in a modern African society, Ama Ata Aidoo, for example, notes that "the position of a woman in Ghana is no less ridiculous than anywhere else."[50] "The few details that differ," she adds, "are interesting only in terms of local color and family times."[51] Her recollections indicate that sexism in African societies is not a recent phenomenon. For example, she recalls "as a child living among adult females that everything which had to do exclusively with being a woman was regarded as dirty."[52] If bell hooks is right about 'talking back' being a sign of equality and vice versa, it should be obvious to those who are familiar with both the traditional and contemporary African society that African women are seldom considered as the equals of men. Bell hooks notes that, "moving from silence into speech is for the oppressed, the colonized, the exploited, and those who stand and struggle side by side a gesture of defiance that heals."[53] "It is that act of speech, of 'talking back,'" she continues, "that is the expression of our movement from object to subject—the liberated voice."[54]

Yet, hooks notes, she was surprised at the extent her fellow blacks will go to deny sexism.[55] The reason, she suggests, has to do with the fear of acknowledging other kinds of oppression and losing the fight against racism:

> Traditionally it has been important for black people to assert that slavery, apartheid, and continued discrimination have not undermined the humanity of black people, that not only has the race been preserved but that the survival of black families and communities are the living testimony of our victory. To acknowledge then that our families and communities have been undermined by sexism would not only require an acknowledgement that racism is not the only form of domination and oppression that affects us as a people; it would mean critically challenging the assumption that our survival as a people depends on creating a cultural climate in which black men can achieve manhood within paradigms constructed by white patriarchy.[56]

5. FEMINISM AND AFRICAN PHILOSOPHY

I am also surprised at the extent to which my fellow Africans and non-Africans too will go to deny sexism. But unlike hooks, I am not in a position to psychologize about those who have either failed to philosophize about sexism in Africa or, having philosophized about it, failed to draw the conclusion that our traditional as well as contemporary 'African conception of women' has been intolerably sexist. Hence, I am not in a position to confirm hooks' thesis that this is due to the fear of admitting that racism is not our only problem. My guess is that African philosophers have been too preoccupied with metaphilosophical problems such as the existence of African philosophy rather than with the more substantive issues that automatically ensure the existence of African philosophy. No one—whether of the ethno-philosophical or professional school of thought—denies that the critique of traditional and contemporary African conceptions of women generates African philosophy. Rather we have been absorbed by the highly speculative and, yet, more empirical issue of whether, in the absence of documentation, people in traditional African societies philosophized. Thus, Tsenay Serequeberhan's recent anthology of essential readings in African philosophy, for example, consists almost exclusively of essays on the existence of African philosophy.[57] If I am right in concluding that sexism in African societies is not a recent phenomenon, then it suggests the possibility that the long-standing tradition of sexism has blinded most of us into taking it for granted and being oblivious to its existence. My suggestion is that, even though African philosophy or at least one version of it indicates that there is sexism of an invidious kind in African societies, there is very little evidence that African philosophers have significantly fought or even addressed it. To do that, I believe we do not need a special kind of feminism; for feminist philosophy, whether liberal, radical, socialist or post-modern is—as Alison Jaggar points out—inspired by a determination that women's concerns, interests, capacities, and achievements should receive full and fair appreciation and evaluation.[58] At least, it ought to be so inspired, if it already is not.

"Feminism", according to Barbara Smith, "is the political theory and practice that struggles to free all women; women of color, working-class women, poor women, disabled women, lesbians, old women—as well as white, economically privileged, heterosexual women."[59] She adds that anything less than this is female self-aggrandizement.[60] Joyce Trebilcot explains that "to be a feminist is to care about women, and it is arbitrary to limit our concern to just those aspects of our suffering and limitations which arise from a particular case."[61]

We do not need a special kind of feminism—call it African feminism or whatever—to tackle issues of sexism in Africa, unless Western or other groups of feminists appropriate feminism to themselves as has been done in the case of philosophy. In the first place, neither feminism nor philosophy is a geographic term. Hence the terms 'African Philosophy' and 'African Feminism' are, stictly speaking, uncalled for unless they satisfiy an important need or help to address some important issue. Secondly, other things being equal, it is only when people appropriate philosophy to themselves that there is such a thing as British, European, or Western philosophy in the sense which generates a debate on African philosophy. But once we have allowed some people to appropriate philosophy to themselves, it is difficult to deny others such as women and people of African descent the right to appropriate parts of philosophy without being, at least, apparently guilty of sexism, racism, or some kind of invidious discrimination. Of course one may categorically deny that other sexes and races did philosophize or were capable of philosophizing. But to do that one needs overwhelming empirical evidence.

I am not denying that it is possible to make sense of the concepts of African Philosophy or African Feminism under some conditions or interpretations. I am merely denying the wisdom of using those concepts in one condition and interpretation, namely when neither philosophy nor feminism has been appropriated by any subgroup of humanity and the qualifiers are chauvinistic and geopolitical. My point is that much of the debate on the existence of African philosophy and what sometimes appears as a fight to recognize African philosophy makes sense, often, because some people claim that they have philosophy while others, especially Africans, do not. The same context is suggested by part of the debate on feminism. Yet, if Smith is right, the problem is not with feminism but those who practise it.[62]

Nothing I have said above should be taken as denying that there are differences, especially physiological, sociological and historical differences, between African and Western women. I do not deny that the victims of sexism are victims of specific forms of sexism under specific historical and social conditions, I merely deny that there are philosophically relevant and morally significant differences to warrant their inferiorization. The statuses, roles, and oppression of women relative to men hardly seem to be significantly different from one race to race, though the forms, modes, and techniques of oppression may vary with time and place. In this respect, all women are, at least in some significant sense, generally the same. But if generally women are everywhere oppressed or discriminated against by men, then all men are, at least in this sense, also generally the same.

In making this assertion I do not mean to suggest that no man is more oppressed than some woman. Neither do I deny that there could have been matriachal societies. If any such society exists, it is apparently neither representative of conditions in our present or past world nor statistically significant. In any case, I have argued that there is little evidence that the African society of the Akans is such a society.

Indeed, the suggestion is that there is overwhelming evidence to the contrary, indicating that the traditional society was invidiously sexist.

Consequently, any argument that denies that there is universal oppression of women on the strength of such premises is, even if valid, unlikely to be sound. So too are the arguments of people like Kwame Nhrumah and Kofi Busia who premise the arguments of their political philosophies on the alleged egalitarianism of the traditional African society.[63]   While Nkrumah argued that we should capture the egalitarianism of the traditional African society by practising socialism, Busia argued for liberal democracy as being most consistent with the egalitarianism of traditional Akan-like societies. But if it is true that these traditional African societies were sexist, they could not be egalitarian. Egalitarian societies are societies in which all human beings are treated equally, but sexist societies are not. To think that the egalitarian, utopian society is one that captures the traditional African society, is to fall victim to romanticism and wishful thinking. This is not to deny that in other respects traditional African societies were very humane. In many respects they were more humane than some of the so-called civilized Western societies that until recently practised slavery as well as racism and sexism and still condone these practices.

NOTES

1. This essay was written as part of a larger project on the parallels between Africana and Feminist Challenges to Western Philosophy which was adopted as the theme of Section 23 of the World Conference of Philosophy held on the 21st-25th July 1991, in Nairobi, Kenya. I am grateful to Professors Kwasi Wiredu, Florence Dolphyne, and others for their comments.

2. Barbara Omolade "Black Women and Feminism" in *Women and Values* by Marilyn Pearsall (ed.), (Belmont, CA: Wadsworth Publishing Co., 1986). Originally in *The Future of Difference* by H. Eisenstein & A. Jardine (ed.), (Boston: G. K. Hall, 1980), 139.

3. Barbara Callaway "Women in Ghana" in *Women in the World: A Comparative Study* by L. B. Ighitzin and Ruth Ross (ed.), (Santa Barbara: American Bibliographical Center-Clio Press, 1976), 199.

4. Dorothy Vellenga "Matriliny, Patriliny, and Class Formation Among Women Cocoa Farmers in Two Rural Areas of Ghana" in *Women and Class in Africa* by C. Robertson & I. Berger, (New York: Africana Publishing Co., 1986), 64.

5. Christine Oppong & Katharine Abu *Seven Roles of Women: Impact of Education, Migration and Employment on Ghanaian Mothers*, (Geneva: ILO, 1987), 27.

6. Omolade, *op. cit.*, 140.

7. Omolade, *ibid.*, 140.

8. *ibid.*

9. Even though in *The Emancipation of Women: An African Pespective* (Accra: Ghana Universities Press, 1991) Florence Dolphyne acknowledges that some African women command a lot of respect in African societies, she admits that "it is true to say that, in general, women in African societies are relegated to a rather subordinate position (*ibid.*, 41-4). The lessons Kwame Appiah draws from incidents that he reports in *In My Father's House* (New York: Oxford University Press, 1992), are that we should (1) never confuse a matrilineal society with a society where women are in public control and (2) never assume that individual women cannot gain power under patriarchy (*ibid.*, 184).

10. Omolade, *ibid.*, 140.

11. See Christine Oppong *Sex Roles, Population and Development in West Africa*, (Portsmouth, NH: Heinemann Educational Books Inc. & ILO, 1986)

12. Omolade, *op. cit.*, 141.

13. Callaway, *op. cit.*, 190 & 194.

14. *ibid.*, 192.

15. *ibid.*, 190.

16. Audrey Smock "From Autonomy to Subordination" in *Women: Roles and Status in Eight Countries* by J. Z. Ciele and A. C. Smock (ed.), (New York: John Wiley & Sons, Inc., 1977), 176.

17. Smock, *ibid.*

18. *ibid.*

19. *ibid.*

20. *ibid.*

21. *ibid.*

22. Kwasi Wiredu *Philosophy and an African Culture*, (Cambridge: Cambridge University Press, 1980), 2.

23. Oppong & Abu, *op. cit.*, 27.

24. Kwame Arhin "The Political and Military Roles of Akan Women" in *Female & Male in West Africa* by Christine Oppong (ed.), (Boston: George Allen & Unwin, 1983).

25. *ibid.*, 91.

26. *ibid.*

27. *ibid.*

28. *ibid.*

29. *ibid.*

30. *ibid.*

31. *ibid.*

32. *ibid.*

33. *ibid.*

34. Felix Odei Akuffo "Teenage Pregnancies and School Drop-outs" in *Sex Roles, Population and Development in West Africa* by Christine Oppong (ed.), (London: Heinemann Educational Books, Inc.,/ILO, 1987), 135.

35. Vellenga, *op. cit.*, 64.

36. *ibid.*, 64.

37. *ibid.*, 75.

38. *ibid.*, 76.

39. *ibid.*, 76.

40. *ibid.*, 76.

41. Claire Robertson "The Death of Makola and Other Tragedies" in *Canadian Journal of African Studies*, Vol. 17, No. 3, 1983, 472.

42. *ibid.*, 469.

43. *ibid.*, 476.

44. 'Kalabule' is a Ghanaian name for a range of unethical business practices including hoarding, profiteering, and the creation of artificial shortages.

45. Atuafari is the name of the teacher I have in mind.

46. C. A. Akrofi *Twi Mmebusem*, (Accra, Ghana: Waterville Publishing House, 1958), 45.

47. *ibid.*

48. *ibid.*
49. See the lyrics of "Lady" by Fela Anikulapo Kuti (Yaka Music, Inc.) re-released on the album "Waiting for the Rain" by Hugh Masekela for Table Mountain and Zomba Productions Ltd., 1985; marketed and distributed by Arista Records, Inc. of New York.
50. Ama Ata Aidoo "GHANA: To Be a Woman" in *Sisterhood is Global* by Robin Morgan (ed.), (New York: Anchor Press/Doubleday, 1984).
51. *ibid.*, 259.
52. *ibid.*
53. bell hooks *Talking Back*, (Boston: South End Press, 1989), 9.
54. *ibid.*
55. *ibid.*, 177-8.
56. *ibid.*, 178.
57. Tsenay Serequeberhan *African Philosophy: The Essential Reading*, (New York: Paragon House, 1991).
58. Alison Jaggar "How Can Philosophy Be Feminist?" in *American Philosophical Association Newsletter on Feminism and Philosophy*, April 1988, 8.
59. Barbara Smith "Racism and Women's Studies" in *All the Women Are White All the Blacks Are Men But Some of Us Are Brave* by G. T. Hall, P. B. Scott & B. Smith (ed.), (Old Westbury, NY: The Feminist Press, 1982), 49.
60. ibid.
61. Joyce Trebilcot "Conceiving Women: Notes on the Logic of Feminism" in *Women and Values* by Marilyn Pearsall (ed.), (Belmont, CA: Wadsworth Publishing Co., 1986). Originally in *Sinister Wisdom*, Vol. 11, Fall 1979, 358.
62. *The Emancipation of Women: An African Perspective*, (Accra, Ghana: Universities Press, 1991), xiii.
63. *ibid.*, xiii.—30
64. Smith, *op. cit.*, 50-1.
65. See Kwame Nkrumah's *Consciencism*, New York: Monthly Review Press, 1970 56-77 and Kofi Abrefa Busia's *Africa in Search of Democracy*, New York: Fredrick A. Praeger Publishers, 1967, 17-34.

Questions for Chapter 16
Feminism and African Philosophy

1. TRUE or FALSE?

    a. One of Safro Kwame's objectives is to undermine the thesis of the universal oppression of women.
    b. According to Safro Kwame, all women are the same but not all men are the same.
    c. According to Safro Kwame, the existence of matrilineal societies in Africa is a myth.
    d. According to Safro Kwame, the status of sexism in Africa should have no bearing on the political philosophy of Nkrumah or Busia.

2. According to Safro Kwame, the Akan society:

    (A) is matriarchal.
    (B) is feminist.
    (C) practices polyandry.
    (D) believes in none of the above.

3. Safro Kwame denies:

    (A) that it is possible to make sense of the concept of African Philosophy.
    (B) that there are differences between African and Western women.
    (C) all of the above.
    (D) none of the above.

4. What, if any, are the difference between Dolphyne and Kwame on feminism?

Index